User's Guide to the Ecu

Ralph J. Mehnert

Ecu Consulting Inc.

Graham & Trotman
A member of Wolters Kluwer Academic Publishers
LONDON/DORDRECHT/BOSTON

Graham & Trotman Limited
Sterling House
66 Wilton Road
London SW1V 1DE
UK

Kluwer Academic Publishers Group
101 Philip Drive
Assinippi Park
Norwell, MA 02061
USA

First published in 1992.

British Library and **Library of Congress Cataloguing-in-Publication Data**
is available upon request.

ISBN 1 85333 742 0

Printed and bound in Great Britain by Hartnolls Ltd, Cornwall

Contents

List of Figures

List of Tables

To my parents.

PART I.

INTRODUCTION

The Member States of the European Community decided in 1985 to transform their 12 economies into the world's single largest economy with already over 340 million citizens. All restrictions on the free movement of goods, persons, services and capital are to be abolished by December 31, 1992 when the almost 300 pieces of legislation necessary to effect the Single Market will be enacted. Until last December, however, an important obstacle to this freedom of movement would have remained in the form of the 12 national currencies of the EC Member States which require citizens and businesses to exchange currencies, pay the corresponding banking fees and deal with complicated accounting and invoicing procedures for their transactions inside the Single Market.

With the success of the 1992 program clearly in sight, the EC now has turned to determining the shape of its union following the economic unification. Negotiations were completed in December 1991 for the Economic and Monetary Union (EMU) with a common central bank and a single EC currency by 1999. The EMU will be the culmination of four decades of efforts to establish monetary coherence and stability in the EC. It will be a significant step toward an even more complete union among its Member States.

This book introduces and explains this single EC currency: the ecu.

Created in 1979 as official unit of account for the European Monetary System (EMS), the ecu has developed into an internationally accepted currency with a market approaching $300 billion. Its name derived from a medieval pan-European coin, it is, quite unexpectedly, playing an important role in the unification of the EC. It has developed from being the "illegitimate child" of the EMS to the very essence of EMU and the *sine qua non* for the European Union.

This book is designed as a "User's Guide" to describe the ecu and its development, composition and uses. The information collected in this book permits the reader to acquire a broad understanding of the ecu. It also includes very specific materials to assist in establishing the ecu in daily transactions of private citizens and corporations, including ecu-denominated financing, accounting and invoicing systems.

Part II discusses the basis of the ecu in the provisions relating to the EMU in the Maastricht Treaty on European Union and the need for a single currency in the EC. Part III introduces the European Monetary System and the role of the ecu therein. Part IV summarizes the historic link between the medieval and the modern ecus. Part V deals with the discussion surrounding the nature of the ecu as a unit of account and a currency. Part VI explains the composition and recomposition of the ecu and the necessary five calculations. Part VII discusses the reasons for the relative exchange rate stability of the ecu. Part VIII describes the official uses of the ecu and Part IX the "missing link" between the official and the private ecus. Part X summarizes the private uses of the ecu. Parts XI and XII examine the private ecu bond and non-bond markets, including loans, futures, options and the ecu clearing system. Part XIII outlines present and future commercial uses for the ecu. Part XIV summarizes the status of the ecu in international institutions, such as IMF, OECD and the World Bank. Part XV discusses potential new applications of the ecu in Central and Eastern European countries. Part XVI presents an overview of the legal status of the ecu in the EC Member States and various other nations. Part XVII lists publications on the ecu for reference and bibliographical purposes.

The most important documents related to the ecu, the EMS and the EMU, including the provisions in the Maastricht Treaty, and national laws and regulations on the ecu and ecu instruments are included in Appendices A and B. Appendix C contains a timetable with the most significant dates in the development of the ecu, the EMS and the EMU. Appendices D, E and F list respectively the addresses for the most important financial institutions in the EC Member States (such as the Ministries of Finance, the central banks and the stock exchanges), for private ecu-related organizations and for the international exchange markets offering ecu instruments. Appendix G contains a sample ecu bond prospectus. A detailed index is provided at the end of this book.

PART II.

ECONOMIC AND MONETARY UNION

A. Economic and Monetary Union: Basis for the Ecu as Single Currency

One of the most important issues regarding the ecu relates to its role as the single EC currency and its basis in the Economic and Monetary Union (EMU). Where did the concept of a single currency arise and what are its bases? The answer lies in the development of the EMU in its different forms since 1957. The concept of EMU has always been a part of the drive toward a united Europe in some form. However, the Treaty of Rome which founded the European *Economic* Community in 1957 only established a system of cooperation in monetary affairs. It did not convey the power to create a monetary union with a central bank and a single currency to the jurisdiction of the EC government. This specific power has developed over the past 35 years in a slow process resulting equally from economic necessity and political determination of the EC Member States.

The European Council first enlarged the "cooperation concept" and created the European Monetary Cooperation Fund (EMCF) in 1973. It was designed ultimately to achieve either the total and unrestricted convertibility of the EC currencies or the introduction of a single currency. The European Unit of Account (EUA) served as unit of account to avoid currency conversions. This artificial basis, to which the EC currencies were "pegged", allowed direct conversions and comparisons between those currencies. The practical "arm" of the EMCF, the "Currency Snake", linked the EC currencies and permitted limited maximum fluctuations. It malfunctioned as a result of the rapid fluctuations of the free-floating exchange rates after the collapse of the Bretton Woods monetary system in the early 1970s.

In response to these exchange rate fluctuations, the EC established the European Monetary System (EMS) in 1979. Although the EC failed to meet its own deadline for the next step, the merger of the EMCF and the EMS into the European Monetary Fund (EMF), a central bank-like federal EC institution, the EMS has very successfully created a zone of monetary stability and economic convergence. Surprisingly, the ecu, the official unit of account for the EMS mechanisms, quickly developed a life of its own as a quasi-currency on the private markets.

The unexpected success of the EMS and the advent of the Single Market spurred a renewed interest in the EMU in the mid-1980s. The main benefits of the EMU for the EC and its Member States include increased efficiency and growth of the Single Market as a result of eliminated exchange rate uncertainty and transaction costs, increased price stability, a new framework for national budgetary policies stressing autonomy, budgetary discipline to avoid excessive deficits, and intra-EC coordination. In addition, the EMU might improve the international foreign exchange system, namely through the introduction of the single EC currency which will permit more entities to transact business in their own national currency, i.e., the ecu. The resulting abolition of the 12 existing national currencies will facilitate and strengthen the international system.

The development of the EMU, however, did not proceed unchallenged. The debates relating to the EMU almost immediately centered around the desired features of such union. In this process, a consensus developed in favor of an independent central monetary institution committed to price stability and subject to democratic accountability. The Committee for the Study of Economic and Monetary Union, created in June 1988 by the European Council and chaired by EC Commission President Jacques Delors, issued its influential *Report on the EMU* in April 1989, which proposed a three-stage plan to establish the EMU which developed into the blueprint for the subsequent negotiations.

Table II.1: Summary of the Delors Report

The Committee on the Study of Economic and Monetary Union presented the Delors Report to the European Council in June 1989, proposing a three-stage process toward the EMU, similar to the prior *Werner Report* in 1970.

Stage I

Stage I is based on consolidating the Single Market and involves:

* the complete removal of physical, technical and fiscal barriers;
* the strengthening of competition policy and the reduction of state aids, such as subsidies to industries;
* the reform of the EC structural funds which offer regional aid and the doubling of their resources;
* closer coordination of economic and monetary policies among the Member States;
* the deregulation of the financial markets and the establishment of a single financial area through the implementation of directives on banking, securities and insurance services;
* the participation of *all* EC currencies in the exchange rate mechanisms of the EMS;
* the removal of all impediments to the private use of the ecu.

Stage II

Stage II is a transitional stage involving the restructuring of the existing EC institutions and the establishment of new institutions, most importantly the European System of Central Banks (ESCB). Throughout Stage II, the ultimate responsibility for policy decisions would remain with the authorities in the Member States.

Stage III

Stage III includes:

* the introduction of irrevocably locked exchange rates;
* the promulgation of binding constraints on the budgetary policies of the Member States;
* further strengthening of EC structural and regional policies;

In addition,

* the EC would act as a single entity in the area of international monetary policies;

In addition to this and other influential reports, the success of the ecu on private markets and fresh support for the unification of the EC prompted the introduction of a previously taboo concept: a single EC currency. The idea found immediate support among many Member States. The EC Commission study *One Market, One Money* in 1990 underscored the economic necessity of such a single currency. The Commission estimated the monetary costs to entities in the EC attributed to the lack of a single currency at ECU 13 to 19 billion per year. At that time, the British government rejected a single currency and proposed the "hard ecu" scheme in which a physical parallel ecu would slowly substitute the existing national currencies.

B. The New EMU-Treaty: Setting the Stage for the Single Currency

After intensive negotiations, the EC Member States agreed in Maastricht on December 10 and 11, 1992, on the provisions for the creation of the EMU, comprising an EC central bank and the ecu as the single EC currency as early as January 1, 1997. The Maastricht Treaty on European Union was signed on February 7, 1992 and must now be ratified by the legislatures in the EC Member States to become effective. The deadline for ratification is January 1, 1993, coinciding with the date of the completion of the Single Market.

The following summarizes the provisions of the new treaty relating to the EMU and, most importantly, to the transformation of the ecu into the single EC currency and the resulting abolition of the existing national currencies. A *caveat* at this point: although the Member States have clearly stated that the decision to create the EMU, including the single currency, is irreversible, two protocols were added to the treaty granting Denmark and the United Kingdom a right to "opt out" of the introduction of the single currency. Britain thereby is permitted to avoid implementing the final stage of the EMU and the single currency. Denmark may hold a public referendum before introducing the single currency. All other members, however, are irrevocably bound by the provisions of the treaty. This solution to the long dissension between Great Britain and most of the remaining Member States preserves the credibility of the decision to create the EMU (and, consequently, permits the ecu to develop fully into the single currency in the transition stage) while providing for national concerns in the case of Great Britain and Denmark.

The treaty provisions set a very tight schedule for the introduction of the EMU, particularly the central bank and its predecessor, and the single EC currency (for the complete text of the provisions concerning the ecu, please see Appendix A). It essentially uses the three-stage approach first introduced in the *Delors Report* in April 1989 (see page 15):

(1) Stage I

Stage I began on July 1, 1989. It comprised increased coordination of the monetary and economic policies among the Member States.

(2) Stage II

Stage II will begin on January 1, 1994. Its most important feature will be the establishment of the predecessor to the EC central bank, the European Monetary Institute (EMI), which will prepare Stage III.

The treaty sets forth the various tasks of the EMI related to the preparation of Stage III. First and foremost, it will establish the regulatory, organizational and logistical framework necessary for the EC central bank, the European System of Central Banks (ESCB), to perform its tasks in Stage III, including the instruments necessary for carrying out the single monetary policy. It will prepare the rules for operations of national banks in the framework of the ESCB and promote the harmonization of procedures for creating statistics. The duties also include the facilitation of the use of the ecu, the promotion of efficient cross-border payments in the EC, supervision of the technical preparation of the ecu bank notes required for Stage III and of the development and functioning of the ecu clearing system. This will result in the usability of the ecu in all types of financial transactions on a pan-European basis even before its transformation into the single EC currency.

(3) Stage III

Stage III will be the actual implementation stage for the central bank and the single EC currency. This stage will begin either on January 1, 1997 or January 1, 1999. The European Council will decide the definitive implementation date according to the following procedure:

(a) By December 31, 1996, the European Council will decide by a weighted majority vote (in the current composition of the EC, the 12 Member States have a total of 76 votes, and an affirmative weighted majority vote would be 54 affirmative votes) whether: (i) a majority of the Member States (currently seven out of the 12 Member States) fulfill the conditions necessary for the adoption of a single currency; and (ii) whether it is appropriate for the EC to enter Stage III.

To provide for an environment in which it will be economically feasible for the EC central bank to carry out its mandate of price stability, the Member States must have achieved a high degree of convergence. Therefore, the eligibility of each Member State will be assessed on the basis of its price stability (the inflation rate must be within 1.5 percentage points of the three Member States with the lowest inflation), long-term interest rate levels (within two percentage points of the Member States with the lowest inflation), a sustainable budget situation (budget deficits of less than 3 percent and government debt of less than 60 percent of the gross domestic product) and participation in the narrow fluctuation band of the EMS (see page 27) for at least two years.

(b) If the EC does not implement the EMU in 1997, then it will automatically begin on January 1, 1999. The European Council will then only determine, by simple majority, which countries will qualify for participation in the EMU. The eligibility of any

Member State which is not permitted to join the EMU will be reassessed periodically.

The treaty clearly states that the ecu will become the single EC currency and that it will retain its name. To ensure the smooth transition of the ecu from its current status as a basket currency (see page 46) into the single EC currency, the treaty provides that the composition of the ecu (see page 48) will not be changed and that the European Council will set the final conversion rates of the national currencies into the ecu. The latter provision will effectively "freeze" the conversion rates of the national currencies in the EC toward the ecu from a certain point onward.

With Stage III, the ecu will become the single EC currency and is to be rapidly introduced as such in the Member States. As a technical matter, however, it is very unlikely that the ecu will substitute the national currencies overnight. The EC will very likely introduce an intermediate, two-currency pricing and payment system in which the ecu would be legal tender throughout the EC while the national currencies would remain legal tender in their respective home countries and would gradually be phased out. The EC central bank will have the exclusive right to mint ecu bank notes under consideration of existing national practices in this respect. The Member States will issue the ecu coins, subject to approval by the central bank. The denominations and technical specifications of all coins will be harmonized to ensure their smooth circulation in the EC.

C. THE NEED FOR A SINGLE CURRENCY

"Without a common currency, the Single Market of the EC will remain a fiction."
Helmut Schmidt, 1988

The EC agreement to proceed with the EMU was surely a political decision. However, underlying this political consensus are a variety of economic reasons and needs which have made EC businesses strong supporters of a single EC currency. From such a political standpoint, the EC needs a central bank to coordinate its monetary policies and to avoid divergences among national monetary policies. The central bank is necessary to take advantage of the Single Market of 1992 and a unified Europe. It alone, however, would not have sufficed. Monetary union, by definition, also includes a single currency. There should be no doubt that only a single currency truly accomplishes monetary union. An economic entity as large as the EC cannot function properly on the basis of 12 or more national currencies even if those currencies maintained fixed exchange rates among each other. The necessity of using different currencies is tedious and uneconomical for businesses and citizens and decreases the potential benefits of the Single Market.

Businesses, and to a rapidly increasing degree, citizens of the EC now support the single currency concept. A recent poll, for example, showed that 60 percent of the polled citizens supported the abolition of national currencies in five to six years.

Figure II.1: European Opinion - Central Bank and Ecu

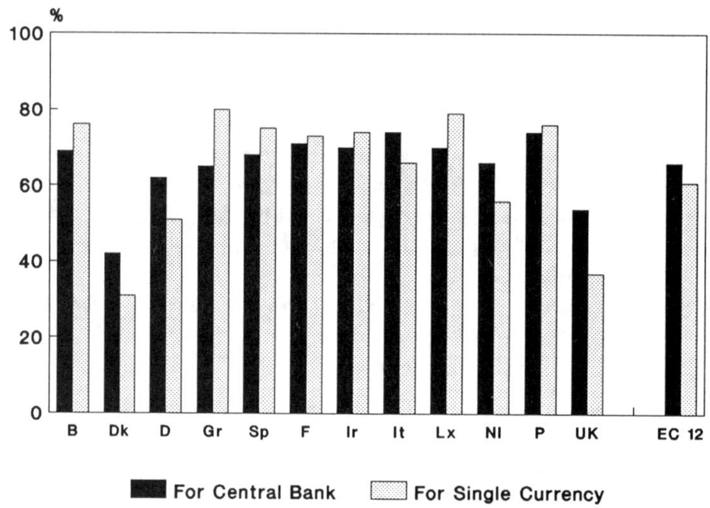

Source: EC Commission

This support is the reason for the unexpected success of the private ecu with which private market initiatives turned the "illegitimate child" into a global currency. The savings associated with such a currency are enormous. Any business will, by definition, support a single currency if for no other reason than to decrease its expenses and increase its profits accordingly. At this point, a word of caution is necessary. Following the decision to create the EMU by 1999, the attitude of citizens in several Member States has drifted away from the unquestioning acceptance of a single currency. Especially German, who for the loss of their stable currency, seem to rethink their attitude toward monetary unification. One reason for this change might be the fact that the theoretical possibility of a single currency - and the abolition of the national currencies - surprisingly fast has become a reality which will have very significant practical consequences for every EC citizen.

A single currency for the largest economic entity in the world is an inevitable necessity. The United States of America introduced its single currency with a central monetary authority at the beginning of this century to take most advantage of its huge internal market and standardize (e.g., facilitate) the payment system under the auspices of one central authority. The EC will introduce its single currency at the end of the same century to make a reality of an old dream: the United States of Europe. However logical such a single currency may seem, its introduction, especially in an entity as diversified as the EC, will not be without significant problems. Despite the obvious economic savings aspects, there are many difficulties, ranging from nationalistic concerns to psychological and very practical considerations. At the forefront of these are the concerns of the Germans who will face the loss of their status symbol Deutsche Mark, with its proverbial stability, and the British whose pound is not only a means of payment but also a symbol of the once mighty British Empire.

D. Problems in Introducing the Single Currency

Despite the progress of recent months, the discussions among the Member States have shown the degree of disagreement and divergence on a number of issues relating to the EMU and the single currency.

One of the most complex issues has always been that of sovereignty. Based on the success of the EMS and the ecu, the establishment of monetary union is less a question of technique than one of politics. The creation of an independent central bank and a single EC currency requires national governments to relinquish their monetary powers to the supranational level. The power to issue money and regulate monetary affairs is one of the most "basic" powers of any nation and its transfer to a more supranational body is more a matter of pride and politics than one of rationality. The reluctance of the British government to agree fully to monetary union and the recent more negative attitudes in Germany are, in a large part, the result of such sovereignty concerns.

The solution to the issue of sovereignty has been in favor of the supranational EC. The EC and the 1992 program are other examples of areas in which the Member States have already relinquished powers to the EC, although the matters involved here did not concern one of the "basic" sovereign powers. Technically, monetary union has only been the first concession of a traditional national power to the EC, and already some Member States have shown uneasiness about this drastic change. Although this step is logical from a practical standpoint, it is also a step into the "unknown" and has not been taken without some lingering doubts by the governments and the people of the Member States. The ability of the Member States to create monetary union, as reluctant and problematic as it may be, is not only of great importance in the monetary field. The ability to relinquish this basic power indicates that the Member States may also be prepared to forsake their national sovereignty in other areas and create the political and military union.

The practical introduction of a single currency with the simultaneous abolition of national currencies might also cause problems. While "sovereignty" might prompt a government to refuse to give up its own currency, citizens of some Member States might resist if their currencies were abolished without proper information and education. The current reaction of some Germans who fear that their stable currency will not only be abolished but also substituted by an unknown and unproven currency, is a prime example of such a fear. Even the remote possibility that the new currency might not have all the attributes of the Deutsche Mark might make a German fear instability and inflation.

Such concerns present significant obstacles and *must* be overcome to render the new currency a success. In addition, citizens will have to get used to new scales of values with the new money. An Italian, for example, would not pay with 1,500 lira, but with 1 ecu - an enormous difference in understanding and doing business. Old traditions and values based on the units of each currency will be altered. Old habits die hard. Many French, for example, still refer to the "old" francs which were abolished years ago. The new EC currency will face similar reactions and will have to establish itself as valid, everyday currency over years to come.

It is therefore of extreme importance that the currency not be introduced by some sort of unannounced overnight operation. The introduction must be preceded by in depth education and familiarization and fears, such as those mentioned above, must be counteracted. After all, it is the general public who must be comfortable with their new currency. Dissatisfaction or non-acceptance would result in economic disaster and - more importantly for the introducing governments - a political nightmare. Fortunately, in the past, limited promotions of ecu in private transactions (see page 133) have been quite successful. They indicated that the introduction of the single currency might actually be less difficult than anticipated because many EC citizens are ready to accept it as their currency. However, tradition and nationalism are very strong separators and the abolition of national currencies will not be greeted with unanimous approval.

The abolition of an existing currency and the introduction of a new one will also carry a hefty price tag: Physical money, coins and notes, will have to be minted and the old money destroyed. Price lists and denominations, catalogues, computer programs and all other items denominated in the old currencies will have to be changed at considerable short-term expense. This whole process, and its costs, has been complicated by the short timetable adopted in the new EMU treaty which provides for the introduction of the single currency in five or seven years. The anticipated long-term savings associated with the single currency, however, might dwarf these costs.

In addition to the far-reaching political consequences for the EC and its citizens, the single currency will have very tangible implications for parties involved in multinational transactions all over the world. As the adoption of the single EC currency entails the abolition of existing national currencies, parties already transacting business or drafting and negotiating contracts denominated in those national currencies should provide for the event of their abolition.

> For example, a contract signed in 1992 with an expected term of 10 years which requires payment in Deutsche Marks should provide for the probability that, by 1999, the Deutsche Mark might not even exist and payments in Deutsche Marks, consequently, would be impossible after this date.

Such contracts should be rewritten or renegotiated to provide for their re-denomination in the new EC currency or the utilization of a third currency, such as the yen or dollar. The process of including such provisions conceptually is an easy task, but its practical execution might well turn out to be an administrative nightmare. Although the renegotiation of existing contracts is a possibility, such a process is costly, disruptive and time-consuming. Therefore, the transition from the old to the new currency might result in significant short-term disruptions for businesses and private individuals alike. Again, it will be extremely important that the parties involved are educated to carry out the necessary steps for the transition well in advance.

Additional concerns pertain to the reaction of world financial markets to the possible abolition of 12 currencies, including the widely-used German mark, British pound and French franc, and to the implications of the creation of the ecu for inflation rates within the EC. Similarly, some EC banks will balk at the prospect of losing enormous current revenues from exchanging EC currencies. Some banks derive millions of dollars in revenue from currency conversions and the same also applies, for example, to the foreign exchange and futures markets in EC currencies. These entities will lose significant business and revenues with the creation of a single currency and the abolition of the national currencies.

These are important issues and possible hurdles which must be overcome before the EMU and the ecu can be successful. Fortunately, on a practical level, the ecu has already developed into a true currency in a number of areas where, despite its lacking official legal tender status, the ecu is well accepted (see page 82).

PART III.

THE EUROPEAN MONETARY SYSTEM

The ecu is an integral part of the European Monetary System (EMS). Its official role is defined within the framework of the EMS whose establishment is the *raison d'etre* for the ecu. Without the EMS, the EC would not have created - would not have needed - the ecu. Officially, there are no ecus outside the EMS at this time. Only those ecus created for the purposes of the EMS are "official" (see page 72). However, as the independent private ecu market based on the definition of the "official" ecu has by far outperformed any of its official functions, an understanding of the EMS and the role of the official ecu is necessary to understand the private ecu.

The EMS provides an important foundation for the EC: exchange rate stability. Its mechanisms ensure that EC currencies fluctuate only to a very limited extent against one another. This decreased fluctuation has resulted in economic growth and stability in Europe and has given new input to the process of integration in the EC. It also makes business transactions involving several EC currencies more predictable and helps limit exchange rate losses.

A. The EMS

The history of the EMS begins in the early 1970s when problems with the international monetary mechanisms and the malfunction of the Snake forced the EC to find alternatives to ensure greater monetary stability and solidarity. Following the determined joint efforts of Helmut Schmidt and Valéry Giscard d'Estaing, the EC established the EMS in 1978 (see Appendix A). It also introduced the European Currency Unit (ecu) as the successor to the EUA and as unit of account for the EMS. A simultaneous agreement between the EC central banks (see Appendix A) set forth the operating procedures, the EMS mechanisms and the features of the ecu. The EMS began to operate on March 13, 1979 with three basic purposes: (i) to provide a zone of monetary stability; (ii) to support closer monetary cooperation; and (iii) to foster economic and monetary unity in Europe.

The EMS operates under the auspices of the European Monetary Cooperation Fund (EMCF). It is based on agreed exchange rates for the 11 participating currencies (all EC currencies except the drachma). A "parity grid" assigns individual central rates in ecu to each currency. These central ecu rates then determine the bilateral exchange rates between any two currencies. The currencies are thereby linked to each other through the ecu (see page 56).

Most importantly, the daily fluctuations of the EMS currencies around their bilateral exchange rates vis-à-vis another currency may not exceed fluctuation margins of plus or minus 2.25 percent (±6 percent for the Spanish peseta, the British pound and the Portuguese escudo). Whenever the bilateral exchange rate of a currency reaches certain limits within those margins, the central banks are required to intervene and to re-establish rates within the margins. The divergence threshold and the divergence indicator are the triggers for these intervention mechanisms.

The divergence indicator determines the relative position of a currency within the fluctuation margins. It is designed to show whether a participating currency is developing an exchange rate significantly different from its prior rate as result of exposure to special influences or the basic exchange rate conditions. For example, a currency could divert 20 percent of its allowed maximum divergence of 2.25 or 6 percent. The divergence threshold is reached at 75 percent of each maximum divergence. As a practical matter, maximum divergence of 2.25 or 6 percent, does not equal the 100 percent divergence in each maximum fluctuation margin. The individual currency for which the indicator is calculated cannot appreciate or depreciate against itself. As a result of the different weights of the currencies, the *actual* maximum divergences will be smaller than the maximum fluctuation margin and will vary among the currencies. In addition, it will be smaller for currencies with high weights than for those with low weights in the ecu basket (See Table III.1). The formula used for this determination is:

(1 - official weight) x 2.25 (or 6.00 for pound, peseta and escudo)

Table III.1: Maximum Divergences and Divergence Thresholds

Currency	Official Weight Jan. 7, 1990	Maximum Divergence	75% Threshold
Pound	12.06%	+ / - 5.276	+ / - 3.957
Krone	2.53%	+ / - 2.193	+ / - 1.645
Franc (F)	19.43%	+ / - 2.193	+ / - 1.360
Escudo	0.78%	+ / - 5.953	+ / - 4.465
Pound (Irl)	1.12%	+ / - 2.225	+ / - 1.669
Lira	9.92%	+ / - 2.027	+ / - 1.520
Guilder	9.94%	+ / - 2.035	+ / - 1.526
Mark	30.53%	+ / - 1.563	+ / - 1.172
Franc (B)	8.14%	+ / - 2.066	+ / - 1.550
Peseta	5.18%	+ / - 5.689	+ / - 4.267

Source: Deutsche Bundesbank

At the time of the creation of the EMS, the general understanding was that the divergence indicator would serve an important purpose for the intervention mechanisms. Experience over the last 13 years, however, has shown that the significance attributed to the divergence indicator was overstated because the EMS has provided the EC central banks with a well-functioning framework for cooperation. This cooperation has developed into a system in which the central banks evaluate the performance of their currencies and engage in necessary interventions even before the divergence thresholds are crossed. Without a real need for determining the threshold the divergence indicator becomes unnecessary.

The EMS has four main technical features: (i) discretionary and mandatory exchange rate and intervention mechanisms - the ERM; (ii) financing and credit mechanisms; (iii) measures to support less prosperous economies; and, most importantly, (iv) the ecu.

There are two types of exchange rate mechanisms (ERM) - discretionary and mandatory. Discretionary mechanisms are triggered by the 75 percent divergence threshold. Whenever the threshold is crossed - when a currency changes value by more than 75 percent of its maximum divergence - the central banks should, and usually will, intervene to bring the rates of the currency closer to its bilateral exchange rate to prevent tensions in the exchange régime. When currencies cross the 100 percent maximum divergence limit, the central banks must engage in mandatory intervention measures and re-establish rates within the fluctuation margins.

The discretionary and mandatory intervention mechanisms operate mainly through the buying and selling of the currency of the affected EMS member state in unlimited amounts by the central banks. For example, if the German mark depreciated beyond its maximum margin against the lira, the Bundesbank would buy marks for lira and the Banca d'Italia would sell lira for marks on the foreign exchange markets. The corresponding increase in the amount of lira available would decrease its value. The simultaneous decrease in marks available would raise the value of the mark on the foreign exchange markets. This would move the bilateral rates between mark and lira closer to their predetermined central rates. Other measures to ease actual or prospective tensions in the exchange rate régime include changes in the countries' domestic monetary policies, changes in the EMS central rates (see page 57) and other measures of economic policy. Should a country be unable to engage in any of these measures, it must inform and consult with the other Member States and the EC government.

Figure III.1: Functioning of the EMS Mechanisms

External Developments
Economic factors result in capital flows from the Netherlands to Denmark
and in exchanges of guilders into kronas.
↓
Effect on the markets:
Increased sales of guilders and increased demand for kronas.
↓
Effect in the EMS:
The guilder moves to the bottom and the krona to the top of the 2.25%-margins.
↓
INTERVENTIONS:
The Dutch central bank sells kronas and swaps kronas for guilders and the Danish central bank sells kronas and borrows guilders for the swap.
↓
Effect on markets:
Increased sales of kronas and increased demand for guilders.
↓
Effect in the EMS:
Guilder and krona move closer to their central rates.

Very short-term, short-term and medium-term financing mechanisms are the second feature of the EMS. Very Short-Term Financing (VSTF) helps EMS members maintain the fluctuation margins for their respective currencies. A central bank can tap credit facilities from other central banks in order to meet its commitments under the ERM and to have available sufficient amounts of currencies needed for the interventions. Short-term monetary support finances temporary deficits in the balances of payments of the Member States. Medium-term financial assistance is granted to EC Member States experiencing difficulties in their balances of payments.

Table III.2: Short-Term Monetary Support

Central Banks	Quotas		%
	Debtor ecu million	Creditor ecu million	
Banque Nationale de Belgique	580	1,160	6.50
Danmarks Nationalbank	260	520	2.91
Deutsche Bundesbank	1,740	3,480	19.51
Bank of Greece	150	300	1.68
Banco de España	725	1,450	8.13
Banque de France	1,740	3,480	19.51
Central Bank of Ireland	100	200	1.12
Banca d'Italia	1,160	2,320	13.00
Nederlandsche Bank	580	1,160	6.50
Banco de Portugal	145	290	1.63
Bank of England	1,740	3,480	19.51
Total EC	8,920	17,840	100.00

Source: EC Commission

The third feature is support to less prosperous member economies in the form of subsidies with a low (3 percent) interest rate. These subsidies are for loans made by the European Investment Bank or under the New Community Instrument (see page 74).

The EC created the official ecu as the fourth and single most important feature of the EMS (see page 28). It is the means of settlement for the EC monetary authorities and institutions permitting them to denominate their receipts and liabilities in ecu instead of any particular EMS currency. It is also the denominator for the ERM, the basis for the divergence indicator, and the denominator for most transactions under credit and financing mechanisms.

The need for the ecu is the result of the mechanisms of the EMS because, just as interventions in the markets, financing and support mechanisms require certain monetary transfers. For example, an EC central bank might lend money to another EC central bank to assist the latter in maintaining its currency within the fluctuation margins. The variety of the EC currencies, currently 12, poses a problem for these transactions. If, for example, the German Bundesbank had to transfer money to the Banca d'Italia, it would transfer Deutsche Marks to Italy. This transfer would require exchanging Deutsche Marks for lira. To avoid such exchanges and the associated administrative and effective costs, the EC created the ecu as a "unit of account" (see page 40).

Although the EC expected the ecu to play a dominant role in the EMS, the actual development of the official functions was disappointing. The monetary authorities traditionally have used either the underlying currencies themselves or have found it more practical to use third currencies for interventions. The German mark, for example, and the United States dollar are very often used for such purposes. The EC continuously attempts to increase the official use of the ecu in the EMS. So far, these efforts have been without positive results.

This underdeveloped official role points to one of the most interesting developments with regard to the ecu. It was initially only supposed to serve as the unit of account for the EMS. Parallel to the official role, and solely because the ecu was created as part of the EMS, it developed into a private and commercially used currency of the free markets. Its roles in some segments of those markets have by far surpassed its official functions (see page 82).

B. Changes in the Ecu Central Rates: Realignments

Realignments are changes in the fixed ecu central rates of the EMS currencies. They become necessary as a result of economic disparities, mostly in terms of inflation, of the individual economies of the Member States.

If and when the exchange rate between any two EMS currencies crosses the divergence threshold or maximum fluctuation limit (see page25), the central banks will first attempt to intervene. If such interventions fail to bring the currencies within the fluctuation margins set around the central bilateral exchange rates, the central rate of the affected currency or currencies will be realigned. The realignment will establish new central rates with new maximum fluctuation limits. The new limits will take into account the movements outside the "old" margins.

Although the central rate of, for example, the alignment of one currency may be necessary at a certain point in time, the nature of the ecu and the link of all currencies through bilateral central rates will also automatically readjust the central rates of all other currencies. If, for example, one currency is revalued against the ecu, the bilateral rates of that currency against all other currencies will automatically change.

In the first years of the EMS, a number of realignments took place and were the cause of concern about the viability of the system. As shown in the following table, the last "real" realignment occurred on January 12, 1987 (the 1990 realignment was a technical measure to account for the decrease of the margins for the lira from 6 to 2.25 percent). This indicates that the proper rates have been established and that the EMS functions very satisfactorily.

Table III.3: EMS Realignments: Changes in the Ecu Central Rates

Currencies	13 Mar 79	24 Sep 79	30 Nov 79	23 Mar 81	05 Oct 81
Guilder	2.72077	2.74748	2.74362	2.81318	2.66382
Franc B/Lx	39.4582	39.8456	39.7897	40.7985	40.7572
Mark	2.51064	2.48557	2.48208	2.54502	2.40989
Krone	7.08592	7.36594	7.72336	7.91917	7.91117
Pound	0.663247	0.649821	0.64891	0.542122	0.601048
Pound (Ir)	0.662638	0.669141	0.668201	0.685145	0.684452
Franc (F)	5.79831	5.85522	5.847	5.99526	6.17443
Lira	1148.18	1159.42	1157.79	1262.92	1300.67

Currencies	22 Feb 82	14 Jun 82	21 Mar 83	18 May 83	17 Sep 84
Guilder	2.67296	2.57971	2.49587	2.52595	2.52595
Franc B/Lx	44.6963	44.9704	44.3662	44.9008	44.9008
Mark	2.41815	2.33379	2.21515	2.24184	2.24184
Krone	8.18382	8.234	8.04412	8.14104	8.14104
Pound	0.557037	0.560453	0.629848	0.587087	0.585992
Pound (Ir)	0.686799	0.691011	0.71705	0.725690	0.725690
Franc (F)	6.19564	6.61387	6.79271	6.87456	6.87456
Lira	1305.13	1350.27	1386.78	1403.49	1403.49
Drachma					87.4813

Currencies	22 Jul 85	07 Apr 86	04 Aug 86	12 Jan 87	07 Jan 90*
Guilder	2.52208	2.40935	2.37833	2.31943	2.30358
Franc B/Lx	44.832	43.6761	43.1139	42.4582	42.1679
Mark	2.2384	2.13834	2.11083	2.05853	2.04446
Krone	8.12857	7.91896	7.81701	7.85212	7.79845
Pound	0.555312	0.630317	0.679256	0.739615	0.738615
Pound (IR)	0.724578	0.712956	0.764976	0.768411	0.76316
Franc (F)	6.86402	6.9628	6.87316	6.90403	6.85684
Lira	1520.6	1496.21	1476.95	1483.58	1529.7
Drachma	100.719	135.659	137.049	150.792	187.984

* Technical realignment as result of the fluctuation margin decrease for the lira.
Source: Commission of the European Communities

As indicated, the last "genuine" realignment took place in January 1987. For over five years, there has been no need to realign the central rates because the EMS mechanisms have resulted in converging exchange rates and provide very successful measures to maintain the currencies within their fluctuation margins. As a result of this development and the decision to proceed even further toward the EMU, including a single EC currency, the Maastricht Treaty provides for the irrevocable fixing of the conversion rates of the national currencies into ecu with the third stage of the EMU in 1997 or 1999. This rate will be the exchange rate for currencies being abolished and the conversion rate for currencies which will be substituted by the ecu as legal tender. At that date, realignments of the ecu central rates will totally cease to exist as an EMS mechanism.

C. Non-EC Countries and the EMS

The EMS has been very successful in stabilizing the exchange rates of the EC currencies. The intervention measures help maintain the currencies within their fluctuation margins. Realignments, the more drastic form of remedying exchange rate problems, have not been used for over five years which indicates the successful functioning of the system. This success prompted Austria and Sweden (both of which have applied for EC membership), Finland, Switzerland (both of which have expressed interest in full EC membership) and Norway to link their currencies to the ecu. Iceland is currently considering engaging in such a step before 1994. Norway linked the krona on October 22, 1990 with a central rate of 7.994 krona per ecu and fluctuation margins of ±2.25 percent. The Swedish krona joined on May 17, 1991 with a central rate of 7.40054 krona and a ±1.5 percent margin. The Finnish markka was linked on June 7, 1991 with a central rate of 4.8758 and a fluctuation margin of ±3 percent. These three currencies have a close relationship with the Danish krona which already is part of the EMS. Following the linking to the ecu, the exchange variability of these currencies has decreased considerably (by 50 percent in the case of the Norwegian and Swedish krona) to the Danish currency.

Although these actions are purely voluntary and unilateral, they indicate the desire of these countries to take advantage of the monetary stability in the EC. On a more important practical level, this linkage also keeps at a minimum exchange rate related losses for the significant trade and business flows between the EC and those countries, including direct and indirect investment. This safeguarding of investments in the EC is especially important in view of the creation of the European Economic Area between the EC and the EFTA nations and the 1992 unification into the Single Market. The linkage of the EFTA currencies will permit all parties to avoid excessive exchange rate losses when dealing in this area. These steps will extend the zone of monetary stability beyond the EC. They will enable businesses to engage in transactions without exposing themselves to serious exchange rate risks. The action by those countries, therefore, is a logical step toward completing the intent of the European Economic Area. In addition, it will assist in a smooth transition of those currencies into the EC monetary union should the respective countries decide to join the EC and/or the EMU at some future date.

PART IV.

FROM MEDIEVAL TO MODERN ECU

The previous two parts introduced two very important factors in the development of the ecu: the striving toward EMU, which will result in the transformation of the ecu into the single EC currency as early as 1997, and the EMS, which itself is the basis for the ecu. The success of the ecu in private markets is independent from its use in the EMS. In the EMS, it is a unit of account. On the private markets, the ecu is a currency.

But it is not the first "European" currency by that name.

The name "ecu" most obviously derives from the abbreviation of the English term "European Currency Unit". The French-speaking Europeans, however, have always regarded the ecu to be the successor to its important and historic namesake, the French "écu d'or".

The first ecus were gold coins minted under Louis IX of France in 1266. On their obverse, they depicted a shield of arms known in Latin as "scutum" which gave the coin its initial name. The French, having difficulties in pronouncing the "sc", added an "e" and changed the name to "escutum", later to "escu" and then to "ecu". Philip III, upon succeeding Louis IX, discontinued the undervalued gold ecus whose use was severely restricted. In 1337, when Philip VI began to mint the écu d'or again, it gained international recognition and was soon used as an international currency in France, the Netherlands, Navarre, Aquitaine and Portugal. During the 15th and 16th centuries, the ecu was virtually the only gold coin struck in Europe. In 1576, Charles V combined the ecu and the franc, the two most important coins in France. This measure stabilized the currencies after the great inflation of the 16th century and established the first monetary system based solely on the ecu.

For centuries, France and other European countries minted gold or silver ecu. The coins would bear different names, such as "écu d'or", "écu à la couronne", "écu au soleil", "écu aux palmes", "écu aux lauriers", "écu porc-épic" or "écu aux insignes". In 1793, the French Republic minted the last of the "old" ecu, the "écu constitutionnel". It was legal tender in France until abolished as means of payment by Napoleon in 1804. The only remaining currency to preserve its Latin origins is the Portuguese escudo.

Reviving the traditional importance of the "old" ecu as the first pan-European currency and the success of the "new" ecu as a private currency, Belgium minted the first "modern" gold and silver ecu coins in 1987 (see page 133). This success also resulted in some confusion on the private markets regarding the use of the name "ECU", the abbreviation format, and of "ecu", the name of the old coin. The EC Commission responded to the conflicting written forms and genders for the ecu, clarified its name in the different languages and dropped the reference to the ecu as an abbreviation in 1988. Although the following forms are only binding in the EC internally, some markets have adopted the terminology in their daily usage.

Table IV.1: The Name of the Ecu

Language	Singular	Plural	Remarks
English	the ecu	the ecus	pronounced as in French, not "EE-SEE-YOU"
French	l'écu	les écus	masculine gender
German	der Ecu	die Ecu	masculine gender
Italian	l'ecu	gli ecu	
Dutch	de ecu	de ecu's	masculine gender; no plural "s" after amounts
Spanish	el ecu	los ecus	
Portuguese	o ecu	os ecus	
Danish	ecuen	ecuerne	after an amount, singular non-specific form "ecu"
Greek	(to) Ecu	(t*a*) Ecu	

Source: EC Commission

The abbreviation for the ecu as a currency symbol, similar to USD, $, FF, DM, is "ECU" in capital letters. Thus, the amount of 100,000 ecus is symbolized by ECU 100,000. On the international foreign exchange markets, the currency abbreviation "XEU" connotes contracts in ecu-denomination (similar to "DEM" for the Deutsche Mark). The European Parliament unsuccessfully proposed the Greek letter "ϵ" as currency symbol for the ecu, similar to "$" for dollars. The final currency symbols and abbreviations will be established with the transformation of the ecu into the single EC currency. In view of the widespread use of the above terms, however, no significant changes should be necessary.

PART V.

A UNIT OF ACCOUNT OR A CURRENCY?

Is the ecu a unit of account, or is it a currency? There have been longstanding discussions about the true *nature* of the ecu. Some will claim the ecu is a currency because it is used as such to a degree rivaling the United States dollar in some segments of the private markets. Others, with equally valid arguments, will maintain that it is merely a unit of account because that, after all, is its only official function.

A. The Ecu as Unit of Account

Described in a rather simplistic way, a "unit of account" is a common denominator for transactions between parties who individually deal in different denominators and who agree to use such a common, specifically defined denominator. Such a unit of account is not a currency or legal tender. It has a certain value which is determined by the participating entities for themselves to transact business without having to engage in frequent currency exchanges.

The concept of establishing units of account to facilitate multi-currency transactions has a long standing tradition in Europe. Such units were first issued by the Bank of Venice in the 12th century. These *zecchino d'oro* enabled medieval merchants to engage in business all over Europe without exchanging their money into the respective local currencies. Instead, they would deposit their individual gold and silver coins with a bank which, in turn, would issue credit in the corresponding units of account. Other widely used units existed in Amsterdam and Hamburg in the 17th century.

The first unit of account used in the EC, namely in the European Payments Union (EPU), was circulated in 1950. Its value was 0.88867088 grams of fine gold, the gold value of one US dollar. A variety of other "units" with widely different bases existed in the framework of the European Economic Community. These included the "Unit of Account" of 1962, the "Farm Unit of Account", the statistical unit of account (EUR), the European Composite Unit (Eurco), the "European Monetary Unit of Account" and the "European Unit of Account" (EUA).

On April 21, 1975, the EC redefined the initially gold-based EUA as a "basket currency". The new EUA then closely resembled the Special Drawing Rights (SDR) still used by the International Monetary Fund. The ecu superseded the EUA in name only on March 13, 1979 as the old EUA-formula remained for the composition of the ecu. The ecu has now replaced the EUA and all preceding units and is the single unit of account in the EC.

EUA and ecu differ from all prior units in that they are not defined by their gold content but as baskets of currencies. In addition, the ecu now performs the functions of a "real" currency in official, private and commercial transactions. The predecessor units, on the other hand, only served as denominators for assets and liabilities which ultimately required settlement in the underlying national currencies.

The development of the ecu is inextricably bound to the founding of the EMS in 1979 (see page 47). The ecu is the center of the EMS and serves as its unit of account. It facilitates transactions in the EMS which otherwise would have to be denominated in the 12 currencies and would require exchange transactions. As explained below, the ecu is a unit of account for the participants in the EMS. Instead of using their individual currencies, those parties agreed to denominate their transactions in a set unit of account: the ecu. The basic idea and reason for the establishment of the ecu, therefore, was its use as a unit of account. The ecu clearly is such a unit but it has also developed further into a currency for certain segments of the private international markets.

B. The Ecu as Currency

"The international status of a currency cannot be decreed. It must be achieved."
Jacques Delors, 1987

The ecu has a very unusual status with regard to being a full currency (see page 158) which results from the generally accepted definitions of currencies. A currency has three non-physical functions: (i) it is a unit of account; (ii) a store of value; and (iii) a settlement medium. In addition, physical money in the form of bills and coins, making it legal tender in the issuing country, and a central bank which supervises the currency and serves as a lender of last resort are traditionally perceived characteristics of a currency. The lack of these latter characteristics, however, does not necessarily prevent a means of payment from being a full currency. Hong Kong, for example, does not have a central bank. The Hong Kong dollar nevertheless is a fully accepted currency.

When viewed in light of the three non-physical functions, the ecu is a full currency. It serves as a unit of account because different parties use the ecu as a denominator for transactions (see page 82). The EC actually created the ecu for that purpose in the EMS. The ecu is a store of value because it is used in the form of accounts, bonds, securities and other financial instruments (see page 86). is The ecu also a medium of settlement because it settles transactions between different parties through book transfers of money (see page 134).

With respect to the two additional characteristics, however, the ecu differs, at present, from the traditional currency definition. First, practically no bills or coins exist and the ecu is not yet legal tender in any country. Second, there is still no supervising central bank. Many experts and the general public perceive the existence of coins and notes as the most important feature of a currency, *i.e.*, a currency without such physical representation is, in their understanding, not a currency at all, because only such coins and notes can validly be tendered for the payments of private and public debts. This narrow *sine qua non* definition, however, overlooks an important aspect and function of modern currencies. Currency not only has the form of physical coins and notes. In fact, most money used in our systems is money in the form of non-physical account balances with commercial and central banks. In European countries, for example, the amount of physical money ranges from 35 percent in Germany to less than 8 percent in Great Britain. This means that between 65 and 92 percent of the money used in those countries is not in the form of coins and notes. Many transactions in modern society, such as cross-boundary payments, do not even lend themselves to the use of physical money anymore. Viewed from a practical standpoint, therefore, the fact that 100 percent of all ecu transactions are currently book transactions without physical money is more a "psychological" and academic barrier than an actual limitation on the ecu itself. These "psychological" shortfalls have had only limited impact on the private ecu in some market segments where it now is accepted as a currency.

However, there is some disagreement on the classifications of the ecu as a currency by the EC Member States and other governments and institutions (see page 158) despite the practical treatment of the ecu as such in some areas. One school of thought ascribes currency classification only to legal tender issued by governmental authorities - the two additional characteristics. Under this definition, the ecu clearly would not be a currency. The German Bundesbank, for example, has held in the past that the ecu lacks essential currency characteristics and, therefore, is not a currency under German law. Generally speaking, however, the broader definition which does not entail legal tender status is becoming more widely accepted. It is also closer to the economic and commercial realities which have ascribed all necessary currency functions to the ecu on the markets.

The ecu is by no means just a "European Folly" or an abstract unit of account without any practical value. It has secured itself a growing position in the international financial markets. From an investor's point of view, it fulfills all the functions of a true currency. As a result, it now stands in second place among the currencies in the international bond markets. It merely lacks the physical component associated with a real currency, namely coins and notes, and a country in which it is accepted as legal tender - both aspects will become reality with the introduction of the ecu as single EC currency as early as 1997. The ecu currently is a fully accepted and traded currency which is not legal tender in any nation. However important these two points appear to be to the international status of a currency, they have not had negative impacts on the use of the ecu. The markets have accepted the ecu as an international currency without any decrees by national or EC governments.

PART VI.

COMPOSITION AND FUNCTIONING

The discussions on the nature of the ecu as a unit of account or currency and the "right" answer on the categorization of the ecu aside, one very important question remains: What exactly is an ecu?

The reason for this question is the composition of the official ecu as a "basket of currencies". This composition is based on rather simple concepts most easily described by comparison with a traditional currency, the French franc. One franc equals . . . one franc. Its value is comprised of a certain amount of gold, foreign exchange reserves and other economic and political assets. Buyers and sellers of francs determine its value every day on the foreign exchange markets. In addition, the franc has a physical form in notes and coins issued as legal tender by the French authorities.

The official ecu, on the other hand, has an entirely different composition. It is "superimposed" over existing currencies to provide a common unit of account in the form of a basket comprised of 12 different currency amounts. Therefore, one ecu does not equal one ecu but the sum of those amounts (see page 48). Although the value of the official ecu indirectly is determined on the foreign exchange markets, its basket composition first requires the determination of the values of the participating currencies.

Figure VI.1: Determination of the Value of the Ecu and the French Franc

Foreign exchange markets determine the value of:

↓

The 12 currencies in the ecu basket

↓

Calculations (see below)

↓ ↓

1 ecu **1 franc**

At this point, the reader should be cautioned about the practical value of the following descriptions and calculations relating to the official ecu. As pointed out, the official ecu is the basis for the private ecu. If the EC had not created the ecu as a unit of account for the EMS, the private ecu would not have developed. In the beginning, both "ecus" had the same value which was calculated according to the basket composition of the official ecu in the manner shown below. However, in the meantime, the private ecu has taken on a life - and exchange and interest rates - of its own (see page 78) and its value now is determined in a manner similar to that of the franc as described above. The calculations of the official ecus which used to apply also to the private ecus have thus lost most of their significance to the user of the latter. The calculations nonetheless are valuable for a general understanding of the evolution of the ecu and some of its problems, as well as, of course, the official ecu itself. The following five steps describe the five calculations necessary for the understanding of the composition of the official ecu, for the calculation of its value and its use in the EMS mechanisms.

A. The Composition and Use of the Official Ecu: Five Calculations

(1) STEP 1: The Ecu is a basket comprised of fixed amounts of each EMS currency

The creators of the EMS faced a significant problem in that each Member State had a distinct currency. Operating with 12 individual currencies, the EMS would have had to engage in extensive exchange and re-exchange transactions. A common denominator was thought to be in the form of a "basket of currencies" which would make exchange transactions obsolete because all parties would deal in the same medium. The "basket"-form ensures that all currencies have an equitable share in the denominator and no single currency is relatively favored in EMS transactions (actually, the ecu is not widely used in the EMS because the Deutsche Mark is the most favored currency for these transactions). The amounts of the individual currencies in the basket are changed infrequently in "recompositions" to accommodate economic changes or to add new currencies to the basket (see page 57). The currencies of all 12 Member States now are included in the ecu basket. Since the last recomposition on September 21, 1989, this basket contains:

Table VI.1: Amount of Each EMS Currency in the Ecu Basket

0.08784	British Pound
0.1976	Danish Krone
1.332	French Francs
1.44	Greek Drachma
0.008552	Irish Pound
151.8	Italian Lira
0.2198	Dutch Guilder
0.6242	German mark
3.301	Belgian Franc
0.13	Luxembourg Franc
6.885	Spanish Peseta
1.393	Portuguese Escudo

Source: EC Commission

(2) STEP 2: The value of one official ecu equals the sum of the currency amounts

Table VI.1 alone does not determine the value of one ecu since simply adding the 12 currency amounts would be like adding "apples and oranges". Therefore, the value of the official ecu must be expressed in terms of a third currency. This is best explained with the above franc-ecu example.

The value of the franc, as determined on the foreign exchange markets, equals . . . the value of the franc. That value depends on many economic and political factors, but it is established directly by the supply and demand mechanisms. In the case of the ecu, the foreign exchange markets will first determine the value of the underlying 12 currencies in a certain third currency and then translate those 12 "sub-values" into the value of the ecu. Apart from this intermediary step, the procedures for French franc and ecu are the same. This, however, means that the ecu does not have an independent value *per se*. One ecu does not equal . . . one ecu directly. This process will change as soon as the ecu is transformed into the single currency for the EC and the national currencies are abolished. To a certain degree, the private ecu already has developed its own exchange rate independent from the rate determined through the basket (see page 78).

The equivalent of the ecu in a third currency equals the sum of the equivalents of the 12 currency amounts in that third currency. For example, to find the corresponding value of the ecu in dollars, the amounts in Table VI.1 must be multiplied by the dollar value of each EMS currency and added together. The EC Commission in Brussels uses this method to determine the *official* value of the ecu each day at 2:15 pm (see Appendix A). It calculates the dollar value for each currency amount in the ecu and adds the values. The official rate is used in the operations of the EMS and for official EC transactions. The Commission publishes the official rates daily in the *Official Journal of the European Communities* for all EC and a number of non-EC currencies, such as the US, Canadian, Australian and New Zealand dollars, the Japanese yen and the Swiss franc.

One important aspect of the daily official rates must be kept in mind. These rates only reflect the official value of the ecu at a certain, arbitrarily chosen point of time (2:15 pm Brussels time). The value of the private ecu (as far as it still is determined in this manner) at a point of time depends on the corresponding exchange rates of the underlying currencies at that very moment. It will vary according to the market forces of supply and demand for any of the currencies.

The following is an example, for the calculation of the dollar value of the ecu. The exchange rates used are of the end of the fictitious "Day X" and not the official rates at 2:15 pm.

Table VI.2: Exchange Rates of the EMS Currencies

One British Pound costs	$1.644
One Danish Krone costs	$0.1508
One French Franc costs	$0.17173
One Greek Drachma costs	$0.006266
One Irish Pound costs	$1.5525
One Italian Lira costs	$0.0007842
One Dutch Guilder costs	$0.5183
One German mark costs	$0.5834
One Belgian Franc costs	$0.02791
One Luxembourg Franc costs	$0.02791
One Spanish Peseta costs	$0.009042
One Portuguese Escudo costs	$0.00666

To find the dollar-value of each currency *amount* in one ecu for Day X, the values of Table VI.1 must be multiplied with those in Table VI.2:

Table VI.3: Calculation I

	Table I X Amount	Table II Currency in $	=	Result I $ per amount
Pound	0.08784	$1.644		$0.144409
Krone	0.1976	$0.1508		$0.029798
Franc (F)	1.332	$0.17173		$0.228744
Drachma	1.44	$0.006266		$0.009023
Pound (Ir)	0.008552	$1.5525		$0.013277
Lira	151.8	$0.0007842		$0.119042
Guilder	0.2198	$0.5183		$0.113922
Mark	0.6242	$0.5834		$0.364158
Franc (B)	3.301	$0.02791		$0.092131
Franc (Lx)	0.13	$0.02791		$0.003628
Peseta	6.885	$0.009042		$0.062254
Escudo	1.393	$0.00666		$0.009277
		TOTAL I		$1.189663

The total of $1.189663 is the actual value of one ecu in dollars at the end of Day X. In comparison, it the official rate should be $1.19674 at 2:15 pm Brussels time on Day X, the difference would show that the official value is frozen at that certain point in time.

(3) STEP 3: The actual value can now be expressed in terms of each EMS currency

The next calculation determines the actual value of one ecu in terms of each of the component currencies. To determine this actual value, the total value of the ecu in dollars -- or Total I in Table VI.3 -- is divided by the value of each currency in dollars -- or Table VI.2. The Commission determines these values with the help of the official ecu and dollar exchange rates (see Steps 1 and 2).

Table VI.4: Calculation II

	Total (Calculation I) One Ecu in $	Table II = Currency in $	Result II Ecu in Currency
Pound	1.189663	$1.644	0.7236392
Krone	1.189663	$0.1508	7.8890119
Franc (F)	1.189663	$0.17173	6.9275199
Drachma	1.189663	$0.006266	189.86003
Pound (Ir)	1.189663	$1.5525	0.7662885
Lira	1.189663	$0.0007842	1517.0402
Guilder	1.189663	$0.5183	2.2953173
Mark	1.189663	$0.5834	2.0391892
Franc (B)	1.189663	$0.02791	42.624973
Franc (Lx)	1.189663	$0.02791	42.624973
Peseta	1.189663	$0.009042	131.57078
Escudo	1.189663	$0.00666	178.62807

In a perfect world, these values would equal the central rates fixed for the purposes of the EMS parity grid as described in Step 5 (see page 55). The actual values on any given day, however, depend on the forces of supply and demand on the foreign exchange markets because, in reality, the dollar exchange rates for each currency fluctuate. For example, on Day X, one ecu was worth $1.189663, one German mark (DM) was worth $0.5834, and thus the actual value of one ecu in German marks was DM2.0391892 for that day. By comparison, the fixed central rate of the German mark in the EMS parity grid is set at DM2.04446. The fixed rate is the "perfect" rate from which the actual rate may deviate by 2.25 percent (6 percent for the peseta, the pound and the escudo) (see page 56).

The actual value of the ecu in terms of the EMS currencies is used for two additional calculations: the relative weight of each currency in the basket (Step 4) and, as outlined above, the divergence of each currency from the fixed central rates in the EMS parity system (Step 5).

(4) STEP 4: The relative weight of each currency in the Ecu basket

The relative weight of each currency in the ecu basket, calculated daily, reflects the relative economic strength of the EC countries and their share in intra-community trade. The greater the weight of a currency, the greater the economic importance of the respective country in the EC. The relative weight of a currency in the basket is determined by dividing the amount of the currency in the basket (Table VI.1) by the actual value of the ecu in terms of that currency (Results II from Table VI.4):

Table VI.5: Calculation III

	Table I Amount	/	Results II Actual Value	=	Weight in % of the basket
Pound	1.189663		0.7236392		12.14
Krone	1.189663		7.8890119		2.50
Franc (F)	1.189663		6.9275199		19.23
Drachma	1.189663		189.86003		0.76
Pound (Ir)	1.189663		0.7662885		1.12
Lira	1.189663		1517.0402		10.01
Guilder	1.189663		2.2953173		9.58
Mark	1.189663		2.0391892		30.61
Franc (B)	1.189663		42.624973		7.74
Franc (Lx)	1.189663		42.624973		0.30
Peseta	1.189663		131.57078		5.23
Escudo	1.189663		178.62807		0.78

Changes in the weights result from two different types of developments. First, they occur when the dollar exchange rate of a currency changes (Table VI.2). As outlined in Step 3, the dollar values of the EMS currencies are used to calculate the ecu value in terms of each currency. That ecu value is then used to calculate the weight in Step 4. Any changes in the dollar exchange value will influence the calculation in Step 3 which then influences the weight in Step 4. The depreciation of a currency against the dollar decreases and the appreciation increases the weight of the currency in the ecu basket. Second, changes in the weights result when the shares of a currency are changed in a recomposition of the ecu basket (see page 57).

For example, a depreciation of the exchange rate of the pound from $1.644 to $1.300, would influence the following calculations:

(a) The value of the ecu in dollars (Calculation I);
(b) The value of the ecu in pounds (Calculation II); and
(c) The weight of the pound in the ecu-basket (Calculation III).

This change would result in the following new values:

(a) Calculation I
0.08784 x 1.3000 = 0.114192
This changes the dollar value of the ecu to $1.159446.

(b) Calculation II
1.159446/1.3000 = 0.8918815 pound per ecu.

(c) Calculation III
0.08784/0.8918815 = 9.85 percent

Thus, the decrease of the pound in relation to the dollar decreases the weight of the pound in the ecu-basket from 12.14 percent to 9.85 percent.

Figure VI.2: Currency Weights in the Ecu Basket (January 7, 1990)

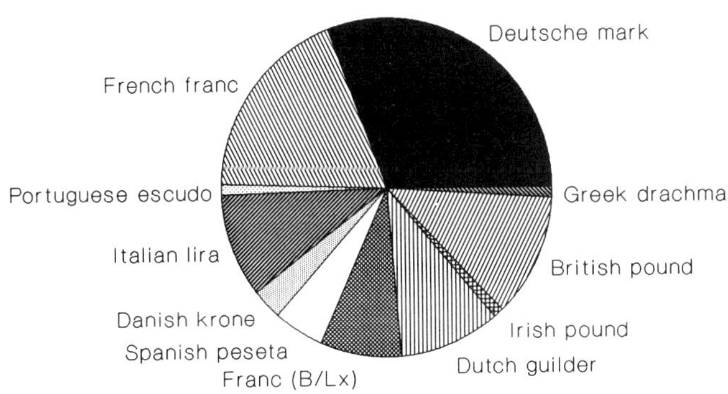

Source: EC Commission

Table VI.6: Changes in the Weights of the EMS Currencies (on realignment and recomposition dates)

	03/13/79	09/24/79	11/30/79	03/23/81	10/05/81
Mark	33.0	33.3	33.4	32.5	34.4
FFranc	19.8	19.7	19.7	19.2	18.6
UKL	13.6	13.6	13.6	16.3	14.7
Guilder	10.5	10.5	10.4	10.2	10.7
BFr/LFr	9.5	9.5	9.6	9.3	9.3
Lira	9.5	9.4	9.4	8.6	8.4
Krone	3.0	3.0	2.8	2.8	2.8
IrL	1.1	1.1	1.1	1.1	1.1

	02/22/82	06/14/82	03/21/83	05/18/83	09/17/84
Mark	34.2	35.5	37.38	36.93	32.70
FFranc	18.6	17.4	16.93	16.73	19.06
UKL	15.9	15.8	14.05	15.07	14.98
Guilder	10.7	11.1	11.46	11.32	10.13
BFr/LFr	8.5	8.5	8.57	8.46	8.57
Lira	8.4	8.1	7.86	7.77	9.98
Krone	2.7	2.6	2.70	2.67	2.69
IrL	1.1	1.1	1.06	1.05	1.20
Drachma					1.31

	7/22/85	4/02/86	8/04/86	1/12/87	9/21/89	1/7/90
Mark	32.12	33.62	34.06	34.93	30.10	30.53
FFranc	19.09	18.81	19.06	18.97	19.00	19.43
UKL	15.81	13.93	12.93	11.87	13.00	12.06
Guilder	10.15	10.63	10.76	11.04	9.40	9.54
BFr/LFr	8.59	8.81	8.93	9.07	7.90	8.14
Lira	9.21	9.36	9.48	9.44	10.15	9.92
Krone	2.69	2.77	2.80	2.79	2.45	2.53
IrL	1.20	1.22	1.14	1.13	1.10	1.12
Drach.	1.14	0.85	0.84	0.76	0.80	0.77
Peseta					5.30	5.18
Escudo					0.80	0.78

Source: EC Commission

(5) STEP 5: The ecu in the EMS parity grid

The last calculation pertains to the use of the ecu in the EMS parity grid. As outlined above, the Commission fixes the central rates in ecus for each EMS currency. These rates represent the fixed values of one ecu in each currency and are somewhat similar to the actual values calculated in Step 3. The rates are adjusted occasionally in "realignments" to represent changed economic conditions (see page 57). The drachma is assigned a "notional central rate" because it does not participate yet in the ERM. Therefore, it does not need a central rate which is used only in the parity grid.

Table VI.7: Central Rates in the EMS

Pound	0.696904
Krone	7.84195
France (F)	6.89509
Drachma	205.311 (notional)
Pound (Ir)	0.767417
Lira	1538.24
Guilder	2.31643
Mark	2.05586
Franc (B)	42.4032
Franc (Lx)	42.4032
Peseta	133.631
Escudo	178.735

Source: EC Commission

With these central rates, a parity grid is established in which the bilateral central *exchange* rates of each currency against each other currency and the fluctuation margins of 2.25 and 6 percent are fixed. The grid is used to determine whether members must engage in intervention mechanisms (see page 28).

The following parity grid was established with the accession of the Portuguese escudo to the ERM on April 6, 1992. It shows the exchange rates in ecus of any two of the EMS currencies against each other.

Table VI.8: EMS Parity Grid - Bilateral Central Rates of the Ecu

	BFranc 42.4032	DKrone 7.84195	DMark 2.05586	Peseta 133.631	FFranc 6.89509	IrPound .767417	Lira 1538.24	Guilder 2.31643	UKPound .696904	Peseta 178.735
BFranc 42.4032	1	5.40723	20.6255	.317316	6.14977	55.2545	.027566	18.3054	60.8451	.237241
DKrone 7.84195	.184938	1	3.81444	.058684	1.13732	10.2186	.005098	3.38536	11.2526	.043875
DMark 2.05586	.048484	.262162	1	.015385	.298163	2.67893	.001337	.887512	2.94999	.011502
Peseta 133.631	3.15144	17.0405	65.0000	1	19.3807	174.131	.086873	57.6883	191.750	.747649
FFranc 6.89509	.162608	.879257	3.35387	.051598	1	8.98480	.004482	2.97660	9.89389	.038577
IrPound .767417	.018098	.097860	.373283	.005743	.111299	1	.000499	.331293	1.10118	.004294
Lira 1538.24	36.2765	196.155	748.222	11.5111	223.092	2004.44	1	664.056	2207.25	8.60626
Guilder 2.31643	.054629	.295390	1.12675	.017335	.335954	3.01848	.001506	1	3.32389	.012960
UKPound .696904	.016435	.088869	.338984	.005215	.101073	.908116	.000453	.300853	1	.003899
Escudo 178.735	4.21513	22.7922	86.9393	1.33753	25.9220	232.905	.116194	77.1597	256.470	1

Source: EC Commission

The parity grid is derived by dividing the value of one ecu in terms of each currency by the corresponding value of each other currency, that is, by dividing the above fixed central rates by each other. For example, 42.4032 Belgian francs per ecu divided by 2.31643 Dutch guilders per ecu equal a bilateral central exchange rate between franc and guilder of 18.3054 francs per 1 guilder, or 0.0546286 guilder per 1 franc. These are considered to be the "perfect" exchange rates between the two currencies. However, as this is not a perfect world, fixed fluctuation margins of 2.25 percent - 6 percent for the peseta, the pound and the escudo - are set around the central exchange rates.

The official rates, as calculated in Step 3 above, must fall between the bilateral central exchange rates and the outer margins. Should the official rates fall outside these margins, the corresponding central banks must intervene. In the franc-guilder example, the currencies may move between 17.8985 and 18.7215 before interventions by the Belgian and Dutch central banks become mandatory. The drachma does not participate in the exchange rate mechanism and its notional central rate is 205.311.

B. Changes in the Composition of the Ecu Basket: Recompositions

Until the decision of the EC Member States to establish the ecu as single EC currency, the ecu was an "open" basket of currencies. This means that the composition of the ecu (the shares of each currency in the basket) could be revised. Recompositions essentially were changes in the fixed currency amounts (weights) in the ecu basket (see page 51). They normally took place in five year intervals. As an extraordinary measure, a Member State whose currency's weight in the ecu had changed by more than 25 percent could also request such a re-examination. The latter type of recomposition, however, was never used.

Recompositions became necessary to compensate for shifts in the relative strength of the individual EC economies and to include new currencies in the basket. Changes in the individual strength of the economies were reflected in corresponding changes in the individual exchange rates. To compensate for such changes, the ecu composition had to be changed.

The EC Council of Ministers determined the new weights for the currencies with the following criteria:

(a) the relative share of the individual Member States in the GDP of the EC; and

(b) the contribution of each Member State to the intra-EC trade; and

(c) the quota of each Member State in the short-term credit mechanism of the EMS.

The EC Council of Ministers apparently also used other non-disclosed, and possibly more political, criteria in its negotiations, which generally made the outcome of the recompositions an unknown factor. This uncertainty resulted in a relative sensitivity of the markets prior to the recomposition dates.

Recompositions, by requirement, could not change the external spot value of the ecu because they were based on changes in the percentage weight of each currency. Thus, although the individual weights of the currencies would change, the total basket always would remain at 100 percent permitting alterations in the weights without disturbing the overnight spot value. This non-disturbing effect of the recomposition could not be explained, however, by the definition of the recomposition process alone. The fact that the ecu markets could normally anticipate the occurrence of such recompositions and, consequently, take possible changes into account even before the actual date probably was the single most important factor responsible for the relative smoothness of this process. Although the overnight value of the ecu would not change, the value would have accounted for such changes in the months before the recomposition when the market participants had sufficient time slowly to adjust their positions.

The weights of the currencies were first examined in September 1979 and no changes were made. The EC revised the basket again on September 17, 1984. At that time, all currencies except the Luxembourg franc were adjusted to represent more accurately the shares of the Member States in the economy of the EC. In the last recomposition on September 21, 1989, all currencies except the pound were adjusted.

The EC also changed the composition to add new currencies to the ecu basket because each Member State had the right to have its currency included in the ecu (this right was revoked in the recent Maastricht Treaty as no currency will be permitted to join before the transformation even if the EC were enlarged). The Greek drachma was incorporated into the basket in September 1984 and the Portuguese escudo and the Spanish peseta in the last recomposition in 1989. Inclusion in the basket does not entail automatic participation in the Exchange Rate Mechanisms of the EMS. The drachma, and until very recently the escudo and the British pound, does not participate in the ERM although it is part of the basket.

Table VI.9: Recompositions of the Ecu Basket

Currency	3/13/79	9/17/84	%-Change	9/21/89	%-Change
British Pound	0.0885	0.0878	- 0.8	0.08784	no change
Danish Krone	0.217	0.219	+ 0.9	0.1976	- 9.78
French Franc	1.15	1.31	+13.9	1.332	+ 1.68
Greek Drachma		1.15	added	1.440	+25.22
Irish Pound	0.00759	0.00871	+14.8	0.008552	- 1.70
Italian Lira	109.0	140.0	+28.4	151.8	+ 8.43
Dutch Guilder	0.286	0.256	-10.5	0.2198	-14.14
German mark	0.828	0.719	-13.2	0.6242	-13.18
Belgian Franc	3.66	3.71	+ 1.4	3.301	-11.03
Luxemb. Franc	0.14	0.14	no change	0.13	- 7.14
Spanish Peseta				6.885	added
Portuguese Escudo				1.393	added

Source: EC Commission

The Maastricht Treaty on the EMU provides that the currency composition of the ecu basket will not be changed. This means that the 1989-recomposition was the last revision of the ecu basket. Once the ecu has become the single EC currency it will, of course, automatically lose its basket status and become a "normal" currency. The decision to freeze the ecu basket at this point will be very advantageous for the development of the ecu in the interim period. Ecu users are now assured of the composition and will not be concerned about a revision and its unknown - and possibly detrimental - outcome. *De facto* the ecu has thereby gone one big step further toward becoming a full currency by any definition.

PART VII.

STABILITY OF THE ECU

The previous chapters dealt with the background and the technical aspects of the ecu. They examined the aspects of the ecu which are of least practical import for a business but are of great importance to the general understanding of the role of the ecu. The following chapters review the more practical applications of the ecu and its use for official, and more importantly, for private purposes. This chapter on the stability of the ecu links the technical and the more practical aspects. This stability is its most tangible advantage over other currencies and explains why it has developed so quickly from a mere unit of account to a full currency.

The relative exchange rate stability of the ecu results from its composition as a basket currency. This composition decreases variability because a total of 24 variables influence the final value. The 12 currency amounts, on the one hand, are fixed by agreement among the EC Member States. The 12 exchange rates, on the other hand, depend on the supply and demand situation on the foreign exchange markets. This composition distinguishes the determination of the value of the ecu from that of any other currency. Provided that such other currency is freely traded, its exchange rates against other currencies depend on supply and demand on the markets. The exchange value of the ecu, in contrast, depends on 12 such situations in addition to the 12 different amounts (see page 46). This means that the value of the ecu will be much less influenced by the supply and demand forces of any *single* one of its component currencies toward a third currency. As a simplified example, the price of the yen in dollars is determined by the supply and demand for the two currencies. There are no other variables. The price of the ecu, in contrast, results from 12 similar supply and demand situations for each of the 12 currencies toward the dollar, the degree of impact of each depends on the amounts in the basket.

The following Table VII.1 shows the monthly variability of certain currencies toward the EMS currencies. In the case of the EMS currencies, except for the Greek drachma, the variability was significantly reduced as result of the EMS mechanisms.

Table VII.1: Monthly Variability of Exchange Rates against EMS Currencies

	Franc (B/Lx)	Krone (Den)	Mark (G)	Franc (Fr)	Pound (Ir)	Lira (It)	Guilder (Neth)	Pound (UK)	Drachma (Gr)	Peseta (Sp)	Escudo (Por)	Dollar (USA)	Yen (Jpn)	Franc (Swi)
1974	0.83	0.64	1.37	1.53	0.78	1.69	0.48	0.71	1.93	1.65	0.49	1.93	1.42	1.70
1975	0.38	0.32	0.54	0.79	1.10	0.80	0.36	1.05	1.81	1.13	0.56	1.89	1.47	0.77
1976	0.85	0.68	1.57	1.23	2.21	3.34	0.77	2.10	0.73	1.08	1.17	0.68	1.11	1.14
1977	0.44	0.81	0.76	0.47	0.96	0.95	0.42	0.90	0.40	2.06	2.41	0.85	1.61	1.51
1978	0.69	0.57	0.77	1.40	1.38	1.03	0.58	1.32	1.82	0.79	2.08	1.84	2.50	2.87
74-78	**0.64**	**0.60**	**1.00**	**1.08**	**1.29**	**1.56**	**0.52**	**1.22**	**1.34**	**1.34**	**1.34**	**1.44**	**1.62**	**1.60**
1979	0.30	0.93	0.37	0.23	0.50	0.64	0.32	1.72	0.96	1.51	1.07	1.13	2.20	0.64
1980	0.19	0.24	0.21	0.26	0.29	0.44	0.20	1.61	1.85	1.17	1.28	2.27	2.89	0.90
1981	0.34	0.30	0.67	0.65	0.29	0.86	0.46	2.39	0.36	0.67	0.98	3.14	2.93	1.57
1982	0.98	0.49	0.73	0.76	0.46	0.46	0.61	1.44	0.91	1.48	1.79	2.49	1.22	1.00
1983	0.24	0.37	0.51	0.50	0.38	0.48	0.18	1.99	2.55	0.98	2.16	1.89	1.64	1.18
79-83	**0.41**	**0.47**	**0.50**	**0.48**	**0.38**	**0.58**	**0.35**	**1.83**	**1.33**	**1.16**	**1.46**	**2.18**	**2.18**	**1.06**
1984	0.22	0.30	0.24	0.08	0.22	0.46	0.10	1.06	1.31	0.77	1.25	2.70	1.62	0.83
1985	0.16	0.15	0.32	0.24	0.20	0.88	0.24	2.04	2.91	0.84	1.29	3.06	1.84	0.93
1986	0.21	0.37	0.31	0.54	1.08	0.15	0.21	2.39	1.22	0.62	1.12	2.07	1.92	1.01
1987	0.18	0.38	0.27	0.27	0.24	0.46	0.21	0.94	0.81	1.05	0.71	2.20	1.64	0.70
1988	0.10	0.26	0.15	0.24	0.16	0.29	0.16	1.18	0.43	0.67	0.23	2.03	1.18	0.44
84-88	**0.17**	**0.29**	**0.26**	**0.27**	**0.38**	**0.45**	**0.18**	**1.52**	**1.34**	**0.79**	**0.92**	**2.41**	**1.64**	**0.78**

Source: EC Commission

Figure VII.1 shows the average annual exchange rates of the Deutsche Mark against the ecu and the US dollar. It clearly shows that the DM/ECU rate is much less volatile than the DM/$ rate. As a result, a German exporter would prefer to use th ecu which has a much lower exchange risk.

Figure VII.1: Exchange Rate of the Deutsche Mark

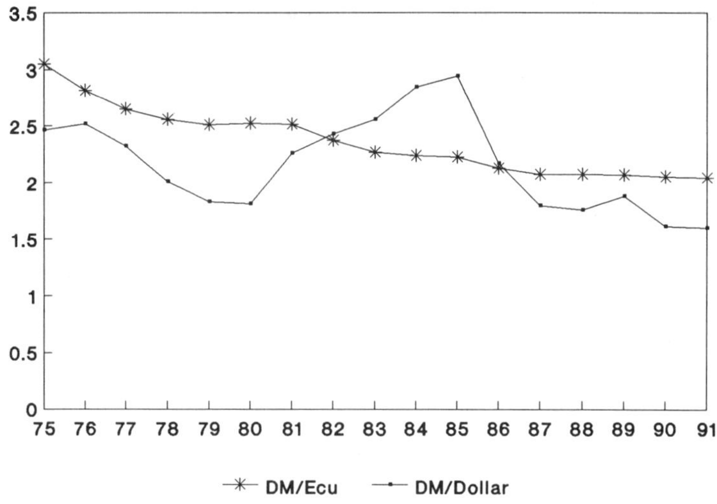

Source: Deutsche Bundesbank

The exchange rate stability of the ecu is reinforced by the somewhat modified negative correlations among the EMS currencies. Although it would be incorrect to assume, for example, that whenever the pound depreciates toward a currency, the mark appreciates against that same currency, some of the EMS currencies very often show opposite exchange rate fluctuations. The latter premise is based on a variety of factors. These include the number of currencies included in the basket, the traditional exchange fluctuations of the individual currencies, differing market interventions by the national authorities, the degree of speculation in the national markets and differences in the economic performance of the individual economies.

Figure VII.2 shows the average annual exchange rates of the ecu and the Deutsche Mark against the dollar. The graph clearly shows that the ECU/$ rate is less volatile than the ECU/$ rate. Again, a German exporter would prefer the ecu which is more stable toward the dollar than the mark.

Figure VII.2: Dollar Rates of the Ecu and the Mark

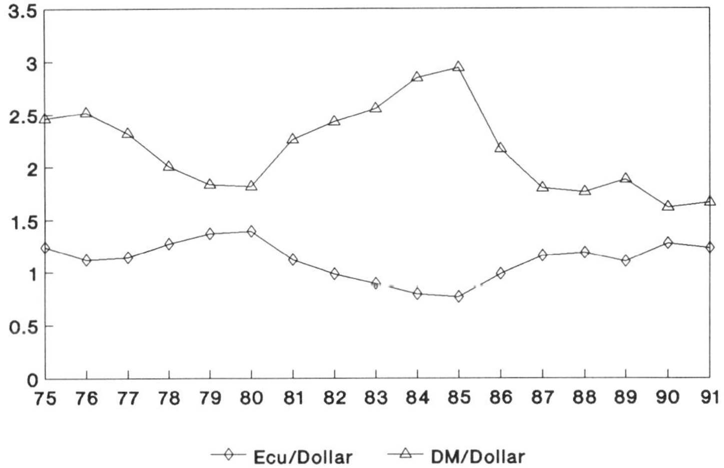

Source: Deutsche Bundesbank

This relative stability is important for investors and businesses interested in using the ecu. It will assist in curbing excessive exchange rate fluctuations and related losses. The following theoretical examples emphasize these reduced fluctuations and losses:

> The German mark accounts for approximately one third of the total ecu basket. If the mark depreciates 10 percent against the dollar, an American investor who purchased at par a security with a DM100 nominal value would lose 10 percent of its dollar value. Using the rates of Day X (see page 49), the investor would have paid \$58.34 (\$0.5834 per mark) for the DM 100-investment before the depreciation. After the depreciation, the investor would receive only \$52.51 if he sold the security and exchanged the DM100 to dollars: loss of \$5.83 or 10 percent.
>
> Had the investor bought an ecu-denominated security, the loss would be approximately be one third of the above 10 percent loss because only one third of the ecu is based on the mark. Using the Day X rates, the investor would have paid \$118.97 for an ECU 100-security. A 10 percent depreciation of the mark

to $0.5251 would result in a $0.0364 decrease in the value of the ecu (to $1.153272). As shown in the following Table VII.2, the amount of the mark in the ecu (0.6242) would then only be worth $2.327767 at an exchange rate of $0.5251 which would decrease the total value of the ecu to $1.153272.

Table VII.2: Calculation IB

	Table I X Amount	Table II = Currency in $	Result I $ per amount
Pound	0.08784	$1.644	$0.144409
Krone	0.1976	$0.1508	$0.029798
Franc (F)	1.332	$0.17173	$0.228744
Drachma	1.44	$0.006266	$0.009023
Pound (Ir)	0.008552	$1.5525	$0.013277
Lira	151.8	$0.0007842	$0.119042
Guilder	0.2198	$0.5183	$0.113922
Mark	0.6242	$0.5251	$0.327767
Franc (B)	3.301	$0.02791	$0.092131
Franc (Lx)	0.13	$0.02791	$0.003628
Peseta	6.885	$0.009042	$0.062254
Escudo	1.393	$0.00666	$0.009277
TOTAL			**$1.153272**

This $3.64 decrease in the value of the ECU 100-security (to $115.33) is a 3.056 percent loss on the investment.

The above calculation will apply as long as the exchange rates of all other currencies against the dollar remain unchanged. If, however, the pound and the French franc (with a combined weight of approximately 30 percent) each simultaneously appreciated by 10 percent against the dollar, the value of the investment would essentially remain constant. As above, the investor would pay $118.97 for the ECU 100-security. The mark would depreciate to $0.5251. However, with the appreciation of the French franc to $0.1889 and the pound to $1.8084, the resulting value of the ecu would be $1.1905836 as shown in Table VII.3. This difference of $0.00092 represents a position change of only +0.078 percent.

Table VII.3: Calculation IC

	Table I X Amount	Table II Currency in $	=	Result I $ per amount
Pound	0.08784	$1.8084		$0.1588498
Krone	0.1976	$0.1508		$0.029798
Franc (F)	1.332	$0.1889		$0.2516148
Drachma	1.44	$0.006266		$0.009023
Pound (Ir)	0.008552	$1.5525		$0.013277
Lira	151.8	$0.0007842		$0.119042
Guilder	0.2198	$0.5183		$0.113922
Mark	0.6242	$0.5251		$0.327767
Franc (B)	3.301	$0.02791		$0.092131
Franc (Lx)	0.13	$0.02791		$0.003628
Peseta	6.885	$0.009042		$0.062254
Escudo	1.393	$0.00666		$0.009277
TOTAL				$1.1905836

Investments denominated in ecu, of course, could appreciate or depreciate if the majority weight of the currencies in the ecu basket would appreciate or depreciate toward a certain currency. In the above example, one third weight of the currencies appreciated while one third of the currencies depreciated. If, in contrast, one quarter weight of the currencies appreciated and one half of the currencies depreciated, the value of the ecu would, of course, depreciate overall.

In essence, the ecu basket composition permits the weighted "averaging out" of appreciations and depreciations. The ecu, therefore, always will be useful for entities whose individual currencies appreciate or depreciate more than the average depreciation or appreciation of the ecu. For example, if currency A and currency B each constituted 25 percent of the ecu basket and currency A would depreciate by 10 percent and currency B by 5 percent, then the ecu itself would depreciate 7.5 percent. In this case, the user of currency A should use the ecu because it depreciates less (7.5 percent) than its currency A (10 percent).

Figure VII.3: Currency Weights in the Ecu Basket

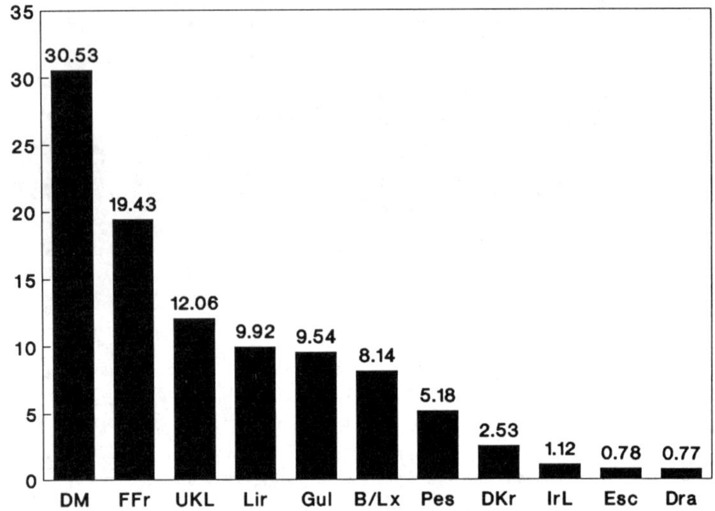

Source: EC Commission

The above description presupposes that only changes occur which pertain to the foreign exchange value of the EC currencies towards the third currency. Changes in those rates will directly affect the value of the ecu. As a result of the basket composition of the ecu, however, changes in the value of the ecu *theoretically* could also result in the past from changes of the composition of the ecu basket in the past which altered the relative weights of the currencies in the basket. In theory, recompositions, by definition, could not change the external spot value of the ecu because they were based on changes in the percentage weight of each currency. Thus, although the individual weight of a currency changed, the total basket always remained at 100 percent permitting alterations in the weights without disturbing the spot value. The change in weights, however, had an indirect impact on the exchange rate *behavior* of the ecu. The overall influence of an appreciation or depreciation of an individual currency on the total value would shift in the case of a recomposition because the relative value would change. The relative weight of a currency impacts the influence of its appreciation or depreciation on the ecu. If, for example, the German mark had a weight of 20 percent, its depreciation of 10 percent would lower the value of the ecu by 2 percent (20 percent of the 10 percent depreciation). If it had a new weight of 50 percent, the value would decrease by 5 percent (i.e., 50 percent of the 10 percent depreciation).

As recompositions changed the weights of the individual currencies in the ecu, the theoretical interest rates calculated for ecu-denominated instruments also would change (see page 93). This rate is close to the average calculated with the weight of the individual currencies. A change in a weight, therefore, would also change the impact of the individual interest rates on that for the ecu. This change in interest rates, in turn, affected the *forward* value of the ecu. The difference between the spot and the forward values takes into account the interest rate for the ecu. A change in that rate will change the forward value proportionally.

The actual effect of a recomposition on the interest rates, however, was always difficult to estimate because the future weights of the individual currencies were not known before a recomposition, because the calculation of the ecu yields became more and more independent from the calculated rates, and because the markets usually took into account the effects of recompositions in advance. In the last recomposition in September 1989, for example, the effect was negligible in part because the financial markets anticipated the recomposition and in part because the EC Commission had already announced the new weights for September 1989 in June of the same year. This gave the markets participants sufficient time to adjust their positions on the forward markets. The concerns related to the impact of recompositions on the exchange and interest notes of the ecu have been alleviated with the Maastricht Treaty which freezes the composition to its current basket. No more recompositions will take place before the transformation of the ecu into the single EC currency.

The relative stability of the ecu with regard to its exchange rates is the result of its basket composition. This stability is an important advantage over other currencies as it gives investors a higher degree of security and predictability. However, two important facts must be kept in mind in this respect. First, with the transformation of the ecu into the single EC currency, this basket-composition will disappear. The ecu will become a "normal" currency, such as the dollar and the yen, whose exchange rates will be determined by supply and demand on the foreign exchange markets. It is, of course, not known whether the ecu will remain a highly stable or will become a more fluctuating currency. However, past experiences indicate that the ecu will be a rather stable currency in the future. The value of the private ecu has already become somewhat independent from that of the official ecu basket (see page 78). This means that the factors inducing stability, namely the 24 variables, have lost some importance. However, these differences are only minimal. Their small degree might indicate that the market regards the ecu as stable even without the basket-composition.

PART VIII.

OFFICIAL USE

The ecu has a "split personality" with regard to its uses and users. One the one hand, it has an official role as unit of account in the EMS and transactional currency for certain European and non-European monetary authorities and institutions. On the other hand, it is a non-official private currency for numerous private users.

The private ecus are linked to the official ecus merely by the fact that they have the same composition. The European Monetary Cooperation Fund (EMCF) only creates official ecus which are used for transactions between the monetary authorities and the various institutions. No private ecus are created by central monetary authorities. This chapter will only deal with the creation of official ecus and their use by the monetary authorities and institutions. These official ecus are of very limited practical use to private parties.

A. The Creation of Official Ecus

Currently the European Monetary Cooperation Fund (EMCF) creates the official ecus. As the EMCF is not the central bank for the EC, the establishment of the EC central bank with the power to issue legal tender will render the following procedures obsolete.

The EC central banks deposit 20 percent of their dollar and gold reserves with the EMCF which, in turn, credits the banks with the corresponding amount of ecus. For this purpose, the EMCF values the dollar reserves and the gold contributions at certain fixed dates before the contribution. Contributions are based on a system of three-month revolving swap transactions, in which the banks receive the ecus and simultaneously sell them back to the EMCF under forward contracts with maturities of three months for the same amount of gold and dollars. The revolving swaps ensure that there will be no gap in the supply of official ecus. If a time-gap between the swaps existed, no ecu could be issued by the EMCF between swaps because no deposits would be available during that time. The swaps also permit adjustments which might be necessary because of changed gold and dollar reserves. More importantly, the swap structure of these contributions has a more "political" reason. At the time the EMCF was established, the EC Member States did not intend to create an EC central bank as a federal entity and to transfer monetary powers from their individual national monetary distribution. The final and irrevocable transfer of these reserves would have conveyed a quasi-central bank status to the EMCF. The revolving swap arrangement, on the other hand, emphasizes the non-final nature of the transfers and the understanding that the EMCF is not considered a central bank.

B. The Official Uses of the Ecu

In the beginning, the EC explicitly restricted the entities permitted to use ecu to the national monetary authorities and the EC institutions. In an effort to enhance the ecu, it expanded the number of entities empowered to use ecus in 1985. Non-EC monetary authorities and international monetary institutions may now be granted the status of "other holder" and acquire, hold and use official ecus.

Despite the rapid growth of the private ecu markets, private parties such as commercial banks, financial institutions, individuals and corporations cannot use the official ecu. That use is limited to the entities granted special status by the EC. Private parties only can use private ecu which are created by the commercial banks. As long as permission to use official ecu is not granted to those private parties, there will be a difference between the official and the private ecu. A link between those two would change the role of the ecu from a unit of account for private parties to a legally accepted unit for transactions: an official currency. As an economic reality, those private parties use the privately-created ecu to a degree which over shadows its official uses (a distinction which, of course, will disappear with the transformation of the ecu into the single EC currency).

The initial functions of the ecu are part of its role in the EMS. It is the means of settlement for the EC monetary authorities. It is the denominator for the Exchange Rate Mechanisms and for operations under the EMS credit mechanisms. It serves as the basis for the divergence indicator (see page 27). The ecu still performs these functions. However, additional official uses have developed within the EC. Its role as an official currency and denominator now comprises:

(a) use as a reserve currency;
(b) use as a means of payment and settlement;
(c) use in the EC budgets, for EC grants, loans and fines, for services and for the salaries of EC officials;
(d) use for statistical purposes;
(e) use in the common agricultural policy;
(f) use by the European Investment Bank;
(g) use in the European Development Fund; and
(h) use as denominator for customs duties.

The use as a reserve currency results from the deposit of the gold and dollar reserves with the EMCF for the creation of official ecu. The central banks report the amounts of issued ecu on their balance sheets and disregard the released gold and dollars amounts for accounting purposes. Thereby, the ecu is transformed into a reserve currency in the hands of the central banks. Approximately 6 percent of the EC central banks' reserves are in ecu.

The ecu is a means of payment and settlement for the EC institutions especially under the Very-Short Term Financing mechanisms of the EMS. The ecu can also be used by the central banks as collateral to obtain funds for intervention purposes. Furthermore, the credit granted under the short-term monetary support programs are denominated in ecu when initial grants are prolonged. Ecu-denomination is used exclusively in the medium-term financial assistance program.

The ecu is the official unit of account and denomination for all EC budgets. This includes the general EC budget as well as the budgets of the individual institutions. The European Coal and Steel Community converted its reserves into ecus in 1987 and 1988. This pool of ECU 1.5 billion played a significant role in the tremendous increase in the ecu bond market. Other uses include grants and loans, fines for infringements of EC provisions and payments for services rendered to the EC by private or corporate specialists. The EC has proposed to pay the salaries of its officials in ecus.

The use of the ecu for statistical purposes by the Statistical Office of the EC (Eurostat) since 1987 now allows the creation of directly comparable statistics.

An important area for the official use of the ecu, although in slightly modified form and under special provisions, is the agricultural pricing mechanisms under the common agricultural policy. Common agricultural prices are fixed in ecus and subsequently converted into the national currencies.

The European Investment Bank (EIB) now denominates its own capital in ecus after it had originally expressed it in ecu equivalents of the Member States' currencies. Payments of new capital and portions of its long-term liabilities, outstanding loans, and an increasing amount of its cash funds, usually money-market issues, are in ecus. The EIB serves as the financing institution for the EC and as agent for certain projects financed by the EC or the European Development Fund under the New Community Instrument (NCI) or the Lomé Conventions. In 1990 alone, the EIB granted loans amounting to ECU 13.4 billion. Under the current Lomé IV Convention alone, the EIB may grant loans of up to ECU 1 billion.

The European Development Fund (EDF) denominates the reserves received from the Member States, as well as expenditures for certain projects in ecus. The EDF was created in 1975 under the Lomé I Convention on the special cooperation between the EC and the now 69 African, Caribbean and Pacific (ACP) countries. Under the current Lomé IV Convention, in effect between 1990 and 1995, the EDF budget increased to almost ECU 11 billion.

Since 1979, the EC expresses specific customs duties and levies in ecus. Tax-free allowances for EC citizens traveling between Member States, as well as refunds, collections and other intra-EC transfers are also denominated in ecus.

The latter three official uses are important to a private business. When participating in certain projects financed by the EC in the ACP nations, or more currently, in Central and Eastern European countries (see Part XV) a business very likely will encounter the ecu. Payments made to or by the EC will be in ecus. Therefore, a business engaging in such projects must be familiar with the ecu in general and must be able to integrate it as a currency in its daily transactions. The same applies to the denomination of custom duties and levies in ecu which will affect a business engaged in exporting from and importing into the EC directly because the duties and levies need to be converted into the national currencies.

PART IX.

OFFICIAL AND PRIVATE ECUS - THE MISSING LINK

In the initial stages of the private ecu, its exchange rate equalled that of the official ecu as determined by the EC Commission (see page 49). The private rates could easily be calculated by using the basket definition of the ecu (see page 47). During the past few years, however, the private ecu has "uncoupled" from its official counterpart, a phenomenon which was not recognized until very recently. Its exchange rates now differ from the value of the official basket in that there are two different exchange rates for the official and the private ecus. The initial divergence of the private rate tended to move around the official basket rates. This closeness indicated a strong dependence of the private ecu in its "infant" years. Since 1990, however, the private rates have moved more and more independently suggesting a de-coupling of the private ecu from the official basket. Similar developments took place with regard to the ecu interest rates (see page 93) which used to be calculable as the weighted average of the national rates.

The theories attempting to explain the divergences are based on the fact that there is no "connection" between the official and the private ecus. This results from the fact that the official ecus are only used (and can only be used) by certain institutions *among* themselves and that the private ecus, on the other hand, are used by private entities. The EMS mechanisms only determine the value of the official ecu, which cannot be traded, and do not establish an exchange rate between the official and the private ecus. This difference in users, in which no cross-use is possible, explains the two different behavior of the rates.

In contrast to other currencies, the private and the official uses of the ecu are clearly separated. The application of the ecu in those two independent "cycles" not only fosters different rates but also aggravates this phenomenon. For example, as central banks cannot intervene in the private ecu markets with the official ecus they hold in their reserves, there is no dominant force (a central bank) which could keep these rates together since the only official rate is fixed. In the case of the Dutch guilder, for example, diverging rates, if at all imaginable, between officially and privately used guilder would be arbitrated immediately. In the case of the ecu, however, such action is not possible because the official ecu cannot be used in the private cycle. Some arbitrage was possible when the Ecu Clearing System (see page 134) required the settlement of the balances by the transfer of the appropriate amounts of the basket currencies. This resulted in a very close exchange rate between the two types of ecus because both were based on the basket definition and were subject to the exchange rate behavior of each basket currency. This procedure, however, was abolished some years ago and induced the "de-coupling" of the ecu and the beginning of the "floating" rate of the private ecu. For the same reason, the difference cannot be remedied by the markets themselves. As a practical matter, the central banks intervene in the private ecu markets with the private ecus they hold in their accounts. Such interventions are not required, however, and are unilateral actions by individual central banks.

The divergences have two main reasons. First, market imperfection not inherent in the official basket but present in the actual market environment might add risk factors to the private ecu. Such factors include transaction costs, lack of competition and non-transparency, as well as the possibility of realignments. Second, the rapid development of the ecu bond market with a wide maturity spectrum, especially with high volume jumbo-issues (see page 94), the success of the EMU negotiations and the resulting increased liquidity of the ecu markets might already have transformed the ecu into a hard currency and made it independent from the official basket.

The missing link between the official and the private ecu puts the ecu user into a somewhat uncertain position. Significant divergences between these two rates should not be expected as there is still at least a perceived connection through the fact that both ecus are based on and developed out of the official ecu basket. The size and continuing spread between the values of the official and the private ecu is, however, reason for some concern. For example, private parties using the private ecu practically always accept the value of the ecu basket as the definition of the calculation of the private ecu used in their transaction. The assumption is that those values will not diverge from one another. The obvious concern, of course, involves the remedy, legal or otherwise, in the case of such diverging rates. Therefore, borrowers and investors in ecu bonds must begin to take divergences into account. The automatic acceptance of the value of the official ecu for interest and capital payments may not be profitable. If the official rate were different from the market rate, the parties may end up paying more or receive fewer ecus upon payment. Instead, parties using the ecu should not automatically accept the official ecu definition and value. They should negotiate this matter and select the potentially more advantageous value.

PART X.

PRIVATE USE

One of the most promising developments in recent monetary history is the acceptance of the ecu as a denominator for private and commercial financing instruments on the international markets. This acceptance is completely independent from the official use of the ecu by monetary institutions. Although initially only contemplated as a denominator and a means of settlement for the EC authorities, the volume of the private ecu markets was estimated at over ECU 100 billion as early as 1985 and now exceeds ECU 200 billion.

This development of the private ecu is important for entities involved in business with the EC. Apart from some limited instances a business will probably not encounter the official ecu in daily transactions. As indicated, the use of official ecus is limited to exposure in transactions which are funded by the EC. The exposure to private ecus, however, may have significantly larger proportions. As will be shown in this and following parts, the ecu has developed into an internationally accepted currency second only to the US dollar in international bond issues.

The private market for the ecu became possible in the early 1980s with ecu accounts opened by certain Belgian banks for EC institutions. These accounts facilitated the cash management of the latter and transfers to the European Investment Bank (EIB). The EIB, in turn, deposited the received and unused ecu assets with Italian banks. The Belgian and Italian banks, however, wanted to use those deposits for which interest accrued. They created an ecu loan and foreign exchange market by granting ecu credits to a limited number of private customers. The customers used the ecu credits and "unbundled" the ecus received by breaking them down into their component national currencies. Similarly, private parties "created" their own ecus by buying and "bundling" the appropriate amounts of the component currencies. The banks also accepted these ecus as deposits. This process of using ecus in private transactions and the establishment of the Ecu Clearing System in 1986 (see page 134) increased the number of individual participants as well as the variety of ecu-denominated banking services. The development from a one-way deposit to a two-way deposit and loan market took place entirely within the private banking system. There is no central supervising authority and the private ecu market is marginally regulated by national central bank regulations. The absence of legal backing, however, is compensated for by the actual treatment of the ecu as a currency by private and commercial users.

There are a number of reasons which explain the favorable development of the ecu despite the lack of official sanctioning. First, the ecu has a very stable exchange rate toward third currencies (see page 62). Second, the interest rates for ecu instruments are between the high rates of "soft" EMS currencies and the lower rates of "hard" EMS currencies (see page 144). Third, as a result of the non-existence of a central monetary authority, there are only a few regulations for the private and commercial uses. The individual central banks established a very basic legal and institutional framework which has made the ecu an extremely attractive investment vehicle. Fourth, individual commercial banks promote the ecu as a means of investment and transfer to their customers. Being relatively independent from national monetary regulations, the ecu has an inherent flexibility which allows monetary institutions to virtually "custom-tailor" to customer needs. Furthermore, the lack of an established home market for ecu products and the resulting relative equality of the banks across the EC enables them to establish their respective clientele and specialization without regard to inherent competitive advantages of the banks in a particular country. Fifth, the use of the ecu by corporations with locations in several EC countries decreases risk exposure and administrative costs for currency management. A corporation can decrease its currency management expenses by using the ecu as sole currency for all transactions instead of the 12 EC currencies.

The following parts discuss the different types of private ecu facilities available at this time. These range from loans and futures to all types of private and commercial banking services. Despite the overall relative success of the ecu, the volume in private and commercial markets is somewhat misleading as its use tends to be centered only on a number of areas. Other applications, while available, are not used to any significant degree. The commercial use of ecu, for example, for invoicing or accounting purposes is still very limited.

There are a number of reasons for the rather restricted use of the ecu in most of the areas of its possible usability, such as in the commercial context and for certain private types of banking services.

The most significant restriction results from the fact that the ecu still is a foreign currency in all EC Member States. As such, it is subject to considerable commission fees and spreads which are payable to banks upon conversion into or out of the ecu. These additional expenses have made is quite costly for businesses to use the ecu to its full extent in their transactions. In addition, these additional expenses cannot be compensated by savings in interest payments for ecu instruments as compared to instruments in many national EC currencies. In the 1980s, the ecu instruments partook in the strength of the Deutsche Mark as a currency and the corresponding lower interest rates of Deutsche Mark instruments which influenced the weighted average interest rates of ecu instruments. With the success of the EMS and the resulting decrease in the disparities between most of the national interest rates (which amounts to less than 1 percent for the most important EC currencies), the additional costs are higher than the interest rates savings. Corporations in the EC thus have been reluctant to switch into the ecu as it basically increases some costs at this time.

This restriction will lose its impact with the transformation of the ecu into the single EC currency. At that point, most of the remaining currencies will disappear and the ecu will become the single legal tender. It then will enjoy the same domestic status in the EC as the dollar enjoys in the United States. By default, its private and commercial uses will increase dramatically. An increased use in most areas should be expected even before the 1997 or 1999 deadlines set by the EC for the creation of the single EC currency. As the ecu is the candidate for that position, private parties might begin to start using the ecu in their daily transactions to prepare for the ultimate transformation. That development, however, is entirely in the hands of the private markets and can only be supported and facilitated, but not demanded, by the EC or national authorities. Therefore, at present, the ecu has a significant status only in a number of areas while its use in others is severely limited.

PART XI.

BOND AND MONEY MARKETS

A. Volume of the Markets

This part discusses the use of the ecu in the bond markets, including government issues of ecu instruments, and the money market. In its private and commercial uses, the ecu has been most successful in these two markets. From the first bond in 1981 until the end of January 1992, over ECU 90 billion have been issued with over ECU 73 billion outstanding.

Figure XI.1: Ecu Bonds (1981 - 1992)

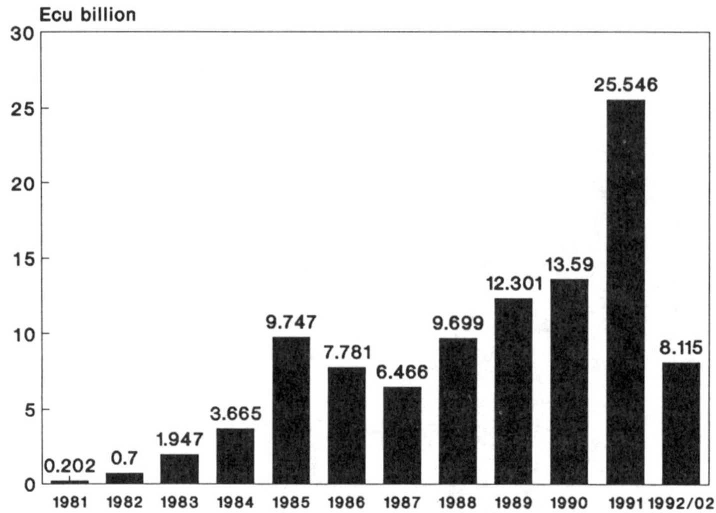

Source: Bourse de Luxembourg/ECU Newsletter

Over ECU 25 billion were issued in 1991 alone. Ecu bonds have secured themselves a significant share in the market for Eurobonds and international bond issues. In 1991, the ecu was the third most used denomination on the international bond markets with three main categories: (i) strictly domestic government bond issues; (ii) domestic/international government bond issues; and (iii) purely international bond issues in the Euromarket.

Table XI.1: Share of the Ecu on the International Bond Market

	1982	1983	1984	1985	1986	1987	1988	1989	1990	1991
$	63.9	57.0	63.6	60.8	54.7	37.9	41.2	41.9	32.2	28.01
Yen	5.2	5.3	5.5	7.8	10.4	13.9	8.4	8.3	14.0	13.20
SFr	15.1	17.5	12.0	9.0	10.4	13.0	11.1	7.5	10.5	3.57
DM	7.1	8.6	6.2	6.7	7.5	8.4	10.1	6.4	7.6	11.00
UKL	2.6	3.9	5.1	4.0	4.8	8.0	9.4	6.8	9.4	10.25
Aus	0.3	0.3	1.8	1.4	5.1	*	3.4	2.3	2.2	*
Ecu	1.1	2.8	2.7	4.2	3.1	4.1	4.9	5.2	8.6	12.23
Cdn	*	*	*	*	2.3	3.4	5.7	4.0	2.8	*
Ecu	#8	#6	#6	#5	#6	#7	#7	#7	#5	#3

* Less than the share of the ecu.

Source: Bank for International Settlements

Figure XI.2: Bond Issues 1991

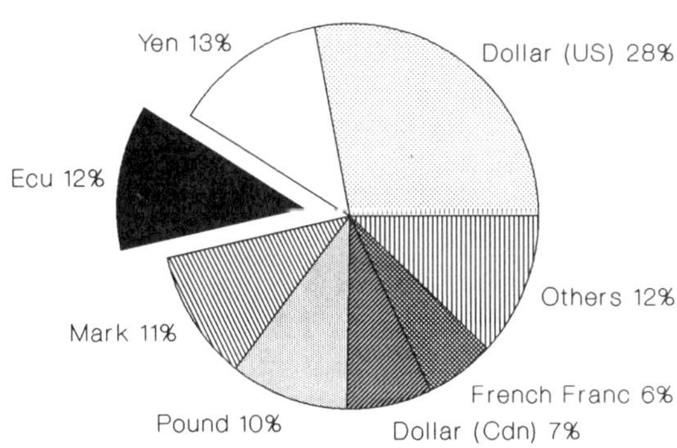

Source: Bourse de Luxembourg

The ecu money market for bank liabilities, medium term notes, certificates of deposit, commercial papers, United Kingdom Treasury bills and Italian BTEs, has been the single fastest growing segment of the ecu market with a total market volume of over ECU 140 billion.

B. Benefits of the Ecu Bond Market

The spectacular increase in ecu issues is the result of the general acceptance of the ecu as an investment currency, its inherent stability and the increased participation of EC governments in the ecu markets to take advantage of its favorable conditions. In addition, ecu bonds are not limited to the size of a domestic market because all ecu issues by definition are "international" issues. The most attractive features of ecu bonds, however, are the relative exchange rate stability of the ecu, its comparably low interest rates and the lack of a home market.

The yield on ecu bonds, as a general rule, is close to the weighted average of the yields for similar instruments in the EC Member States. This means that the ecu interest rate will stand between the higher interest rates of countries like Greece, Italy and Spain and the lower interest rates of countries like Germany, Belgium and the Netherlands. Although the rates will be closer to the lower rates, resulting from the higher weight of low-rate currencies in the ecu basket (approximately 67 percent), they will still be higher than those and substantially lower than the rates of the high-interest rate countries. In addition, the basket composition of the ecu and the determination of ecu bond interest rates permits borrowers or investors to participate indirectly in the markets in each EC Member State, including the smaller markets with high yield issues, without subjecting themselves to exchange rate risks, withholding taxes or frequent illiquidity on the secondary markets.

Ecu bonds are valuable to investors from countries with domestic interest rates lower than those of the ecu who do not want to subject their investment to higher exchange rate fluctuations as a trade-off for a higher risk-return. A German investor, for example, might prefer an 8 percent-investment with a minimal exchange risk to its domestic 7 percent-investment in mark with no exchange risk. The investor probably would avoid the 12 percent-investment in Greek drachma with the high exchange rate exposure (especially because Greece does not participate in the Exchange Rate Mechanisms of the EMS).

The issuers of ecu bonds, on the other hand, particularly from high interest rate countries such as Greece, will prefer an ecu investment with a much lower interest rate than a comparable investment in the national currency.

Apart from the fact that such an investment will probably be sold more easily because it is deemed to be more secure, the lower interest rate results in much lower interest payments by the issuer.

The third advantage is the lack of a true home market. It enables private banks to "custom tailor" ecu securities to a high degree. An issuer can take advantage of this special feature of the ecu market and adapt its debt instruments to the underlying financing need without domestic restrictions on the form of such instruments.

Figure XI.3 shows that the main issuers of ecu bonds are banking and financial entities (47 percent), followed by corporations (21 percent), government entities (18 percent) and institutional entities (14 percent).

Figure XI.3: Ecu Bond Issuers 1991

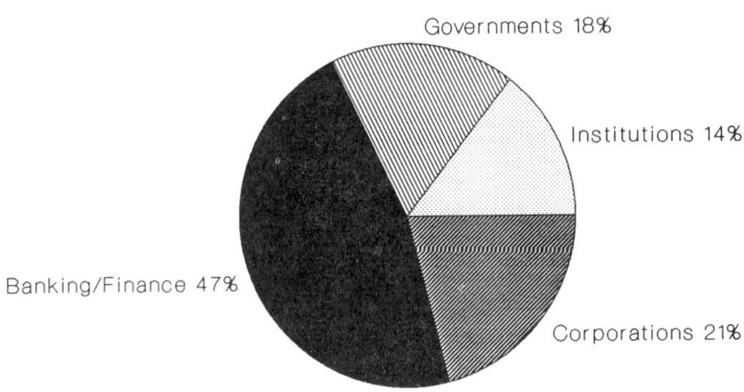

Source: Bourse de Luxembourg

Almost three quarters of ecu bond issuers (72 percent) are located in the EC. They comprise issuers in EC countries (54 percent), as well as EC institutions (18 percent).

Figure XI.4: Ecu Bonds - Issuer Location 1991

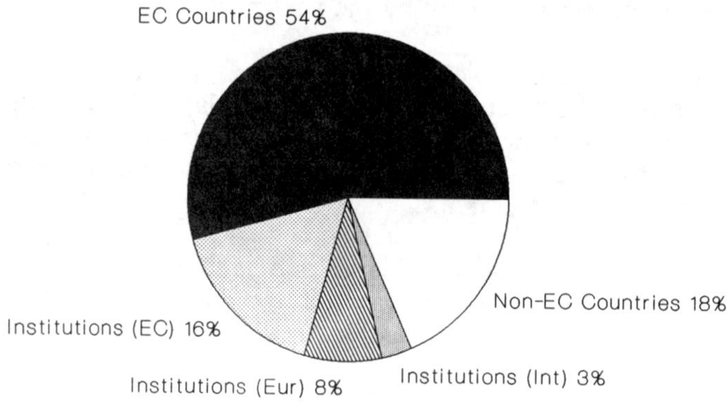

Source: Bourse de Luxembourg

The ecu bond market developed in three main phases. In the initial phase, bonds were denominated in a variety of "units of accounts", such as the European Unit of Account and the European Composite Unit (see page 40). These bonds enabled the issuer (i.e., the borrower of the bond amount) to select one of the underlying currencies for the purchase of the bond, whereas the investor selected a currency for interest and capital payments. In the second phase, French, Italian and Belgian entities issued special bonds linked to the ecu. These issues tied the bonds which were denominated in national currencies to the ecu as a "reference currency" and guaranteed higher repayments should the investor's national currency depreciate. In the present phase ecu bond issues are true ecu bonds in the form of Eurobonds. The bonds are denominated in ecu, as opposed to the "indexing" in the second phase. As there is no domestic market for ecu bonds, all ecu bonds are "Eurobond" issues with some special provisions to take into account the special composition of the ecu.

Table XI.2: Ecu Bonds 1981 - 1991

Country/Institution	Number of Issues
EC Institutions	110
Italy	67
France	153
Germany	20
United Kingdom	18
Belgium	31
Luxembourg	7
Denmark	25
Ireland	10
Netherlands	23
Spain	5
Portugal	1
Greece	1
TOTAL EC	471
European Institutions	23
Austria	22
Norway	7
Sweden	33
Finland	29
Hungary	1
Switzerland	3
USA	73
Canada	14
Japan	65
Australia	13
Other	37
Internat. Institutions	21
TOTAL WORLD	812

Source: Bourse de Luxembourg

Table XI.2 gives a comprehensive overview of the distribution in respect to the country of origin by total number and amount of ecu-bonds issued between 1981 and 1991.

C. Special Technical Issues Regarding Ecu Bonds

Ecu bonds comply with the requirements for Eurobond issues in syndication and documentation. They are issued by international syndicates of financial institutions which manage the bond and carry out the underwriting and the sales of the issues. As with most Eurobond issues, formal regulations regarding the primary markets for ecu bonds are simply non-existent. The syndicate will announce the final terms of an individual issue and invite prospective underwriters by a telex setting forth all the terms and conditions. The settlement takes place after a subscription period of usually between five and 10 days. By that time, the underwriters will have determined the market interest in the individual issue. Most issues are listed on the stock exchanges in London and Luxembourg, a few in Madrid and Amsterdam. Standard denominations are ECU 1,000, 10,000 or 100,000. All payments and repayments are made in ecus. After the sale to an individual investor, the bonds will be deposited in the Euroclear or Cedel systems (see page 110) for the investor or a financial institution. Payments for ecu bonds generally are not subject to any withholding taxes.

The following additional provisions for ecu Eurobonds account for the special nature of the ecu as a basket currency (see also Appendix G for a sample ecu-bond prospectus):

(a) As used in the bond market, the ecu is typically defined according to the "official definition" (see page 48).

(b) Provisions are included to determine how the value of the ecu will be calculated if the official definition of the basket is changed in a recomposition.

(c) Stipulations are added to set the conditions for the selection of a currency for interest and capital payments in the event the ecu ceases to exist.

(d) It is generally determined that the new definitions and values of the ecu following realignments apply to all transactions under the issued bonds.

From a technical standpoint, the above four special provisions are the only features that differentiate an ecu Eurobond from a traditional Eurobond. These special provisions relate exclusively to the special status of the ecu as a basket currency. In view of the evolving divergence between the exchange rates of the private and official ecu, the above provisions must be carefully reviewed. In particular the automatic acceptance of the official value might have adverse financial implications (see page 23). These special provisions and the concerns related to the different values of the official and private ecus will, of course, disappear with the transformation of the ecu into the single EC currency. At that time, the ecu will be treated like any other currency and the basket status will have ceased.

D. Interest Rate Determination

One of the more complex issues with regard to the ecu bond market is the determination of the interest rate for ecu instruments. The interest rate for a financial instrument in a "normal" currency, of course, is determined by the supply and demand characteristics of the markets for the instruments in that currency. If such a market is well developed, a certain kind of bond will have a number of desirable characteristics and will be the "benchmark" issue for that currency. The interest rate of this issue will serve as a reference point for similar instruments. Usually, such a benchmark issue emanates from a national government, such as the OATs in France, the Bunds in Germany and the Treasury securities in the United States.

In the past, the ecu bond market lacked such benchmark issues. Market participants developed theoretical yields and composite ecu yield curves for the analysis and evaluation of ecu bonds, the most prominent of which is the Paribas Theoretical Yield Index. Theoretical curves take into account the corresponding yield curves of the component EC currencies while composite yields are calculated with the weights of the individual currencies in the ecu basket and their national interest rates. Although this calculation will not result in an average rate of all the EC currencies, the ecu yield will always be lower than the highest rate and higher than the lowest rate of the currencies in the basket. The majority of the basket currencies, namely the mark, the guilder and the French, Belgian and Luxembourg francs, are quite stable. Their lower interest rates will influence the weighted average and result in relatively lower rates for the ecu (see page 144).

In practice, however, these calculations of the theoretical yield are imprecise and fall short of accounting for all variables. Following the increased interest in the ecu and the now certain developments toward the EMU, ecu bond yields have differed from those determined by the theoretical curve. This difference may be based on certain market expectations and a "hardening" of the ecu into an independent currency. This difference is accentuated by the increasing degree of independence of the private ecu as compared to the official ecu. The theoretical close link between those two ecu, based on their common composition only, has increasingly diminished as the ecu takes on a life of its own (see page 78).

The need for theoretical yields has decreased with the issuing of true benchmark issues since 1989. A number of highly liquid, large-volume sovereign jumbo issues of ecu bonds with volumes of over ECU 1 billion each now provides an independent yield curve for the ecu. Although the market still suffers from occasional illiquidity, the issues have significantly improved and changed the ecu bond market in general. New issuers and investors can orient themselves at the yields of those issues.

Table XI.3: Ecu Benchmark Issues

MATURITY	AMOUNT	ISSUER	COUPON	MATURITY
3-month	1,000 Million	Italy	FRN	10/2005
	3,600 Million	Great Britain	variable	variable
6-month	4,800 Million	Great Britain	variable	variable
5-Year	1,000 Million	Spain	9.00 %	5/1996
	1,250 Million	Belgium	9.125%	3/1996
7-Year	928 Million	France	8.50 %	5/1997
	1,125 Million	EIB	10.00 %	2/1997
	1,000 Million	Italy	10.375%	7/1997
10-Year	2,708 Million	France	9.50 %	4/2000
	1,000 Million	Italy	10.75 %	4/2000
	1,150 Million	EIB	10.00 %	1/2001
	1,500 Million	France	10.00 %	2/2001
	2,500 Million	Great Britain	10.00 %	2/2001
	949 Million	France	8.50 %	3/2002
20-Year	2,500 Million	Italy	9.25 %	3/2011

A benchmark issue essentially has three features. First, it is usually the instrument with the lowest risk (highest rating) on the market. Therefore, it has the lowest yield with which the issuers of new instruments can determine their interest rates. Second, these low risk issues give the best indications of the interest rate trend in the market. Third, their correlation to market development makes these issues good hedges against exchange rate variability.

E. Types of Ecu Bonds

The ecu bond market offers most of the bond types available in traditional bond markets. They range from fixed rate bonds to floating rate notes, zero coupon and partly paid bonds. One type of bond unique to the ecu are Titres Participatifs in which a portion of the yield is linked to the profit of the issuing entity. The following is an overview of the types of ecu bonds and their most important characteristics.

Fixed Rate Bonds in ecus represent by far the largest share of the ecu bond market. Approximately 85 to 90 percent of all ecu bond issues bear a rate that is fixed until the maturity of the issue.

Adjustable Rate Bonds in ecu have adjustable coupons at certain dates or regular intervals of three, five or six years. The adjustment of the interest rate takes place at the investor's or the issuer's option or upon negotiation between the parties. Almost all adjustable rate bonds have put and call options which can be exercised simultaneously on the coupon adjustment days. These options provide a hedge for both parties against conditions which might make the bond less attractive.

Zero Coupon Bonds pay all accrued interest in a lump sum at the maturity of the instrument. Such bonds are generally attractive for investors from countries with lower tax rates for capital gains. The lump sum would be characterized as a capital gain. A major problem for zero coupon bonds in foreign currencies occurs when the exchange rate between the investor's currency and the denomination of the security has changed so as to decrease the amount of return when the bond matures. This problem is partially eliminated with the use of the ecu. Its relative exchange rate stability ensures that such losses are limited.

Partly Paid Bonds enable an investor to pay part of the purchase price initially and the remainder at a later date. This kind of bond is favored by foreign investors who anticipate an improvement in the exchange rate of their currency against the currency in which the bond is denominated between the initial and the later payments. If their currency appreciated, for example, they would actually have to pay less of their own currency to purchase the rest of the bond. The relative exchange rate stability of the ecu makes such bonds relatively rare.

Floating Rate Notes (FRN) are comparable to adjustable rate bonds in that the interest rate changes over the maturity of the bond. The rates for floating rate bonds are indexed to other specified rates. In the case of ecu floating rate bonds, the interest rates are usually indexed to, and calculated as a spread over, the London Interbank Offer Rates (LIBOR) or the ECU Interbank Offered Rates (EIBOR). The interest rate "adjustments" take place every three or six months. At those intervals, the bond will bear the new rate as indexed over the LIBOR or EIBOR rates. Some of the ecu floating bond issues provide for a maximum cap on the interest rates to be paid by the issuer.

Saint Gobain Titres Participatifs are a type of bond unique to the ecu in which a portion of the yield is linked to the profit of the issuing entity. Those issues tend to be perpetual, i.e., with no maturity date. The investors usually have put options to end their investment. This type of bond guarantees the investor the highest rate between long-term and short-term ecu investments plus an added bonus in the form of a portion of the profits of the issuer.

The Saint Gobain issue bears a six-month yield equal to the greater of either a 3/8 percent spread over the six-month LIBOR on ecu deposits or the yield of long-term bonds less 0.5 basis points PLUS a variable spread which is defined as a function of St. Gobain's profits.

Convertible Bonds permit the conversion of the bond either into other bonds or into shares. Convertible bonds are very attractive for issuers as they afford a much lower interest coupon as a result of the profit expectations upon conversion. The ecu is an ideal currency for such bonds because the investor faces lower foreign exchange risks.

Bond-convertible issues are usually issued with variable initial interest rates and conversion into bonds with fixed interest rates. An investor will profit from the conversion if the adjustable rates fall below the fixed rates. Equity-convertible issues allow the investor to convert the ecu bond into shares denominated in national currencies. The investor will profit when the market price of the share increases at an amount exceeding the overall expenses sustained by the investor.

Cum Warrant Bonds give the investor the right to purchase either additional bonds (debt warrants) or additional shares (equity warrants) of the issuer or its subsidiaries at a fixed price. There also are "naked warrants" in which the investor will not have to purchase an underlying bond to obtain the sole warrant.

Currency Warrants and Convertible Ecu Bonds are issued in a currency other than the ecu, usually the US dollar. They include warrants which allow the investor to purchase other ecu bonds or include options to convert the dollar issue into ecu floating rate notes with characteristics similar to the underlying dollar issue. The ecu currency warrants provide the investor with a hedge against depreciations in the dollar exchange rate.

In October 1987, the EC issued Ecu-"Schuldscheine" which are negotiable and privately placed instruments in the form of bank credits. This traditional German means of investment has a circulation similar to that of bonds.

Figure XI.5: Ecu Bond Types 1991

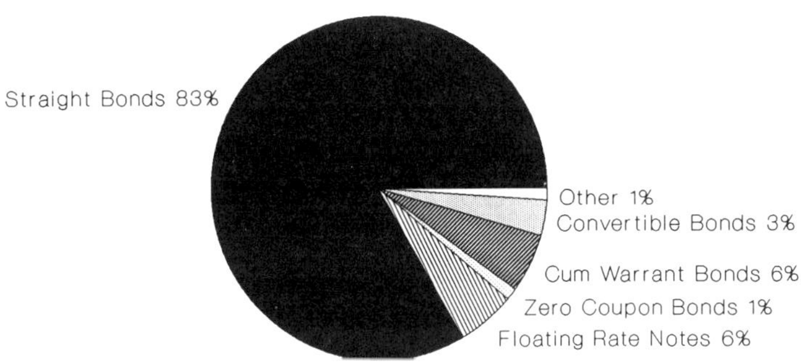

Source: Bourse de Luxembourg

The availability of the various types of ecu bonds indicates the important status of the ecu as an international investment currency. One additional observation, however, is critical. As indicated above, there truly is no home market for ecu instruments. The corresponding lack of limiting regulations on the types of ecu bonds issued is of great advantage for the ecu market. This lack of regulations permits the underwriting syndicates to provide borrowers with custom-tailored bonds. This means that the ecu bond prospectus can take into account certain idiosyncracies and special requirements unavailable to bonds in other currencies, which encourages the use of the ecu for novel financing instruments. The Titres Participatifs are a prime example. The ecu is not only an important new currency in the international financial market but also a means to develop cutting-edge methods of financing in general.

F. The Government Debt Market

Traditionally, the ecu market was split equally between issues by corporations and issues by government entities. The latter include national and local governments, supranational institutions and government enterprises. The ecu bond market has changed significantly during the past two years. Issues by government entities now represent approximately 75 percent of the primary market in ecu bonds. Sovereign governments have found the ecu market especially attractive because of the often lower interest rates compared to their national currencies. The increase in sovereign issues also significantly increased the average size of new ecu bonds. Issuers of ecu bonds (or borrowers of the bond-amounts) are distinguished according to the nature of the issuer or its geographic location.

As a result of the proportionally large share of multinational institutions, sovereign governments, agencies and government-supported companies among the issuers of ecu bonds, the average rating for those issues is relatively high. In a recent listing of the 54 most liquid ecu bonds, 45 carried explicit AAA ratings. Sovereign issuers are typically rated AA or AAA. In addition, corporate issuers generally have high ratings in order to find suitable swap-partners for their issues.

While the market in long-term ecu bonds developed rapidly after the first ecu-bond issue in 1981, the market in short-term ecu-denominated instruments was practically non-existent until 1987 when the first higher-volume ecu government debt instruments entered the market.

The launch of ecu-denominated Treasury certificates (CTE) by the Italian Treasury in 1982 was the very first ecu-denominated government debt instrument. In late 1986, the Greek government issued its first state bond with an ecu clause which permitted repayment in ecu if the bonds were purchased in a currency other than the drachma. The CTE, however, remained the only genuine government ecu instrument until the introduction of ecu floating rate stock by the Irish government in September 1987.

In August 1988 and January 1992, respectively, the Treasury of the United Kingdom introduced its ecu Treasury bill and note programs. The French treasury followed with its first ecu-denominated treasury bill program on April 11, 1989. The Spanish government launched its first ecu bonds in April 1990. These Treasury instruments link the markets for short-term papers and ecu bonds.

Of all the ecu issues of government debt instruments by EC Member States, the Italian, French and British issues are by far the most extensive. There have also been ecu-bond issues by non-EC nations, such as New Zealand, Sweden, Finland and South Africa. The following text only summarizes the ecu government debt programs in selected EC Member States.

Government ecu bond issues have captured the lion's share of the ecu bond market. The creation of liquid jumbo benchmark issues with high ratings has been one of the major reasons for the spectacular increase in the volume of the ecu bond market.

(1) Italy

The Italian government issues Treasury certificates (CTE), Treasury bills (BTE) and bonds in ecu-denomination. CTE in ecus are medium and long-term straight bonds which were first issued in 1982. They generally mature between four and eight years. Between 1982 and September 1990, the Italian government launched 31 issues of CTE. For the relevant information notice by the Bank of Italy, see Appendix B.

Figure XI.6: Italian Ecu Treasury Certificates

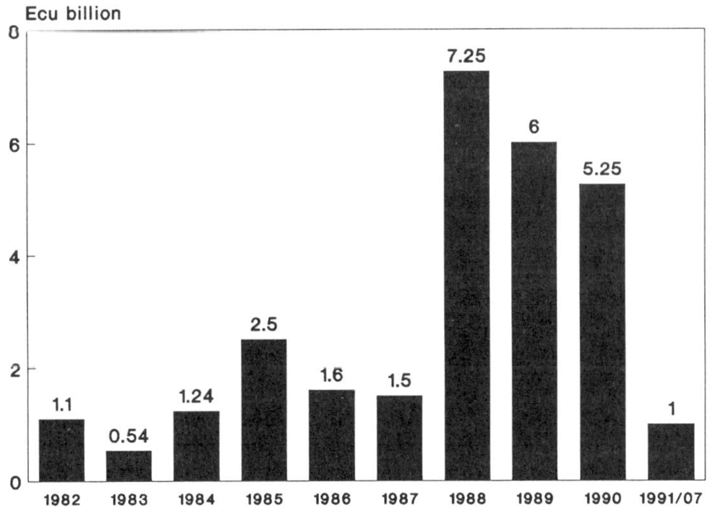

Source: EBA Newsletter

The Italian Treasury introduced Treasury bills (BTE) in ecus in October 1987. BTEs generally have maturities of 12 months. The introduction of BTEs filled the gap of short-term government instruments in ecu. For the relevant information notice by the Bank of Italy, see Appendix B. These BTEs are domestic instruments in Italy which makes a 12.5 percent withholding tax applicable for interest paid to Italian residents. This tax will not be withheld for foreign purchasers of such bonds.

Figure XI.7: Italian Ecu Treasury Notes

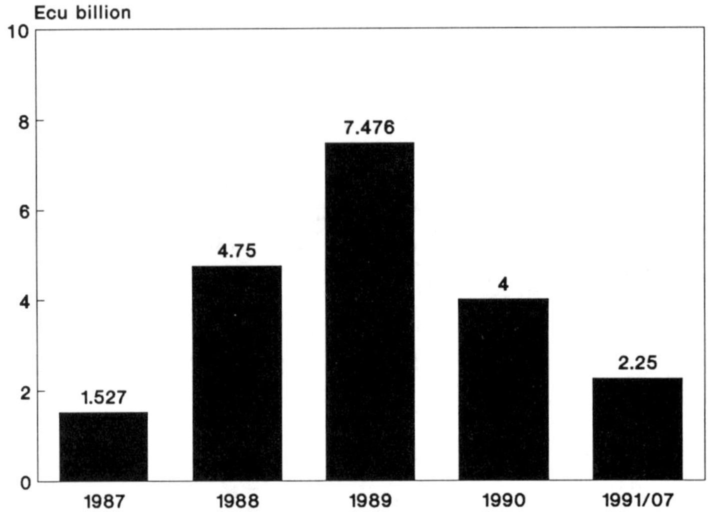

Source: EBA Newsletter

(2) Greece

The Greek government issued the first bond with an ecu clause in November 1986. In these bonds, the drachma is pegged to the exchange rate of the ecu. The bonds can be bought with drachma or with foreign currencies. The payment of the interest and of the principal takes place in drachma in the first case, and in ecu in the latter case. Only the first issues had a fixed offered amount. All subsequent issues were demand-based with no limit on the total amount to be issued. These bonds are in bearer form with nominal values of ECU 1,000, 2,000, 5,000, 10,000, and 20,000. For the announcement of the Greek government for the September 1989 issue, please see Appendix B.

Table XI.4: Greek Government Bonds with Ecu Clauses

Issue Date	Maturity	Coupon	Dr/Ecu	Ecu million
24/11/86	3	8.00	140.6	166
25/02/87	3	8.00	149.9	107
18/05/87	3	8.20	153.0	111
15/5/89	3	9.75	177.1	275
31/5/89	3	9.75	177.1	216
15/9/89	3	9.50	178.7	322
16/10/89	3	9.75	179.6	401
20/11/89	3	10.00	182.3	224
15/12/89	3	10.50	187.2	100
16/1/90	1	12.00	190.0	959
2/4/90	1	11.50	196.6	665
15/5/90	2	11.25	201.8	178
29/6/90	1 ½	11.00	202.0	178
21/11/90	2	10.90	211.70	229
	3	11	211.70	98
17/12/90	2	10.70	213.90	174
	3	10.80	213.90	10
	4	11	213.90	17
16/01/91	1	11	217.80	636
	2	11	217.80	63
	3	11	217.80	10
	4	11	217.80	14
28/02/91	2	9.90	221.20	117
	3	10	221.20	7
	4	10.10	221.20	37
28/03/91	2	10	222.73	262
	3	10.15	222.73	21
	4	10.25	222.73	36
15/04/91	1	10	224.10	368
15/07/91	2	10.10	224.40	67
	3	10.25	224.40	8
	4	10.40	224.40	5

Source: Bank of Greece

On January 16, 1992, the Greek government announced the issuance of a new series of one, two and three-year ecu-linked bonds for a total of ECU 479 million.

(3) Ireland

The Irish government launched its first ecu instrument, the Irish Pound-Ecu Floating Rate Stock 1993, in September 1987. This stock is a government "gilt edged" instrument which also incorporates a hedge against the decrease of the Irish pound against the ecu. The entire ECU 100 million issue will be redeemed on March 31, 1993. For the Information Memorandum of the Irish Department of Finance, see Appendix B.

(4) United Kingdom

In an effort to promote the use of the ecu and to develop London into a major financial center for the ecu, the United Kingdom has been at the forefront of developing the ecu market and new ecu instruments. After establishing a suitable infrastructure, the British Treasury announced its ecu Treasury bill program, initially valued at ECU 1 and 2 billion, in 1988. At that time, the British pound did not take part in the exchange rate mechanisms of the EMS. This program complements the short-term market in ecu-denominated securities which had been only partially served by the Italian issues.

These Treasury bills are money market instruments issued at a discount by the Bank of England on behalf of the British Treasury. The Bank of England carries out monthly tenders for the Treasury bills which have maturities of one, three and six months. As a result of the success of this program, the Bank of England revised and changed the program on March 28, 1989 following the initial six tenders. Ecu Treasury bills are now available in smaller denominations of ECU 10,000 and 50,000 in addition to the denominations of ECU 100,000, 500,000, and 1,000,000, 5,000,000 and 10,000,000. The Bank of England also extended the entire program beyond the initial six months. The announcement by the Bank of England is reprinted in Appendix B.

The initial program based on the monthly issuance of ECU 300 million in 1-month, ECU 300 million in 3-month and ECU 400 million in 6-month bills. This program has been modified and no 1-month bills were offered between July 1991 and March 1992. In addition, for the auction on February 14, 1992, the government increased the amount of 3-month bills issuable to ECU 500 million.

Figure XI.8: United Kingdom Ecu Treasury Bills

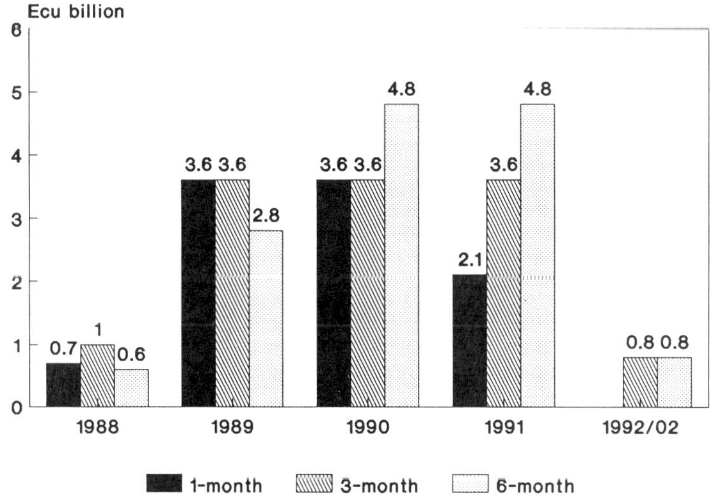

Source: UK Treasury

A secondary market is not well developed for these Treasury securities because most purchasers hold the bonds until their maturity. Trading in the secondary market predominantly takes place among the 27 market-makers selected by the Bank of England.

In addition to the above treasury bill program, the British authorities now allow the gilt edged market-makers who deal in British government gilt edged securities to enter the ecu markets and offer a wide range of ecu-denominated instruments and hedging instruments in EC currencies. The second step to promote the ecu market in London was the issue of a 10-year fixed ecu bond by the British government in February 1991. This ECU 2.75 billion ecu gilt issue was the largest fixed rate issue ever on the international bond market. It was closed in only seven days after pricing and has developed into an actively traded low-yielding 10-year benchmark issue.

In January 1992, the government also announced the issuance of three-year Treasury notes, to be sold in auctions, to fill the maturity gap between six months and five years. These notes, available in denominations of ECU 1,000, ECU 10,000, ECU 100,000 and ECU 1,000,000, will be tendered

(5) France

On April 11, 1989 the French Minister of Economy, Finance and Budget announced the first Obligations Assimilables du Trésor (OAT) of ECU 1 billion. This issue has a maturity date of May 12, 1997 and an interest coupon of 8.5 percent. The government placed an additional ECU 1 billion between July 1989 and March 1992. This issue provided the basis for the ecu futures contract at the MATIF (see page 123). Approximately ECU 1 billion of this issue already have been swapped into a later 8.5 percent ecu OAT issue (with a maturity of February 2002) to ensure liquidity for the MATIF contract.

The second, and now most liquid, OAT followed in April of 1990. It is payable on April 25, 2000, with a coupon of 9.5 percent and six tranches (April, June, September and October 1990 and July and September 1991) totaling over ECU 3.2 billion. Société Générale issued put and call options on this OAT issue.

The third OAT issue of November 1991 with an interest rate of 10 percent with a maturity in 2001 was the first OAT ecu jumbo-issue sold in a single tranche. It was sold through a syndicate and immediately included in the delivery list for the MATIF ecu futures contract (see page 123).

The fourth OAT has an interest rate of 8.5 percent and matures in 2007. These issues followed the Finance Act of 1989 which had authorized the Minister of Finance to launch long, medium and short-term securities in ecu denomination. For a reprint of this act, please see Appendix B. France has announced the issuance of 15 percent of its government debt in ecus and, by the end of March 1992, had issued ECU 9.3 billion in ecu OAT.

The French OATs have attracted three types of investors: long-term investors, such as insurance companies, mutual funds and private investors, interested in the conservative nature of the investment in OAT; medium-term, mainly currency-sensitive Asian investors; and short-term investors, namely arbitrageurs, attracted by the high degree of transparency and liquidity of the OAT market.

In November 1990, the French Electricity Board, Electricité de France introduced the first issue exchanging a new and old ecu bonds. This bond issue replaces a number of smaller, older ecu bonds by a new single and very liquid ecu bond. The offer was a huge success and will be very important for the development of a more liquid ecu-denominated market.

(6) Spain

In April 1990, the Spanish government issued its first "Bonos de Estado" in ecu. This ECU 500 million benchmark issue has a maturity of five years and carries a 10.75 percent interest rate.

(7) Belgium

The Belgian Treasury announced in March 1991 that it would enter the ecu Treasury market in 1992 with two new ecu instruments which will be issued domestically for resident and foreign investors. Belgium, which has issued over ECU 2 billion in ecu Eurobonds so far, will now sell short-term Euro commercial paper and a Treasury instrument similar to the French OAT.

(8) Denmark

In early 1992, the Danish government issued an ecu-bond with a maturity of 10 years and a coupon of 8.5 percent, totaling ECU 1 billion.

G. Swaps

The ecu financial markets are characterized by a significant volume of swap transactions. The currency swap market and the interest swap market was one of the most important developments on the financial market in the 1980's. In 1990 alone, the International Swap Dealers Association estimated the total volume of interest rate swaps at $2,311.5 billion and currency swaps of $1,155.1 billion. The ecu accounted for approximately $40.3 and $47.8 billion respectively.

Table XI.5: Currency Swaps Volume 1987 - 1990 (in US dollar equivalent)

Currency	1987	1988	1989	1990
Dollar (US)	162,606	269,477	354,166	428,355
Dollar (Aus)	20,438	32,637	61,768	77,407
Franc (B)	1,330	1,867	2,997	5,695
Dollar (Cdn)	13,881	29,259	32,580	56,919
Mark	21,377	33,979	53,839	72,310
Guilder	3,987	6,164	10,132	13,109
Ecu	**18,718**	**24,497**	**39,948**	**47,832**
Franc (F)	4,827	5,178	8,435	13,398
Dollar (HK)	197	390	583	639
Dollar (NZ)	8,074	7,473	5,818	5,815
Pound	10,506	17,704	33,466	49,041
Franc (Swiss)	39,928	73,983	64,823	92,084
Yen	59,746	131,033	201,145	244,787

Source: International Swap Dealers Association

Table XI.6: Interest Rate Swaps Volume 1987 - 1990 (in US dollar equivalent)

Currency	1987	1988	1989	1990
Dollar (US)	541,517	728,166	993,746	1,272,653
Dollar (Aus)	10,688	29,341	67,599	67,342
Franc (B)	185	554	835	3,523
Dollar (Cdn)	6,494	15,771	29,169	68,292
Mark	31,640	56,466	84,620	193,365
Guilder	1,086	2,086	5,979	13,743
Ecu	**3,221**	**9,197**	**18,988**	**40,367**
Franc (F)	11,195	18,871	42,016	61,582
Dollar (HK)	1,336	2,348	2,149	2,428
Dollar (NZ)	292	2,042	444	1,013
Pound	29,706	52,265	100,417	242,089
Franc (Swiss)	5,031	14,610	28,605	80,539
Yen	40,498	78,488	128,022	231,942

Source: International Swap Dealers Association

The increase in volume of ecu swaps is attributed to the significant growth of the ecu bond market. Issuers of ecu bonds, especially large corporations, which have no ultimate use for the ecus raised by the issue swap them for other currencies. Other issuers profit from the spreads between the yields available in the different currencies or on the basis of favorable exchange rate expectations. On the secondary markets, swaps provide efficient risk management of foreign currency positions because of the more advantageous exchange rate risk at conversion.

Approximately 30 percent of all ecu bonds are swap issues. The majority are cross-currency swaps in which the parties exchange interest and capital payments in different currencies. Counter-currencies for ecu swaps include the US and Canadian dollars, Swiss and French francs and the German mark. A minority of swaps are based on different interest rates. They are usually cross-currency fixed to fixed or to floating interest rate swaps. On the bond market, swaps are used to arbitrage the competitive advantages of the parties in their respective home markets. Ecu swap issues are often advantageous to non-European borrowers as they do not require ratings as high as normal on the Eurobond rating market. A borrower in country X thereby could borrow at the favorable conditions in country Y by negotiating a swap with an entity in country Y which had a competitive advantage in that market. Borrowers with a low credit standing, for example, can avoid the higher risk premium with a swap with a higher-rated borrower.

Counter-parties to the swaps of new ecu bond issues are typically European companies unable to launch ecu issues directly because of their insufficient credit standing or agencies and corporations who have large dollar liabilities and seek to hedge their currency exposure. Swaps of new ecu issues are facilitated by the fact that credit differentials in the ecu market are narrower than in the Euro-dollar market. This means, for example, that an "A" rated company may obtain better terms in an ecu instrument than in the Euro-dollar market where the lower rating would count more.

Since 1984, ecu swaps have also included asset swaps for the purchase of ecu bonds. The purchaser of the ecu bonds swaps its interest and final capital repayment for payments of interest and repayments in a third currency. This might result in a greater yield than a direct investment in the third currency. The other party to this transaction usually needs ecu to repay an ecu obligation. The spread in the yields between the instruments results in decreased financing costs to such a party.

H. Main Purchasers - Primary Markets

Ecu bonds are purchased by a variety of investors from different countries for a multitude of purposes. They include retail, institutional and arbitrage investors. Traditionally, the ecu bond market was primarily retail-driven. Individual retail investors in France, Italy, Belgium, the Netherlands, Luxembourg and Switzerland, such as the famous "Belgian dentist", used to be the main purchasers of ecu instruments. This purchaser base has shifted dramatically toward more sophisticated institutional investors which purchase large portions of newly-issued ecu bonds and investors from non-EC countries. These include central monetary authorities, insurance companies, namely in Japan and the United States, pension funds and French SICAVs.

Table XI.7: Top Managers of Euro-Ecu Issues 1991

Rank	Manager
1	Banque Paribas
2	Morgan Stanley International
3	Credit Suisse First Boston
4	Nomura Securities
5	Banesto
6	Goldman Sachs International
7	JP Morgan
8	Swiss Bank Corporation
9	Nikko
10	Deutsche Bank
11	Crédit Commercial de France
	Banco di Roma
	Dresdner Bank

Source: Bourse de Luxembourg

Investors from countries with strong currencies and, therefore, lower interest rates, can profit from the generally higher ecu interest rate which typically stands between the highest and lowest rates of the Member States. Investors from countries with weaker currencies, on the other hand, can safeguard their investments from possible depreciations of their national currency. Ecu bonds are now widely used by private and institutional investors to diversify exchange rate risks and take advantage of the relative high rating of the securities. Their features render them very important alternative investments providing relative exchange rate stability and attractive interest rates.

Table XI.8: Top Issuers of Ecu Bonds 1990-1991

Rank	Issuer	Ecu million	Issues
1	European Investment Bank	7796.46	58
2	Republic of Italy	6428.00	11
3	EEC	4567.93	32
4	Crédit Local de France	2911.49	23
5	Kingdom of Belgium	2052.62	5
6	World Bank	1733.00	16
7	Crédit Foncier de France	1710.51	18
8	Svensk Exportkredit	1667.72	19
9	Eurofirma	1382.51	14
10	Kingdom of Denmark	1362.72	10

Source: Bourse de Luxembourg

I. The Secondary Markets

Following the initial issuance of ecu bonds, trading takes place on the secondary market. The most important requirement here is liquidity, i.e., a sufficient number of sellers and buyers for a certain bond issue to provide a functioning market. This liquidity also depends on the number of market-makers, securities firms which actively trade in ecu instruments. Initially, the secondary markets for ecu bonds suffered from chronic illiquidity. This has changed since the introduction of the benchmark jumbo issues which more than doubled the secondary trading volume in 1991.

The secondary market for ecu instruments is very similar to that for instruments denominated in other important currencies, such as the mark, yen and dollar. The clearing for the Eurobond issues takes place through Cedel and Euroclear, the two computerized settlement houses for Eurobonds.

The market differentiates between reporting dealers and market-makers. Reporting dealers are also market-makers, while market-makers need not be reporting dealers. The reporting dealer must comply with certain rules and reporting requirements concerning trading sizes and activities and the highest, lowest and closing prices per day. There are currently 27 recognized market-makers and 28 reporting dealers. The larger market-makers typically deal in about 60 to 70 ecu issues. The smallest securities firms quote about 40 to 50 issues. The minimum trading amount between these market-makers is ECU 100,000. The number of market-makers has expanded slowly since the first transactions in this market in 1982. At that time, the market was concentrated in Belgium and Luxembourg and the market-makers were mainly Belgian and Luxembourg banks. Between 1983 and 1986, a number of French, Japanese, American and British securities firms entered the sector. The number of market-makers had increased to 31 by the stock market crash on October 19, 1987. It then significantly decreased to approximately 15 securities houses. Since late 1988, however, the number of market-makers has steadily increased, especially in London.

J. The Ecu Money Market

The ecu money market for bank liabilities, medium-term notes, certificates of deposit and commercial papers (including also United Kingdom Treasury bills and Italian BTEs, please see pages 100 and 102) has been the single fastest growing segment of the ecu market. This increase can be traced back: to the stability of the ecu which has rendered it a preferred currency for entities interested in stable denominators to decrease foreign exchange risks; to the substantially increased number of jumbo-issues of ecu money market instruments by national governments, namely the United Kingdom and Italy; and to the fresh political support for the EMU and the transformation of the ecu into the single EC currency.

This expansion has been fueled mainly by the significant increase in the interbank deposit market for ecu which now account for almost 90 percent of the ecu money market. The Italian and British issues follow with a share of approximately 8 percent. Medium Term Notes, Certificates of Deposit and commercial papers constitute the remainder of the market.

Despite the significant growth of the ecu in the money markets, there have been two substantial obstacles to the further development of these products. First, the lack of demand for ecu assets from corporations - which generally have no ultimate use for the ecu in cash management, as means of payment or commercial settlement currency at this time (see page 140) - has limited the access to ecu money markets to financial institutions and governments. In addition, almost all corporations which borrow in ecus still swap the ecus received into their national currencies and do not deposit these ecus in the banking system to "use" them in their transactions. Second, there is no thoroughly developed liquid secondary market for the British and Italian money market instruments. Most of the trade takes place on the primary markets among the market-makers. The non-accessibility of these instruments through the secondary markets has turned into a major obstacle for the ecu in this segment.

Table XI.9: The Structure of the Ecu Banking Market (in ecu billion)

					Assets					
Vis-à-vis	**82IV**	**83IV**	**84IV**	**85IV**	**86IV**	**87IV**	**88IV**	**89IV**	**90IV**	**91II**
Total	**5.68**	**12.09**	**39.8**	**61.1**	**75.4**	**80.8**	**100.0**	**128.3**	**148.5**	**173.7**
- non-res.			25.4	42.9	55.3	59.3	73.3	96.7	113.9	131.8
- residents			14.4	18.2	20.1	21.5	26.7	31.6	34.6	41.9
Non-Banks		**1.33**	**11.2**	**13.9**	**16.9**	**21.5**	**24.5**	30.8	**34.3**	**44.7**
- non-res.			4.4	7.9	10.3	13.0	15.4	19.9	23.7	28.0
- residents			6.8	6.0	6.6	8.5	9.1	10.9	10.6	16.7
Bank Sector		**10.76**	**28.6**	**47.2**	**58.5**	**59.3**	**75.5**	**97.5**	**114.2**	**129.0**
- non-res.			21.0	35.0	45.0	46.3	57.9	76.8	90.2	103.8
- residents			7.6	12.2	13.5	13.0	17.6	20.7	24.0	25.1
TOTAL	**5.68**	**12.09**	**39.8**	**61.1**	**75.4**	**80.8**	**100.0**	**128.3**	**148.5**	**173.7**

					Liabilities					
Vis-à-vis	**82IV**	**83IV**	**84IV**	**85IV**	**86IV**	**87IV**	**88IV**	**89IV**	**90IV**	**91II**
Total	**6.72**	**14.38**	**31.3**	**54.5**	**64.7**	**66.5**	**85.9**	**116.9**	**147.7**	**178.8**
- non-res.			22.5	38.9	48.4	50.2	64.6	88.4	115.4	139.3
- residents			8.8	15.6	16.3	16.3	21.3	28.5	32.3	40.5
Non-Banks		**4.71**	**2.8**	**7.2**	**6.7**	**7.2**	**7.7**	**18.6**	**22.6**	**28.3**
- non-res.			1.5	3.6	3.2	4.1	4.5	11.7	14.5	18.3
- residents			1.3	3.6	3.5	3.1	3.2	6.9	8.1	10.7
Bank Sector		**9.67**	**28.5**	**47.3**	**58.0**	**59.3**	**78.2**	**98.3**	**125.1**	**150.1**
- non-res.			21.0	35.3	45.2	46.1	60.1	76.7	100.9	121.0
- residents			7.5	12.0	12.8	13.2	18.1	21.6	24.2	29.8
Comp. Curr.			**8.5**	**6.6**		**14.3**	**14.1**	**11.4**	**0.8**	**-6.1**
TOTAL	**6.72**	**14.38**	**39.8**	**61.1**	**64.7**	**80.8**	**100.0**	**128.3**	**148.5**	**173.7**

Source: Bank for International Settlements

The various ecu money market instruments available at this time include ecu deposits, commercial papers, certificates of deposit and Medium Term

Notes. The United Kingdom Treasury bills and the Italian BTEs were discussed earlier as government debt instruments.

The ecu deposit market constitutes approximately 88 percent of the ecu money market and is mainly located in London, Paris and Milan. The majority of deposits are between banks (ECU 124 billion in March 1991) and less than 10 percent are between banks and non-banks. Again, this dichotomy is the result of the very limited use of the ecu in the commercial area which, in turn, limits the amount of ecu deposit transactions by corporations.

Ecu commercial papers and certificates of deposits account for approximately 8 percent of the total ecu money market. Their secondary market is rather illiquid and, as the primary market for these instruments, is predominantly demand driven, resulting in somewhat erratic market behavior. As in other money market segments, corporations have only recently developed a stronger interest in these instruments.

Medium Term Notes, on the other hand, have developed into a high growth segment of the money market instruments. With maturities of between one and nine years (generally, however, of less than two years), they fill the segment between the bond market and the traditional money markets.

PART XII.

PRIVATE NON-BOND MARKETS

A. Loans

The market for ecu loans has grown steadily since 1981. Private parties, as well as the governments of some EC Member States, such as France, and local governments, use these syndicated ecu loans which have amounts between ECU 10 and 450 million and maturities between 1.5 and 10 years. Typical amounts are between ECU 10 and 150 million with maturities from five to eight years. Interest rates are expressed as it spreads over vary in accordance to EIBOR, PIBOR or LIBOR rates (Ecu, Paris or London Interbank Offered Rates).

Figure XII.1: Ecu Loans

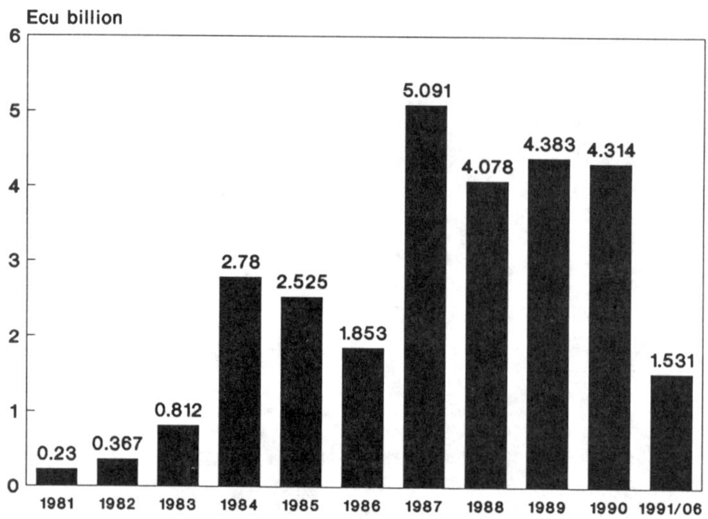

Source: Ecu Newsletter

Ecu loans are available in a number of different types. They range from Euroloans to revolving credit lines and term loans. The funds for Euroloans were historically raised entirely outside of the country of the debtor. These loans now also include internationally syndicated loans. An Ecu Commercial Paper are ecu "promissory notes" usually issued at a discount. Revolving lines of credit are loan facilities enabling the borrower to use a loan in full or in part up to a maximum amount during the lifetime of the credit arrangement. Term loans, on the other hand, are paid out in full and are repaid in full or in scheduled installments. Credit lines for suppliers and exporters and multiple loan facilities typically are comprised of a revolving credit line which can be used in various ways, including bankers acceptances or cash advances. Some ecu loans are part of multi-currency loan facilities in which other currencies also are utilized.

Despite the increasing use of ecu loans, this market is still of very limited use for most entities. There are two main reasons for this limitation. First, most smaller entities cannot participate in this market because the traditional minimum loan amount is ECU 10 million per loan. This substantial minimum only satisfies borrowers with substantial capital needs, i.e., large corporations or public entities. A small corporation, on the other hand, with financing needs in any amount below ECU 10 million cannot obtain ecu loans. Second, only entities using ecus in their daily transactions can use the proceeds of the ecu loans directly without re-exchange. Unless it borrows the ecus through an ecu loan and then immediately exchanges them for another currency, an entity must be able to use the underlying ecus. Only large corporations or governments which use the ecus to pay obligations or to make certain investments will be able to use the ecu proceeds in this way. Entities with no means to use the ecu proceeds directly have to exchange the ecus - and incur the substantial fees and possible exchange rate related losses. For these entities it will be more advantageous at this time to borrow directly in the currency which they need for payments and financing.

B. Futures and Options

The development and introduction of ecu futures and options soon followed the issue of the first ecu bonds and loans. Seven major exchanges in Europe and the United States have offered or are currently offering ecu futures and options. The European Options Exchange (EOE) in Amsterdam launched the first option on the ecu in 1985. The New York Cotton Exchange (NYCE), the Philadelphia Board of Trade (PBOT) and the Chicago Mercantile Exchange (CME) introduced ecu futures and the Philadelphia Stock Exchange (PHLX) introduced ecu options in 1986 The London International Financial Futures Exchange (LIFFE) offered a three-month interest rate futures contract denominated in ecu in 1989 and an ecu bond futures contract in 1991. The Marché à Terme des Instruments Financiers (MATIF) in Paris introduced a 10-year ecu-futures contract in 1990. In addition, the Chicago Board of Trade (CBOT) obtained government approval for a three-month ecu interbank interest rate contract in 1991. This contract has not yet been launched.

Generally speaking, most of the earlier of these instruments were not very successful and have not been used extensively. The EOE contract, for example, was delisted soon after its introduction. There are two probable major reasons for this disappointing performance. First, despite the popularity of the ecu in a number of market segments, the actual *number* of users of ecu instruments is rather small. This naturally limits the potential quantitative demand for options and futures as hedging instruments for entities using the ecu. Second, and more important, the composition of the ecu and its resulting foreign exchange stability do not require futures and options for hedging purposes to the same degree as for other currencies. The success of the ecu as a stable currency thus might be the main obstacle to its success in the futures and options markets.

Despite this development, there has always been a perceived need for an ecu hedging vehicle. As the use of ecus in international trade and finance increases and the composition of the ecu as a basket disappears, the corresponding increase in the exposure of the ecu as a currency will warrant the introduction of futures and options as common hedging instruments. Apart from its use for basic payment hedging, an ecu futures contract can serve as a proxy for hedging many currencies which do not have individual active and liquid forward contracts and as hedge for ecu bonds. For example, a potential purchaser of an ecu bond can hedge against the rise in the value of the ecu by buying an ecu futures contract prior to the purchase. The owner of the bond would sell contracts to hedge against a decline in the value of the ecu prior to the sale of the bond. Ecu futures also can hedge the interest payments of ecu bonds. Although, resulting from its stability, the fluctuations of the ecu are more limited than that of other currencies, some fluctuations can be expected and hedging might be advantageous.

The following is an example of a simple payment hedge against another currency:

An importer in the United States and an exporter in Spain contract for the sale of goods from Spain to the United States. The contract is denominated in ecu as the Spanish company wants to take advantage of the peseta/ecu rate which is relatively more stable than the peseta/dollar rate. The importer receives the goods on September 1, the payment of ECU 1,250,000 is due on December 1 and the importer will sell the goods for dollars. At the end of the period, on December 1, the importer will have to pay the balance on the ecu account to the Spanish exporter. The exchange rate between the ecu and the dollar might change between September 1 and December 1. The United States importer might suffer a loss as a result of the appreciation of the ecu against the dollar in which case it will have to spend more dollars to buy the necessary ecus. To avoid such exchange losses before the payment on December 1, the importer in the United States will buy 10 ecu futures contracts of ECU 125,000 on September 1 for delivery on December 1 at a fixed price. On December 1, the importer will offset any loss it might have incurred from the changed exchange rates by the gain realized from the increased value of the futures contract.

Table XII.1: Hedging Transaction with Ecu Futures

Futures transaction			
Number of contracts purchased at CME: 10			
Increase in value of ecu: 20% (from $1.4000 to 1.6800 per ecu)			
Purchased	Sept. 1	1.4000 $/ECU	
Sold	Dec. 1	1.6800 $/ECU	
Gain per contract		0.2800 $/ECU	
Total gain for futures transactions			
10 x 125.000 x 0.2800		=	$350,000
Cash transaction			
Dollar value of ECU 1,250,000			
Sept. 1 (1.4000$/ECU)		=	$1,750,000
Dec. 1 (1.6800$/ECU)		=	$2,100,000
Increase in cost		=	$ 350,000
Loss in cash transaction		=	$ 350,000
Gain in futures transaction		=	$ 350,000
Net Gain		=	$ 0

The above transaction, of course, is a simplified example of an ecu hedge. As a result of different interest rates for ecu and dollar instruments, there will be a difference between the ecu spot exchange rate and the ecu futures price. This difference (the basis) will make the balance of the gains and losses less than perfect. In addition, there will be fees charged by the brokers and traders for the purchase and sale of the futures contracts and the foreign exchange. However, as in every hedge, the basic idea is to decrease exchange rate exposure. Although such exposure might be minimal in the case of the ecu, the availability of ecu futures and options permits concerned parties to take advantage of ecu hedging.

As indicated, there have been seven exchanges in Europe and the United States which have listed ecu futures or options contracts. The following is a short overview of the characteristics of the contracts still in existence. Again, it is important to note that the trading volume for some of these instruments is negligible at this time. A party interested in using ecu futures or options should realize that there might not be a liquid market for such instruments for purchase or sale. The volume at these exchanges should increase following the transformation of the ecu into the single EC currency. Until such time, however, trading will remain limited for some instruments.

The European Options Exchange (EOE) in Amsterdam launched the first ecu/dollar option on December 5, 1985. The contract has been delisted for lack of trade.

The Financial Instruments Exchange (FINEX), a division of the New York Cotton Exchange, offers ecu futures and options contracts.

Table XII.2: Finex Ecu Futures Contract Specifications

Underlying trade	US$/ecu spot exchange rate
Contract size	ECU 100,000
Quotation	Cents per ecu
Minimum price fluctuation	US$ 10.00 per contract
Maximum price fluctuation	Prior day's settlement +/- 200 ticks (no limit during last 30 minutes of trade). Establishment of new limits of +/- 200 ticks should the price hit ecu old limit and remain within 100 ticks of that limit for 15 minutes (the new limit will be at +/- 200 ticks the previous limit)
Expiration months	March, June, September and December
Last day of trading	Two business days before third Wednesday of expiration month
Settlement date	Third Wednesday of expiration month
Trading hours (local time)	7:00 pm-10:00 pm and 11:30 pm-3:00 pm (Daylight Savings hours: 7:00 pm-11:00 pm and 12:30 am-3:00 pm
Date of launch	January 7, 1986
Settlement	Physical delivery of ecus.

Table XII.3: Finex Ecu Option Contract Specifications

Contract size	One FINEX ecu futures contract (ECU100,000)
Quotation	Cents per ecu
Minimum price fluctuation	US$ 10.00 per contract
Maximum price fluctuation	None
Contract months	March, June, September and December and two nearest months
Last day of trading	Two Fridays before third Wednesday of expiration month
Trading hours (local time)	7:00 pm-10:00 pm and 11:30 pm-3:00 pm (Daylight Savings hours: 7:00 pm-11:00 pm and 12:30 am-3:00 pm
Exercise	Until 5:00 pm on the last trading day

The Chicago Mercantile Exchange (CME) introduced its ecu futures contract on January 15, 1986.

Table XII.4: CME Ecu Futures Contract Specifications

Underlying trade	US$/ecu spot exchange rate
Contract size	ECU 125,000
Quotation	Cents per ecu
Minimum price fluctuation	US$ 12.50 per contract
Maximum price fluctuation	None
Position limits	4,000 contracts
Expiration months	March, June, September and December
Last day of trading	Two business days before third Wednesday of expiration month
Settlement date	Third Wednesday of expiration month
Delivery	Physical ecu
Trading hours (local time)	7:20 am-1:30 pm
Date of launch	January 15, 1986

The Philadelphia Stock Exchange (PHLX) opened the trade in ecu options on February 12; 1986.

Table XII.5: PHLX Ecu Futures Contract Specifications

Underlying trade	US$/ecu spot exchange rate
Contract size	ECU 62,500
Quotation	Cents per ecu
Option type	American
Strike price interval	2 cents
Minimum price fluctuation	US$ 6.25 per contract
Maximum price fluctuation	None
Position limits	6,000 contracts
Expiration months	March, June, September and December + 2 additional near months
Last day of trading	Friday before third Wednesday of expiration month
Settlement date	Third Wednesday of expiration month
Delivery	Physical ecu
Trading hours (local time)	8:30 am-2:30 pm
Date of launch	February 12, 1986

The Philadelphia Board of Trade (PBOT) launched its ecu futures contract on August 8, 1986.

Table XII.6: PBOT Ecu Futures Contract Specifications

Underlying trade	US$/ecu spot exchange rate
Contract size	ECU 125,000
Quotation	Cents per ecu
Minimum price fluctuation	US$ 12.50 per contract
Maximum price fluctuation	None
Position limits	4,000 contracts
Expiration months	March, June, September and December (+ 2 additional months)
Last day of trading	Friday before third Wednesday of expiration month
Settlement date	Third Wednesday of expiration month
Delivery	Physical ecu
Trading hours (local time)	8:00 am-2:30 pm
Date of launch	August 8, 1986

The London International Financial Futures Exchange (LIFFE) introduced a three-month ecu interest rate futures contract on October 28, 1989. This contract is based on the bid/offer midpoint forward-forward interest rate for the ecu. It allows an entity to engage in liability risk management by limiting the exposure to rising interest rates and asset risk management by limiting the exposure to falling interest rates.

Table XII.7: LIFFE Three-Month Ecu Interest Rate Futures Contract

Contract size	ECU 1,000,000
Delivery months	March, June, September, December
Delivery day	First business after the last trading day
Last trading Day	11:00 am, two business days prior to third Wednesday of delivery month
Quotation	100.00 minus implied rate of interest
Minimum price	0.01 (ECU 25)
Trading hours (London time)	8:05 am to 4:05 pm
Contract standard	Cash settlement based on the Exchange Delivery Settlement Price (EDSP)
Exchange delivery Settlement price	Based on the British Bankers' Association Interest Settlement Rate (BBAISR) for three-month ecu deposits at 11.00 a.m. on the last trading day. The settlement price will be 100.00 minus the BBAISR.
Date of launch	October 28, 1989

The ecu interest rate contract is traded on an index basis, like other Eurocurrency futures, which is calculated by subtracting an implied interest rate from 100. For example, a price of 92.5 implies an interest rate of 7.5 percent. With the rise in the interest expectations, the price will decrease and vice versa.

Investors who will invest in three-month ecu deposits or ecu treasury certificates at some point in the future will buy this contract in anticipation of a decline in interest rates. Such a decline in interest rates will lower the interest of the ecu deposits or treasury certificates and, thereby, the investor's profit. The profit realized on the sale of the futures contract, however, will compensate for this drop in the interest revenue. The overall profit on the futures contract will correspond to the lower interest rates.

This contract is the first exchange-traded hedging instrument on the interest rates of ecu instruments. Generale Bank, Kredietbank N.V. and Istituto Bancario San Paolo di Torino are the designated market-makers.

In March 1991, the LIFFE also introduced a bond futures contract. As result of the minimal trading volume of this contract, the LIFFE made important changes to the specifications, most notably in the bond issues permitted for delivery, effective from March 1992.

Table XII.8: LIFFE Ecu Bond Futures Contract Specifications

Contract Size	ECU 200,000 nominal value Ecu bond with 9 percent annual coupon
Delivery Months	March, June, September and December
Quotation	Per ECU 100 nominal value
Minimum Price Movement	ECU 0.01 (ECU 20)
Delivery day	20th calendar day of delivery month
Last trading day	Same as LIFFE Bund contract (11:00 a.m. Brussels)
Trading hours	8:00 am-4:15 pm (London time)
Deliverable Bonds	Delivery may be made of any Deliverable Ecu Bond on the list for such bonds for a particular delivery month (see following text for inclusion)
Date of launch	March 6, 1991

To be included in the LIFFE Deliverable Bonds list, a particular issue must:

(a) be a direct, unsubordinated debt obligation of a sovereign country or its government;
(b) have an aggregate amount of at least ECU 1 billion, solely payable in ecus;
(c) have a remaining maturity of between 6 and 10 years with a single redemption date;
(d) be not callable;
(e) not bear an investor put option except for default events;

(f) bear a single, fixed interest rate with annual or semi-annual payments in ecus;
(g) be fully paid and eligible for secondary trading;
(h) deliverable through Cedel or Euroclear;
(i) not be subject to withholding tax; and
(j) listed or quoted on a stock exchange.

The final determination regarding the inclusion of a particular bond is in the discretion of LIFFE.

The Marché à Terme des Instruments Financiers (MATIF) in Paris introduced a 10-year ecu bond future on October 18, 1990. At the expiration of the future, the seller selects the bond to be delivered to the buyer from a "basket of securities". This basket contains bonds issued by sovereign governments and international institutions

Table XII.9: MATIF Ecu Futures Contract Specifications

Contract	national issue
Nominal value	ECU 100,000
Interest coupon	10%
Maturity	10 years
Delivery	ecu-denominated bonds with fixed interest rates, amortized at expiration and issued by national governments and supra-national institutions
Deliverable bonds	OAT 8.5% 1997; OAT 9.5% 2000; OAT 9.5% 2001; UK 9.125% 2001
Quotation	in percent with two decimal points
Minimum price fluctuation	0.02% or ECU 20
Expiration months	two successive quarterly expirations (March, June, September and December)
Closing day	four trading days before the last trading day
Opening date	the working day which follows the 15th of the delivery month
Maximum price fluctuation	150 base points
Trading hours	9:00 am to 4:00 pm (local time)
Launch date	October 18, 1990

In late 1990, the Commodity Futures Trading Commission of the United States approved a new ecu bond futures contract as hedging instrument at the Chicago Board of Trade (CBOT). This contract is based on three-month ecu interbank interest rates similar to the LIFFE and MATIF contracts. The trade has not yet been introduced at the CBOT and the following are merely the expected characteristics of this contract.

Table XII.10: CBOT Ecu Futures Contract Specifications

Underlying trade	Bond with annual coupon of 9%
Contract size	ECU 100,000 nominal value
Quotation	Per ECU 100 par value
Minimum price fluctuation	ECU 0.01 = ECU 10 per contract
Delivery months	March, June, September and December
Delivery/Settlement Day	20th calendar day of delivery month (if not an Ecu Clearing day, then the following day which is a market and clearing day)
Last day of trading	11:00 am Brussels time on same last trading day as LIFFE Bund contract
Delivery	Any ecu bond on Qualification List for delivery month
Trading hours (London time)	8:00 am - 4:15 pm
Date of launch	pending

The CBOT contract requires the delivery of a ecu bond on the CBOT Qualification List for the respective delivery month for the settlement of the futures contract. Bonds must have the following characteristics on the delivery date to be eligible for that list:

(a) issued by, or direct obligation of, a national government (domestic or sovereign Euroissue) or a supranational entity;
(b) aggregate amount of at least ECU 1 billion and repayable in ecus;
(c) implicit or explicit AAA or Aaa Standard & Poor's or Moody's rating;
(d) initial maturity of less than 12 years and a remaining maturity between six and 10 years;
(e) single redemption date;
(f) non-callable other than withholding tax call;
(g) no investor put except related to events of default;

(h) interest payment in exclusively in ecu at fixed rate annually or semi-annually;
(i) fully paid and eligible for trade in secondary markets;
(j) deliverable through Euroclear or Cedel;
(k) not subject to withholding taxes; and
(l) listed or quoted on a stock exchange.

C. Ecu Foreign Exchange Markets

The ecu is officially quoted on the exchange markets in almost all EC Member States as well as without official rates in London and Dublin. Trading in spot and forward ecu is concentrated in the Paris, Brussels, London and Luxembourg markets. The ecu, like the British pound, is a currency whose quotation is expressed in terms of dollars per ecu and not in terms of ecu per dollar.

Table XII.11: Ecu Foreign Exchange Markets

Exchange	First Quotation
MILAN AND ROME	March 15, 1984
PARIS	June 4, 1984
BRUSSELS	September 3, 1984
COPENHAGEN	September 17, 1984
ATHENS	January 24, 1985
OSLO	January 3, 1985
AMSTERDAM	July 1, 1985
LISBON	August 15, 1985
STOCKHOLM	October 1, 1985
VIENNA	January 2, 1986
MADRID	July 1, 1986

Source: Centre Ecu et Prospective d'Intégration Monétaire Européenne

On the spot market, the majority of ecu transactions involve the German mark and the United States dollar as counter-currencies. The central banks of the EC Member States, the EC institutions and the European Investment Bank are the most active parties on this market. The underlying transactions include interventions by the central banks (as most EMS interventions are undertaken in marks and dollars, see page 31) and the management and diversification of the currency portfolios of the central banks. The predominant position of the official institutions on this market is based on the fact that only very few private parties can use ecu in their daily transactions. For example, only very few corporations use the ecu as denominator for payments or other business transactions. Therefore, those entities will not require to trade ecus for their national currencies to make certain payments. A Belgian importer, for example, who negotiates with an American exporter to pay the price for the goods imported in US dollars would have to exchange its Belgian francs into dollars at the foreign exchange markets to effectuate the payment. As only few corporations invoice in ecu at this time, such conversion is not necessary with regard to the ecu. With the transformation of the ecu into the single EC currency and the increasing use of ecus in commercial transactions which will require the exchange of national currencies into ecus, the ecu foreign exchange markets should experience a dramatic increase in users and volume.

Table XII.12: Currency Composition of the Foreign Exchange Markets (April 1989)

Currency	Percentage Share
US dollar	45.0
Deutsche Mark	12.5
Yen	13.0
Pound Sterling	7.5
Swiss franc	6.0
Australian dollar	2.0
French franc	1.5
Canadian dollar	1.0
Ecu	0.5
Others	11.0

Source: BIS

There are no regularly published reports on the quantity of ecu traded on the spot markets. Estimates now exceed a daily aggregate of ECU 10 billion with approximately ECU 8 billion in London alone. The increase in the number of brokers in the spot ecu market has resulted in an uninterrupted availability of bid and offer quotations. The bid/offer spread is generally lower for the relatively stable ecu than for other currencies because it does not need to account for possible significant fluctuations.

Market-makers determine the bid and offer spot rates for the ecu by calculating them with the bid and offer rates of the EC currencies in terms of a third currency in the same way the EC Commission calculates the official rate of the ecu (see page 50). The dollar/ecu spreads range from ECU 0.003 to 0.007 for amounts below $20 million and ECU 0.001 to 0.0015 for higher volumes.

The forward ecu exchange market is concentrated in Brussels, Paris, Dublin, Stockholm, New York and London. The volume on this market is still very limited. The trade focuses almost exclusively on exchanges of ecu for dollar. Generally, the transactions are in amounts of over ECU 25 million with maturities of up to six months.

The ecu spot and forward exchange markets are important for the development of the private ecu. They provide instant "cash" ecus to central banks and other institutions. However, only with the increased use of commercial ecus at or possibly before the final transformation of the ecu in the single EC currency, will this market gain importance for corporations and eventually rival that of the dollar. At present, the spot and foreign exchange markets account only for about 1 percent of global foreign exchange transactions and are only accessible to large corporations and public entities with the need for significant amounts of ecus. Smaller entities cannot fully utilize spot and forward transactions because of the adverse structure of the markets and the fact that those entities often do not even require spot and forward ecus for their normal business transactions.

D. Ecu Investment Funds

The ecu is a very advantageous currency for investors, private or institutional, who are looking for a safe investment in a foreign currency with stable exchange rates. As outlined, the ecu has both of those characteristics as a result of its nature as a basket currency and the quantity of the issuers of ecu bonds and similar instruments. Investors who are interested in investing in a wide array of ecu instruments are interested in ecu-denominated investment funds. The increasing demand prompted large commercial banks in Europe and the United States to create a sizable number of such funds with portfolios consisting partially or entirely of ecu bonds, money market and other financial instruments in their branches in Luxembourg, France and the Channel Islands. Since October 1984, the number of such investment funds has grown at a rapid pace with fund sizes ranging from ECU 167,000 to over ECU 200 million. Some are composed of ecu-denominated assets but valued and subscribed in French franc. The funds are generally divided into four classes according to their investments:

(a) funds composed of instruments denominated in ecus or its component currencies;
(b) general funds without specialized focus on ecu instruments which invest partly in ecus;
(c) general funds without specialized focus on ecu instruments which are denominated in ecus; and
(d) umbrella funds which include ecu funds.

Like investment funds in other currencies, ecu funds provide significant risk management opportunities through the wide range of their investments. Ecu funds are particularly interesting for investors in foreign currency funds because they are not subject to significant exchange rate losses. In addition, the generally favorable ecu interest rates enable investors to invest in competitively priced low-risk instruments.

E. Insurance in Ecu-Denomination

There have been attempts in recent years to introduce the ecu for insurance and re-insurance contracts. Although the market for such contracts is very limited at this time, some ecu contracts have been issued. The transformation of the ecu into the single EC currency will significantly increase the number of offering insurance carriers, the types of contracts offered, the types of risks covered and the number of insured parties.

There are two main reasons for the current growing interest in ecu insurance contracts. First, the inherent stability of the ecu makes it a very valuable currency for insurance companies as it decreases fluctuation losses while allowing the insurer to offer foreign currency contracts. Resulting from the increasing international business, foreign currency policies are an important features in the product mix of insurance companies. Second, an increase in ecu securities and other instruments on the commercial and private markets will increase the need for ecu insurance contracts. An entity engaging in an ecu transaction, for example, will also need insurance contracts (denominated in the same currency to avoid conversion losses or inadequate coverage) to safeguard the investment. The fastest growth of ecu insurance contracts should be expected in the commercial area where corporate treasurers will seek ecu insurance coverage as soon as the ecu becomes a widely used commercial currency. Again, the need for such ecu coverage will only become acute either when ecu-denominated assets have to be protected or when there is an independent ecu insurance market which offers more favorable terms than insurance in other currency denominations.

Greater labor mobility across Europe should increase the interest in ecu life insurance contracts for private parties. The payment in ecus of the insurance amount, for example, will not subject an insured United States citizen living in Spain to potential exchange rate fluctuations or conversion risks between a dollar insurance payment and the peseta.

Another potential area for the ecu is re-insurance contracts. Reinsurance companies often cannot predict the currency in which claims ultimately are payable. Ecu re-insurance contracts would reduce exposure to foreign exchange risk. The ecu would also make the establishment of a pan-European insurance claim settlement system possible in which all participants such as brokers, customers and insurance companies would use the ecu as their sole currency.

The European Space Agency (ESA) already uses ecu insurance contracts. The ESA is an international organization among European nations which promotes cooperation in space research, technology and the implementation of a European space program. Before 1984, ESA contracted space insurance in United States dollars. The significant exchange rate fluctuations of the dollar resulted in inadequate insurance coverage because the lesser amount of dollars received did not cover the insurance claims which typically were denominated in other, namely European, currencies. As a result, the ESA changed the denomination of its insurance contracts and used a combination of ecus and dollars for its main projects until 1987/88. In June 1988, however, the ESA convinced its insurance carrier to sell the first pure ecu space insurance. A "pure" ecu insurance contract essentially contains the same provisions as contracts in other currencies. The main difference is the ecu denomination of the premium and coverage payments, the valuation of the insured property and the deductible amount. By using ecu-denomination, the insured party, especially when located in the EC, can significantly reduce foreign exchange exposure because the amount of national currency received upon exchange of the ecu will hardly change during the life of the policy as result of the stability of the ecu value through the EMS.

A number of other insurance companies now offer ecu contracts. These include Assicuriazioni Generali di Triëste in Italy, Union des Assurances de Paris in France and Assurantieconcern De Stad Rotterdam in the Netherlands. In addition, Verenigde Provinciën in Belgium and Le Foyer in Luxembourg provide travel insurance for Eurocard holders.

At this time, only large entities, such as ESA, use these contracts. A new market, however, is developing for private life insurance contracts as described above. Such contracts may be of interest not only for private parties living in different EC countries, but also for employers who are interested in providing adequate and relatively exchange risk-free insurance coverage for their employees. The EC Commission supports the use of the ecu for life insurance. Its recent common position on the new non-life insurance directive and the Third Life Insurance Directive of 1991 give the ecu a preferred status in this field.

F. Other Private Ecu Uses

The ecu has made other inroads into the lives of EC citizens. Private ecu services offered by a growing number of financial institutions comprise traveler's checks, credit cards, mortgages (some Italian banks denominate up to 30 percent of their new mortgages in ecus) and sight, time and savings accounts. The ecu is particularly advantageous for the private customer. The alternative, known in its full extent to every traveler in Europe, is a diverse and sobering assortment of traveler's checks and banknotes in at least a dozen denominations.

In a recent study, a European consumer organization researched the various means of payment available to travelers in the EC. The study showed that users of traveler's checks, credit cards, Eurocheques and international postchecks are subject to substantial fees in the form of additional commissions, brokerage fees and increased conversion rates. The prime example for such fees, which stresses the need for a single EC currency, is the use of cash for travel purposes. According to the study, a traveler starting in Belgium with 50,000 Belgian francs would, after traveling to each EC country and merely exchanging the cash into local currencies, return to Belgium with 25,241 Belgian francs. This loss of 49.5 percent is attributable mainly to transaction fees and, to a small extent, to exchange fluctuations.

A number of European banks now offer sight accounts, time accounts and savings accounts in ecus. Although the number of ecu accounts is still very small, the transformation of the ecu into the single EC currency, by necessity, will dramatically increase the number of banks offering such accounts and, of course, the number of users. In essence, all accounts currently denominated in a national currency in the EC which will be abolished and substituted by the ecu will have to be changed into ecu accounts. Ultimately, all accounts for the 340+ million citizens and all EC businesses will be in ecus.

One of the major problems currently related to ecu accounts is the transaction costs charged by banks for ecu transactions. These ranged from 1.15 to over 4.6 percent per transaction in 1989.

Table XII.13: Transaction Costs in Ecus on Ecu Accounts (Survey of Six Banks in Luxembourg, November 1989)

	Amount of Transaction Involved					
	ECU 100		ECU1000		ECU10000	
	Min	Max	Min	Max	Min	Max
Receipt of ecu transfer	0	1.73	0	1.73	0	15.01
Number of banks	(5)	(1)	(5)	(1)	(5)	(1)
Conversion of transfers	0	1.15	0.5	4.62	10	46.20
Number of banks	(1)	(1)	(1)	(1)	(2)	(1)
Ecu transfer - same bank	0	1.73	0	1.73	0	15.01
Number of banks	(5)	(1)	(5)	(1)	(5)	(1)
Ecu transfer - local bank	1.15	4.65	1.73	4.65	3.23	39.72
Number of banks	(1)	(1)	(1)	(1)	(1)	(1)
SWIFT transfer abroad	1.15	4.65	1.73	4.65	3.23	39.72
Number of banks	(2)	(2)	(2)	(2)	(1)	(1)

Source: European Investment Bank

These fees should decrease with the increase in the number of ecu accounts and in the interbank competition following the transformation of the ecu. At this point, however, account transfers in ecus still are considered "special services" to a limited number of customers in a market with limited competition. Therefore, the banks are currently able to charge substantially higher fees for such services. In order to promote and facilitate the use of ecus, San Paolo Bank reduced its fees for ecu transactions by 50 percent in June 1991.

Société du Chèque de Voyage and Thomas Cook issued the first ecu traveler's checks in 1985. These checks are purchased in the buyer's national currency and are then negotiated with affiliated banks or businesses for payment in the national currency in the foreign country. About 90 percent of the payments are made at affiliated banks. They might become a viable competitor to the United States dollar as a means of international private payment, especially after the transformation of the ecu into the single EC currency.

The advantages of ecu traveler's checks are essentially fourfold. First, the users of such checks can take advantage of the periodically fixed rate of the ecu against the EC currencies when traveling through EC countries. Second, users from countries with weak national currencies can avoid exchange losses on cashing such checks because the value of the ecu will not change. If such users had bought checks in their own currencies, a possible devaluation would decrease the amount of currency available at a later point of time in the foreign country. Third, all major banks in the EC and other western European countries, as well as an increasing number of retail stores accept the ecu as a currency for payment. This facilitates currency management for the traveling party. In this respect, it must be kept in mind, however, that this system will require the retailer to offer its goods, and to accept payment, in ecu. This results in increased administrative expenses, monetary as well as intangible, to the retailer. This problem can only be solved by introducing the ecu as sole legal tender, at which point the retailer will only have to deal with one currency. Fourth, the ecu also can be exchanged into any of the basket currencies at relatively stable rates. In this case, however, the exchanging entity would possibly charge substantial conversion fees and costs. In general, ecu traveler's checks provide the traveler with the convenience of one currency, the general facilitation of international travel, savings in the form of decreased exchange rate fees and security as a result of the inherent stability.

The first ecu credit cards were issued in Luxembourg in September 1983. Balancing and settlement procedures are carried out in ecu via an ecu current account. Payments, of course, can still only be made by the owner in its national currency as physical ecu money, coins and notes, do not yet exist.

Visa International and Eurocard International have accepted the ecu as an official denominator for payments and transactions. The 1.5 million businesses which accept these cards can now transact business in ecus. Also, the traditional Eurocheque guarantee has been extended to the ecu for ECU 170 per check as of January 1, 1991. This action has included the ecu as valid currency for payments in the pan-European Eurocheque system even though the amount of ecu Eurocheques is still very limited.

The ecu is also slowly gaining importance as a denominator for the pricing of goods at the retail level in some EC countries. Usually, such pricing takes the form of parallel pricing with the national currency and the ecu. Although still limited, it is prominent in Belgium and Luxembourg. The governments of those two Member States strongly support the use of the ecu for this purpose. A prime example was the Luxembourg government's decision to declare November 1989 as "ecu month". All residents and nonresidents were encouraged to use ecus for payments of all kinds. This measure was quite successful with up to 10 percent of transactions being conducted in ecus during that month. A similar action took place in the town of Bellême in Normandy. For two days in June 1991, payments for goods and services could be made with specially minted ecu coins. These coins were also freely exchangeable into any EC currency. The success of these programs, albeit limited in time and area, indicates that some EC citizens are actually prepared to accept the ecu as their daily currency.

A related private use of the ecu is the denomination of court judgments and the corresponding enforcements of judgements. The availability of judgments in foreign currencies depends on national laws as the ecu will be subject to the same restrictions as any other foreign currency. Once such an ecu judgment is rendered, the enforcement and possible foreclosure of levied property will also have to take place in ecus. The use of ecus in this area provides the judgment recipient with exchange rate stability and ensures that the amount finally received equals that set forth in the judgment and is not decreased by intermediate rate losses.

An area with increasing interest in the use of ecus is the $800 billion pension industry in Europe. With increasing intra-EC mobility as a result of the creation of the Single Market, companies and employees are searching for a denominator for their pension plans which can both decrease exchange risk to the provider and stability for the recipient of the pension who might relocate from country to country and might be subject to foreign exchange related losses.

G. Ecu Coins

A psychological shortfall of the ecu has always been the lack of physical ecu money. In 1984, to promote the ecu and to make Europeans more aware of their membership in the EMS, the European Parliament called on the Member States to issue metal ecu coins under the authority of EMCF. The Member States and the European institutions, however, never reached an agreement on this issue.

The situation changed in March 1987, when the Belgian Royal Mint issued the first "modern" gold and silver ecu coins. It minted 2 million five-ecu silver coins and 200,000 50-ecu gold coins for distribution in Europe, the United States, Canada, Japan, Australia and South East Asia. Royal decrees authorized the minting and provided the ecu with full exchange value and legal tender status in the Kingdom of Belgium (see Appendix B). The minting was very successful (as a convenient side-effect, the sale of the ecu coins resulted in a net gain of 2 to 3 billion Belgian francs for the Belgian Treasury). The coins have turned into a sought-after item for numismatics and are now traded at a price much higher than the issue value. The obverse of the coins shows the same portrait of Charles V which appeared on silver coins minted in Bruges between 1540 and 1548. Charles, born in 1500, was crowned Emperor of the Holy Roman Empire of German Nations in 1519. He introduced a new monetary system in 1521 as part of which the silver florin was minted in 1540 in an effort to introduce a single coin and currency for the entire market (see page 36).

Since the first issue, a number of other countries and repeat issues of ecu coins have followed. Belgium minted a second issue of ECU 50 and 25 gold coins in 1989. In the same year, Spain minted ECU 10, 50 and 100 gold and ECU 1 and 5 silver coins. In 1990, Ireland, France and Belgium introduced ecu coins. Ireland issued ECU 50 gold and ECU 10 silver coins. The French coins have a double value designation in ecu and franc. Ecu gold and platinum coins are valued at ECU70/FF500 and silver coins at ECU15/FF100. The most recent Belgian coins are ECU 10 and 20 gold coins. Although these coins have legal tender status, they are more valuable as collector items at present. And although they are far from being the single EC currency, they represent a very important step in this direction as the issuing countries accept these coins as legal tender in their respective territories. At this point the problem is that the Belgium coins are not legal tender in France, for example. Once the ecu becomes the single EC currency, ecu notes issued by the new central bank and coins issued by the Member States will be legal tender in all Member States.

H. The Ecu Clearing System

At this point, mention must be made of an extremely important factor in the development of the private ecu: the Ecu Clearing System. This highly advanced system represents the technical side of transactions in ecus by providing a settlement mechanism for ecu payments and transactions. As more ecu-denominated products become available, more payments are being made in ecus between private parties. These parties will approach their respective financial institutions and request the making or receiving of ecu payments. In order to facilitate the multitude of such incoming and outgoing transactions, a number of banks established the Ecu Clearing System as their interbank payments and settlement system.

The Ecu Clearing System has been instrumental in the development of the private and commercial ecu markets. It is a multilateral clearing system for transactions in private ecu among 44 commercial clearing banks, the Bank for International Settlements (BIS) and the Society for Worldwide International Financial Telecommunications (SWIFT). The system began operations on October 1, 1986 after a study on the feasibility of a multilateral clearing system for private ecu payments had been proposed by the EC Commission to the European Investment Bank and five commercial banks in 1983. These banks then formed the MESA-Group (Mutual Ecu Settlement Account). Thirteen more commercial banks joined these six institutions, founding the Ecu Banking Association (EBA) in Paris on September 17, 1985. The member institutions of the EBA now are located in all EC Member States, Austria, Switzerland, Scandinavia, the United States and Japan.

The clearing system entails a two-phase settlement procedure: the initial *netting* and the final *settlement* phases, both transacted on Brussels time. The BIS maintains a clearing and an ecu sight account for each participant. It acts as the clearing agent and the "bank for the clearing banks" in that it undertakes the technical clearing transactions and maintains the accounts in its books but it does not act as a lender of last resort and does not carry out any central bank functions for the clearing members. One of the express roles of the new EC central bank (and the interim EMI) will be the establishment of a pan-EC clearing system which will very likely take over the role of the current private Ecu Clearing System. The new system would, of course, be much larger and transact a tremendous number of settlements on a daily basis. At the moment, however, the private Ecu Clearing System is the only - and an extremely well-functioning and successful - settlement mechanism for the ecu with a monthly turnover of ECU 750 billion. Its success has prompted some Eastern and Central European countries to study the feasibility of a very similar, ecu-based clearing system (see page 153) to assist their fledgling market economies.

The initial clearing system among the EBA banks operated on a "next day value" basis in which only payments valued the next day would be cleared on a certain business day. This procedure was changed in 1988 and the clearing now operates on a "same day value" basis. As a result of the numerous and varying bank holidays in the different Member States, the clearing system was faced with a potentially large number of days on which no clearing would be possible. Special arrangements have decreased the number of non-clearing days significantly from approximately 25 to seven per year.

Table XII.14: The Settlement Procedures of the Ecu Clearing System

Time	Action
until 11:00 am	Customers must submit payment orders to their respective clearing banks.
2:00 pm	Preliminary cut-off: SWIFT calculates the preliminary netting balances
2:10 pm	SWIFT reports the preliminary netting balances to the clearing members
2:10 pm - 3:15 pm	Netting phase: The clearing members engage in pre-settlement transfers
3:15 pm	Final cut-off: SWIFT calculates the final netting balances on the BIS clearing account
3:15 pm - 3:45 pm	Settlement phase: The banks deposit funds on the sight accounts at BIS
3:45 pm	Final clearing: BIS balances the clearing accounts

Source: Ecu Banking Association

The netting phase serves as pre-settlement mechanism among the commercial banks. Each clearing bank allows its customers to transact ecu payments with same day value, usually until 11:00 a.m. Brussels time. If the netting results in a positive preliminary balance, when a clearing number has received more ecu than it has transferred to other members, an ecu asset results. This asset balance can be lent or sold to other members. In this phase, the banks attempt to pre-settle or at least diminish their positive or negative balances.

The BIS-maintained clearing account is then debited or credited with the final balance determined in the netting phase. The balances state the residual liabilities or claims of the members against each other following the transactions after the preliminary balance.

These final netting balances established at 3:15 pm are settled in the settlement stage. At 3:45 pm, the BIS settles the balances on the clearing accounts with the funds available in the ecu sight accounts of the respective banks. The BIS credits or debits each clearing account with the respective final netting balance and settles that balance by crediting or debiting the respective balance of the sight account.

The transfers to reduce balances can take the form of other money market transactions, such as taking loans or arbitrage. The netting balances, of course, could be reduced by transferring certain amounts of the individual currencies which make up the ecu basket from the ecu debtor to the ecu creditor member. Such transfers, however, are very costly and complicated. Until 1988, the system permitted the settlement of the balances through such transfers. This practice has been abolished (with some far-reaching consequences (see page 78)).

To avoid the difficulties associated with negotiating an interest rate for ecu lending transactions to balance the BIS accounts in the relatively short time-span, the clearing members have agreed to a fixed formula for calculating the interest base for such loans. In essence, this formula is calculated during the two days before each value date and results in the submission of each clearing bank's Ecu Interbank Offer Rates (EIBOR) and Ecu Interbank Bid Rates (EIBID) which will be averaged by BIS into a mean rate (EIMEAN) prior to the preliminary cut-off time on the corresponding value date. The clearing members use the EIMEAN-rate for positions of up to ECU 100 million, the EIBOR-rate for short-term positions of over ECU 100 million and the EIBID-rate for long-term positions of over ECU 100 million. This procedure eliminates lengthy negotiations and ensures the smooth functioning of the settlement mechanism.

The ecu clearing system has been very successful: the number of settled payments more than tripled from 39,103 during October 1987 (a daily average of 1,777) to 129,666 during October 1991, or 5638 per day.

Figure XII.2: Ecu Clearing System Volume

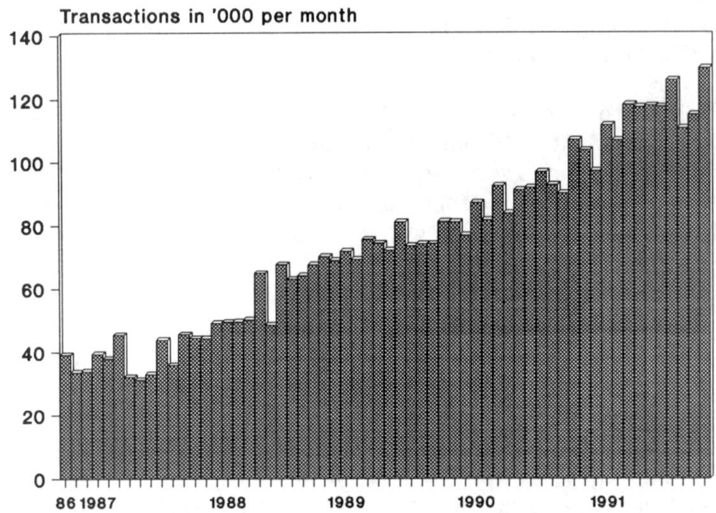

Source: Ecu Banking Association

This well-functioning and experienced clearing system will encourage an increase in the use of private and commercial ecus and will facilitate the transformation of the ecu into the single EC currency. The success of the system, however, has created an unforeseen problem as the system is running at full capacity and is reaching its technical limits. This has resulted in recommendations to change the settlement procedures from the current "position clearing", in which the payments are not final until the completion of all clearing operations, to a "payment system" with facilities guaranteeing the settlement. In the latter, payments would be finalized through debits and credits to current accounts up to the amount of each member's fixed commitment to the system. Bilateral credit lines, a last resort standby credit line of ECU 5 million per member and collateralized credit lines with central banks would guarantee the settlement of the balances. The Banque de France and the Bank of England have already expressed interest in providing such collateralized credit lines for cash or securities collateral. This modification of the system could ensure that the development of the ecu would not be impeded - at least from a technical standpoint - until the creation of a clearing system under the auspices of an EC institution.

PART XIII.

COMMERCIAL USE

Another possible significant area of use for the private ecu is for commercial purposes, such as payments, invoicing, accounting and other transactions by businesses which, of course, do not include the use of physical ecu money until the introduction of the ecu as the single EC currency. Despite some initial interest in the ecu as a commercial currency, its development in commercial transactions did not parallel the growth of the other private ecu markets.

There are a number of reasons for this different development. Most importantly, the lack of private end-users of ecu which resulted from its non-legal tender status has prevented the ecu from becoming a credible means of payment and transactions for most corporations. The lack of a central bank responsible for the ecu and the sometimes negative attitude of some authorities in the EC Member States toward the ecu as a fully fledged currency also hindered some potential commercial users from introducing it in their transactions. In addition, the initial characteristics of the ecu market for financial instruments, namely relative illiquidity and the non-completeness of the array of available financing instruments, stifled commercial uses. Other obstacles to the increased use of the ecu particularly in the commercial area are the lack of a definite legal basis for ecu-denominated bills of exchange and the fact that most Member States do not permit the denomination of official corporate accounts in ecus even though some (namely the Netherlands, Luxembourg, Great Britain and, to a limited extent, Greece) permit reporting in ecus parallel to the national currency. As an incentive for the use of ecus by corporations, the 1990 EC Council Directive on annual accounts permits small and medium-sized businesses in the EC to publish their accounts in ecus.

Corporations usually also cannot pay taxes in ecus or have their tax liabilities assessed in ecus. Another significant obstacle to the commercial use of the ecu is the inability of corporations to have their Value Added Tax liability assessed and denominated in ecus. This means that a corporation which potentially is interested in using ecus for its transactions with other entities would be required to translate the ecus received into the national currency in order to pay its VAT liability to its government. It would be easier for such corporations to transact its business in the national currency from the beginning to avoid this conversion and the related administrative expenses.

In recent years, however, commercial entities have become more interested in the ecu. This new interest results from the increased acceptance of the ecu, the efforts to create the EMU with the ecu as its single currency, the higher degree of information and the availability of virtually any type of financial instrument in ecus.

The following discussion of potential ecu uses for commercial purposes must be evaluated in light of the fact that the ecu will become the single EC currency as early as 1997. With this transformation and the concurrent abolition of existing national currencies, the discussion of whether and how the ecu is an advantageous currency for commercial purposes will be meaningless. At that time, there will be no alternative for EC entities than to use the ecu for all commercial purposes unless they decide to use not-yet-abolished or non-EC currencies. The discussion below, however, is important for businesses interested in introducing the ecu for commercial purposes before the transformation date. The ecu will very likely gain much importance and volume over the years leading to the transformation as it will not simply turn into an important currency on the eve of its transformation. Businesses, therefore, are well advised to introduce and utilize ecus for commercial uses as soon as possible and not to wait until that magic date.

For a commercial user, the ecu essentially has two major advantages: (i) the decrease of exchange and interest rate related risks; and (ii) the reduction of transaction costs. The more important of the two is the foreign exchange stability of the ecu. Its basket composition reduces exchange and interest rate variations (see page 62). This reduction decreases the loss exposure for a commercial user. Compared to the volatility of major world currencies, namely the dollar and the yen, the ecu is a stable and less risky currency for investment and business transactions.

The second significant potential benefit relates to the simplification of exchange transactions and the corresponding decrease in administrative costs. Generally speaking, any company that transacts business outside its home country will be required to deal in different currencies. A company transacting business in all EC Member States, for example, will have to buy and sell 12 different currencies to effect all of its transactions. This results in administrative costs, costs from the exposure to exchange rate related risks, expenses in the form of commissions and fees, opportunity costs and complicated pricing policies, cash and currency management. The out-of-pocket expenses for the conversion of EC currencies and the necessary hedging transactions are substantial for multinational corporations. The former are estimated at $13 billion and the latter at $2 billion annually. They include financial costs in the form of the currencies' bid/ask spreads and banking fees. Such costs average between 0.15 and 0.2 percent for EC corporations. In addition, the need to employ more individuals to supervise multi-currency transactions and other opportunity costs impose extra expenses on corporations. The EC Commission has estimated the in-house costs alone to amounts to 0.1 percent of the GDP of the EC. By definition, the introduction of the ecu as the single EC currency and the abolition of the underlying national currencies will result in substantial savings and a significant facilitation of corporate finance. These costs, of course, are also income for other businesses, namely the financial industry. For those, the introduction of the single EC currency will bear substantial losses in income.

In addition to the internal and cost-saving advantages, the commercial ecu can be a very important currency for the external relations of a corporation. Not only is the ecu a stable currency but it is also a neutral currency because there is no home market and monetary authority for the ecu. These characteristics might give the ecu certain advantages as a currency for the import and export business. Exporters, who would prefer the denomination of their outstanding accounts in a strong currency, and importers, who would benefit from a weak currency, can use the ecu as a compromise currency provided, of course, that they are in a position to negotiate such ecu payments or receipts. The ecu thereby provides a more equal distribution of exchange and interest rate risks. The neutrality factor, on the other hand, is important for foreign partners to a business transaction who might shy away from using a particular national currency, in which case, for psychological reasons, the ecu might be a very attractive alternative.

Corporations can already use the ecu as a book denominator for internal and external invoicing, export and corporate financing and for accounting purposes. Companies with subsidiaries and business transactions in various European countries can introduce ecu-based internal invoicing systems which could simplify the maintenance of "scales of charges" for transactions between branches, the corporation and customers. It would be unnecessary, for example, to denominate the prices and charges in the individual currencies of the countries in which the branches, the parent or the customers are located. Every transaction, price or charge will simply be in ecus. There will be no intermediate conversion costs as there is no need for currency conversions until the balancing of the accounts and the final conversion of the balance into a national currency. As a result of the relative stability of the ecu, the ecu scales are not subject to frequent adjustments. If the scales were based on the Deutsche Mark or French franc, for example, revisions would be necessary with every appreciation and depreciation of the currencies against each other. Similarly, the use of ecu for accounting purposes facilitates the accounting and decreases administrative costs for multinational corporations. Paribas Capital Markets London, for example, the investment banking subsidiary of the French Banque Paribas, recently switched its internal accounting to ecus to prepare for the single currency.

Export financing is generally cheaper in ecus than in other "hard" currencies. This has increased the share of the ecu in the foreign trade between Italy,

France, the United States, Germany, Sweden, and some Central and Eastern European countries (see page 144). The ecu, for example, is included as export credit agreement currency of the Organization for Economic Cooperation and Development (OECD).

Table XIII.1: Commercial Interest Reference Rates (January 1992)

Currency of Credit	12/15/91 - 1/14/92	11/15/91 - 12/14/91
Japanese Yen	6.70	6.70
US Dollar (<5 years)	7.52	7.77
US Dollar (>5 years)	7.92	8.17
SwFranc (<5 years)	8.30	8.30
SwFranc (>5 years)	8.55	8.55
Canadian Dollar	9.10	9.50
New Zealand Dollar	9.49	9.57
Ecu	**9.60**	**9.49**
Austrian Schilling	9.63	9.62
German Mark	9.68	9.75
Netherlands Guilder	9.90	9.90
Australian Dollar	10.00	9.96
Belgian Franc	10.20	10.15
French Franc	10.20	10.20
Irish Pound	10.42	10.40
Norwegian Krone	10.59	10.80
Danish Krone	10.70	10.50
Pound Sterling	10.85	10.79
Swedish Krona	11.15	11.26
Finnish Mark	11.20	10.70
Italian Lira	12.06	12.02
Spanish Peseta	12.79	12.62

Source: OECD

The OECD Credit Arrangements set minimum interest rates for export credits that receive official subventions. They are the lower of matrix minimums for poor countries or the fixed Commercial Interest Reference Rates (CIRR) for rich countries. CIRR are set for each participating currency in monthly intervals. In the February 1992 rate structure, the ecu rate (9.60 percent) stood between the extremes (6.70 percent for credits in Japanese Yen and

12.79 percent for credits in Spanish peseta). This meant that financing for countries with interest rates of over 9.60 percent would have been cheaper if the ecu had been the currency of credit especially for entities in the EC because they would not have been subject to fluctuation losses as a result of the fixed ecu rates.

Because of the composition of the ecu, interest rates for ecu-denominated financing instruments, such as bonds and loans, generally fall between the high rates of "soft" currencies and the low rates of "hard" currency instruments (see page 93). Borrowers from countries with such high interest rates prefer the relatively lower rates of ecu instruments. Investors from countries with low interest rates favor the relatively higher interest return in combination with the stability of the ecu. This stability also decreases expenditures and losses for hedging and exchange rate fluctuations. The value of ecu-denominated future payments and revenues are not subject to extreme fluctuations, and hedging and exchange rate losses will be kept at a minimum (see page 62).

While this interest and exchange rate stability is a clear advantage, the ecu is currently used only to a very limited degree in export finance because corporations still prefer to raise funds in the same currency in which they invoice. As invoicing in ecu is very limited, export financing in ecu is also limited. The decreasing number of swapable ecu bonds (see page 105), which allow a corporate bond issuer to swap the ecu raised for the currency needed, further limits the use of the ecu in this area.

A third area of commercial use is for treasury management for which the combining of ecu assets and liabilities results in more stability and predictability in general. The availability of ecu futures and options make the ecu an effective hedge against other currencies. Corporate treasurers can also use the ecu as a means of portfolio investment and diversification. This use has increased somewhat because of the more liquid market in ecu-denominated financial instruments. Ecu deposit and current accounts help corporate treasurers with the management of their cash reserves. A small number of corporations now denominate their balance sheets in ecus and their national currencies. The ecu thereby is used as an international reference currency which allows direct comparisons between the balance sheets of different companies or their subsidiaries. The use of the ecu as *sole* denominator for balance sheets of EC corporations, however, is limited because the ecu usually does not have the appropriate legal status in the Member States.

Although corporations interested in ecu financing generally use ecu loans and bonds, another way to raise funds is through ecu shares. To date, such shares are available only at the Luxembourg Stock Exchange. The issuance of ecu shares allows investors from all Member States to invest in companies without subjecting themselves to exchange rate fluctuations or transaction costs and provides corporations with a much broader market for capitalization purposes. It would, of course, subject the investor to the costs of converting the share-investment back into the investor's currency at the termination of the investment. Proposals have been introduced for the issuance of "European Depository Receipts", similar to the American Depository Receipts, for which the shares of European companies would be deposited with banks and then re-issued in ecu denomination.

Despite the general limitations, a few entities have already used the ecu as denominator for commercial applications. Over 40 leading companies in Europe, for example, now publish their corporate accounts in ecus parallel to their national currencies. The primary example is the French Saint Gobain conglomerate with approximately 105 subsidiaries, which has used ecus for intra-group accounting, transfers and payments since 1980.

The International Air Transportation Association (IATA) and Eurocontrol, the European air control organization, denominate billing and other transactions between 24 African and European airlines in ecus. In December 1990, the International Union of Railways adopted a new ecu-based pricing system. Although railway tickets will not be sold for ecus, the railway tariffs will be quoted in ecus in a new price scale, Europrix, through a computerized booking system. CIMACOREM (Conférence Internationale Madagascar, Les Comores, Réunion et Maurice), an international shipping conference, has used ecus since 1977 when it still was the EUA. The Conference replaced the Swiss and French francs in some freight rates with the ecu. Fiat, the Italian car manufacturer with over 400 companies in over 50 countries is using the ecu internally and in its joint venture with the Soviet Ministry for the Automobile Industry (see page 156). Générale Banque and Moscow Narodni Bank denominated their financing for Sherotel hotel near Moscow in ecus. These are merely some examples of the steadily growing number of companies using the ecu for commercial purposes.

Although this area is still very underdeveloped, any business interested in commercial transactions in more than one country in the EC should consider using the ecu for invoicing and accounting purposes. The establishment of an ecu commercial practice is not complicated and, as outlined, the costs of not using the ecu can be significant even for smaller businesses. With the greater availability of the ecu, businesses will find themselves confronted with more business partners using ecus in their transactions. This and the increasing liquidity of the ecu markets will make it necessary and easy for a business to establish an ecu-based invoicing and accounting system even before the upcoming transformation of the ecu into the single EC currency and the abolition of national currencies.

PART XIV.

THE ECU IN INTERNATIONAL INSTITUTIONS

As the ecu developed into a currency for private parties and sovereign governments, a number of international institutions also adopted or accepted it as a currency for certain purposes. To a large degree, such acceptance resulted from the significantly increased use of ecus on certain markets, namely the bond market. This increased the instances in which such institutions were confronted with ecus for financing or payment purposes. In addition, some of these institutions, namely the World Bank and the European Bank for Reconstruction and Development, have become significant participants in ecu financing and have found in the ecu a reliable and stable denominator for international debt issues.

The ecu, upon transformation into the single EC currency, will become much more important for those institutions, especially in view of the fact that many of the currencies now used, such as the Deutsche Mark, British pound and French franc, will disappear. The following is a short overview of the institutions which currently accept or use the ecu. It is provided as a guide for parties which transact business with such institutions and are interested in the possibility of using ecus for their purposes. Any limitations which the institutions might impose on the ecu at the moment are very likely to disappear over the next few years.

A. International Monetary Fund

The International Monetary Fund (IMF) has implicitly accepted the ecu as a currency since 1984 when it began to exclude the gold and dollar deposits of the EC central banks with the EMCF from their assets for the calculations determining the apportionment of Special Drawing Rights. Instead, it now includes the ecu created through these deposits in the foreign exchange reserves and thereby has, at least theoretically, accepted the ecu as a currency.

The IMF will face an interesting problem related to its Special Drawing Rights (SDR) and the introduction of the ecu as single EC currency in the contemporaneous abolition of national currencies. The SDR is currently defined as a basket of currencies containing certain amounts of US dollar, Japanese yen, German mark, British pound and French franc. The SDR definition will have to be revised to account for the abolition of mark, franc and pound as early as 1997. The IMF would either have to limit the SDR definition to the remaining two currencies, dollar and yen, plus the ecu (arguably *the* most important three global currencies) or create a new SDR containing different additional currencies. The effect of such a redefinition on the overall stability of the SDR, of course, is not foreseeable. However, it is quite possible that an SDR based only on three currencies, namely dollar, yen and ecu, might be more volatile than the current SDR which is based on five currencies. In this respect, the same features that make the ecu more stable at the moment - its broad basket composition - could make a smaller-basket SDR more unstable.

B. Bank for Reconstruction and Development - World Bank

The Bank for Reconstruction and Development (World Bank) rejected an ecu tender in 1986 when an Italian company submitted ecus for a project in Hungary. Following negotiations between the EC Commission and the World Bank, the World Bank, while not recognizing the ecu as a currency *per se*, agreed not to raise objections to its use in tenders and payments.

Despite this initial objection regarding the ecu use for program payments, the World Bank is a very active borrower on the ecu markets. Between 1980 and the end of 1991, it launched ecu bonds totaling ECU 1,733 million.

C. Organization for Economic Cooperation and Development

The Organization for Economic Cooperation and Development (OECD) implicitly recognizes the ecu as a currency. It treats the ecu as an export credit agreement currency and establishes Commercial Interest Reference Rates (CIRR) for ecu credits (see page 143).

D. European Bank for Reconstruction and Development

The establishment of the European Bank for Reconstruction and Development (EBRD) provided additional impetus for the use of the ecu. The EBRD fosters the transition of Central and Eastern European countries toward open market-oriented economies and promotes private and entrepreneurial initiatives. The EBRD agreement includes a number of provisions for the use of ecus. The authorized original capital stock, for example, is ECU 10 billion. Fifty percent of the payments for the capital stock must be made in ecus, US dollars or Japanese yen. In fact, 60 percent of the payments made in 1991 were denominated in ecus. Although the parties establishing the EBRD did not agree to the exclusive use of the ecu in its transactions, the fact that the ecu is among the three major listed *currencies* shows that it has already been accepted as such by the EBRD.

The EBRD has also become a significant new participant on the ecu markets. Based in London, a major ecu center, the EBRD issued its first ECU 500 million straight ecu bond (with a coupon of 8.875 percent) in October 1991. The EBRD expects to issue 60 percent of its capital needs in ecus, 35 percent in dollars and five percent in yen.

E. International Bank for Economic Cooperation

The International Bank for Economic Cooperation (IBEC) terminated its role as a rouble-based clearing house for the former COMECON member nations on January 1, 1991. The IBEC now will focus on commercial banking activities in convertible foreign currencies. In a move indicating the acceptance of the ecu in formerly communist nations, the IBEC re-denominated its capital in ecus in December 1990.

PART XV.

THE ECU IN EASTERN EUROPE

Following the demise of the communist governments, the ecu has the opportunity to develop into an important denominator for financial transactions with Central and Eastern European countries. It is generally understood that one of the major weaknesses for the development of free market systems in those countries is the lack of convertible currencies. The legal tenders of these countries are usually not convertible, at all (such as the rouble), or only semi-convertible (such as the Polish zloty). This lack of convertible currencies has prevented many western businesses from establishing more solid relationships with their Central and Eastern European counterparts. Those businesses are interested in receiving payments for delivered goods and repatriating profits from business ventures in "hard", convertible currencies. As those countries themselves do not have such hard and convertible legal tender and their foreign currency reserves are insufficient, western businesses have been very cautious in their approach to such new business relationships. The governments of those countries, on the other hand, while not being able to make their currencies convertible overnight, are looking to receive payments for goods exported, mainly raw materials, in convertible, but stable currencies. Payments received in volatile currencies, such as the dollar, might subject those countries to significant foreign exchange losses.

The convertibility of currencies is an important prerequisite for free market systems for other reasons because it ensures that the prevailing price structure results in the most efficient and complete integration and use of resources. Freely convertible currencies can assist Eastern and Central European countries in opening their domestic markets to achieve better economies of scale and to take advantage of the incentive from foreign competition. In addition, convertibility is an important factor in preventing the total disintegration of trade among the Eastern and Central European countries which has diminished greatly as result of the demise of the rouble-payments system of the former COMECON. The ecu has three different main uses for such countries: (i) as "peg" for the national currencies; (ii) as denominator for an ecu-based payment and clearing system; and (iii) as trading currency.

To assist in the establishment of freely convertible currencies, Eastern and Central European countries should "peg" their currencies to the stable ecu at fixed exchange rates. The ecu would thereby serve as a strong "anchor" for their national currencies, which, in connection with appropriate monetary policies, decrease of inflation and limitations on budgetary deficits, would ultimately result in freely convertible and stable currencies for those countries. There is, however, one concern related to such a peg to the ecu because the ecu currently does not have a market as liquid as other possible anchors, namely the Deutsche Mark and the United States dollar, which enables these governments to carry out financing transactions in ecus. The growth of the ecu-denominated market in recent years and the decision of the EC to transform it into the single EC currency, however, should alleviate such concerns. The Czechoslovakian government has already taken a step in this direction by pegging its koruna to the ecu.

San Paolo Bank has contacted several institutions in Eastern and Central European countries to study the implementation - and ultimately finalize an agreement for the establishment - of a multilateral ecu-based payment system for these nations. One bank each from Hungary, Poland and Czechoslovakia, and possibly banks from the Commonwealth of Independent States, would participate in the system with the assistance of Western European banks. The planned system would be very similar to the existing Ecu Clearing System (see page 134). The Ecu Banking Association, which established and monitors the ecu clearing system, has been actively involved in this project.

The system would attempt to avoid hard-currency shortages in - and the total collapse of - the trade among Eastern and Central European countries, establish a new and efficient payment system to replace the now defunct rouble-based system and implement restrictions on the use of hard currency reserves. The system would centralize the management of the accounting and clearing procedures in its netting and clearing phases.

While any convertible western currency could be used as monetary standard for the payments system in Eastern and Central European countries, the ecu is most advantageous because it is stable and neutral. Other freely convertible currencies, namely the United States dollar, are very volatile and therefore could not provide a stable basis for the payments system. The ecu should be adopted as a standard of value for the system and as a denominator (or later currency) for the settlement of the balances in the netting and settlement phases of the clearing process. In addition, the experience of the very successful existing ecu clearing system can be used to establish and maintain a similarly successful system for Eastern and Central European countries.

Even before the fall of the Berlin Wall and the opening of the Iron Curtain in 1989, a number of Central and Eastern European countries looked at the ecu for finance and trade transactions. With the end of the Cold War, the ecu has shown great potential for developing into the currency of choice for east-west trade and the external transactions of those countries. A number of governments and institutions now actively promote the role of the ecu as a means of payment and possibly as the catalyst for converting the socialist economics into free markets.

The ecu combines the advantages of a convertible currency with the relative exchange rate stability required by Central and Eastern European governments as well as western businesses. The general advantages of the ecu apply to Eastern European countries to an even higher degree. This encompasses its inherent exchange and interest rate stability and the simplification of cross-border transactions which are even more important to the eastern bloc countries which hardly can afford foreign exchange rate losses. Foreign exchange stability is almost perfect with regard to EC currencies which are linked through the ecu in the EMS. As by far most of the aid to these countries is received from the EC, the ecu, next to the Deutsche Mark, is developing into a currency of choice for transactions in these countries.

In addition to those general factors, the ecu entails some specific advantages for Eastern European countries. The first concerns the general non-convertibility of eastern currencies. The former socialist countries can transact international business only in foreign currencies which, in turn, subject them to open foreign exchange positions. The relatively stable ecu would at least decrease the risk of extreme exchange rate losses.

Second, the acceptance and use of the ecu by Eastern and Central European countries will open new and innovative markets for financial instruments and will permit the diversification of their currency portfolios. It might also assist in the establishment of national capital markets. The former USSR, Hungary and Poland have used it as denominator for loans, bonds and other financial instruments. Inter-Europa Bank and Magyar Tavkozlesi Vallalat in Hungary, Export Development Bank in Poland and Vnesheconombank in the former Soviet Union, for example, borrowed in ecus in 1990.

Third, the number of ecu-denominated financial support payments flowing to Eastern European countries is steadily increasing. This includes the financial support by the EC, by the national governments of the Member States and, lately, the programs by the European Bank for Reconstruction and Development (which plans to denominate 60 percent of its distributions in ecus). The increasing use of ecu for financial support for Eastern European countries should not be underestimated. It will "force" the eastern governments as well as western businesses to deal with the ecu on a practical level. As approximately 80 percent of all aid to the members of the Commonwealth of Independent States comes from the EC, acquaintance with the ecu is necessary should the transactions involve loans or grants from the EC.

Fourth, the differential between the interest rates for the ecu and the Commercial Interest Reference Rate (CIRR) as determined by the OECD, is much smaller than that between the CIRR and the interest rates for many other foreign currencies (see page 143). This translates into interest rate savings for Eastern European countries. These savings could be of great importance to eastern governments and western businesses alike. A western business with the need to raise capital for investment in Eastern Europe, for example, could raise such capital in ecus at a lower cost than its national currency. This would directly decrease interest expenditures.

The fifth and most futuristic factor relates to the fact that the use of the ecu by Eastern European countries is not only necessary because the EC is a significant trading partner for these countries, but more importantly, because it will prepare certain Eastern European countries for a possible later joining of the EC. The ecu will be the single currency for the EC by the time any of these countries will be admitted as an EC member.

Despite the obvious advantages, the ecu also has a drawback, albeit psychological. The governments and people in Central and Eastern European countries had for decades to live with their practically worthless currencies. At this point, they are looking to substitute these by a hard and liquid means of payment. This, for many, implies physical money, such as coins and notes, and no questions about the "true currency status" of such a means of payment. The ecu, of course, does not yet have such coins and notes and the debates about its currency status are still ongoing. From this point of view, therefore, the ecu might encounter problems in this area for the next few years. With the transformation of the ecu into the single currency, however, these problems will disappear and Central and Eastern European countries should be very willing to accept the ecu completely.

As indicated earlier, the former Soviet Union and Hungary have already used the ecu as denominator for a variety of financial instruments. The National Bank of Hungary treats the ecu as a convertible currency, permits ecu accounts and has quoted the ecu since October 1985. In addition, Hungary issued its first ecu-bond in 1991. Similarly, the former Soviet Union used the ecu as a unit of account in its bilateral trade transactions. Several banks in Eastern and Central European countries, such as Hungary, Poland and the former USSR, have used ecu loans in the past.

In a model transaction, the Soviet Ministry for the Automobile Industry and the Italian car manufacturer Fiat use the ecu in a joint venture established in early December 1989. The parties agreed jointly to produce 300,000 cars in the Soviet Union, an estimated total investment of ECU 1.2 billion. The joint venture was set up to operate within a "currency enclave" in which all transactions are denominated in ecus.

The ecu is of great interest for the development of the trade between western nations and Eastern and Central European countries. Although a substantial amount of those relations will still be factored in the traditional currencies, such as the German mark and the dollar, the share of ecu transactions will increase rapidly in the near future especially with the abolition of the EC currencies. The single most important reason for this development will be the denomination of a significant portion of aid flowing to Central and Eastern European countries in ecus. This fact will make it necessary for any business interested in transaction with Eastern European countries to strongly consider the ecu as denominator for such transactions.

PART XVI.

THE LEGAL STATUS OF THE ECU AS A CURRENCY

The distinction between official and private ecu involves more than differences in markets and users. As shown above, the ecu legally can only serve as a unit of account for private parties. The official use in transactions is limited to certain monetary authorities and governments. Until December 1991, there had been no legal basis, such as an EC agreement conferring legal tender status on the ecu, for the private use of ecus by private parties. The recent Maastricht Treaty among the EC Member States establishing the EMU now includes provisions for the transformation of the ecu into the single EC currency. This legal tender status, however, will not be conveyed until 1997 at the earliest. In the meantime, while the difference between the private and the official ecus continues, some segments of the private and commercial ecu markets have flourished over the past decade. The non-existence of a basis for the private ecu as "legally accepted" currency, however, resulted in initial differences in the treatment of the ecu as a full currency by the EC authorities, the EC Member States and non-EC entities.

These differences were generally based on the composition of the ecu as a basket of currencies. For non-EC nations, the acceptance of the ecu as a currency is procedurally uncomplicated. The ecu itself, as well as the individual currencies in the basket, are currencies entirely foreign to such non-EC nations. Therefore, the ecu can be granted foreign currency status usually either by decree or implicit acceptance. It is merely a question of whether the monetary or governmental authorities issue such regulations or whether the features of the ecu make it automatically acceptable as a currency in such a country. The EC Member States had to confront a quite different situation. Problems arose because part of the ecu basket is the currency of the individual Member State seeking to convey foreign currency status. A Member State treats its own legal tender as a foreign currency when it accepts the entire ecu as foreign currency. Conversely, the ecu also includes 11 additional shares of currencies foreign to each EC member. If the ecu were accepted as legal tender in the country, these foreign currencies would also be accepted as legal tender. Although with differing interpretations, all EC Member States have opted to grant the ecu foreign currency status explicitly, *de jure*, or implicitly *de facto* by a corresponding instrument of the national monetary authority. By implication, the share of domestic currency in the ecu basket is thereby treated as a foreign currency for the purposes of the ecu definition.

One important observation must be made with regard to the foreign currency status of the ecu in the EC Member States. As result of the recent EMU treaty, the ecu will be transformed into the single EC currency. It will, over time, substitute all national currencies and become the single legal tender for the entire EC. Once this transformation takes place in each individual

Member State, the ecu, of course, will lose its foreign currency status in each such Member State and become its sole legal tender.

The following are short summaries of the status of the ecu in each of the EC Member States and various non-EC countries. They include the dates of the classifying instruments and of the first quotation at the national exchange, when applicable. Other information relates to the fixing procedures and the use of ecu by the national governments. These summaries are intended only as overviews of the status of the ecu in various countries. The classifying instruments are included in Appendix B for more detailed information.

A. Belgium and Luxembourg

Belgium and Luxembourg officially classify the ecu as a currency as all other foreign currencies according to the rules of the Institute Belgo-Luxembourgeois du Change (IBLC). The instruments classifying the ecu as a currency were promulgated on March 1, 1982, and October 1, 1983. The Brussels Stock Exchange first quoted the ecu on September 3, 1984. The fixing for the official quotation takes place at 1:30 pm. The official exchange rate is the average bid/offer rate. The IBLC undertakes interventions on behalf of the ecu.

There are no investment and financing restrictions on ecu-denominated instruments in Belgium and Luxembourg. All ecu financial instruments are permitted and, if public issues, require IBLC approval.

Belgium has issued some public debt in the form of Euro-obligations in ecus but announced a Treasury instrument program similar to the French OAT for launch in 1992. Luxembourg has issued no Treasury bills but denominates approximately 25 percent of its public debt in ecu.

The Luxembourg government declared November 1989 as "ecu month". Residents and non-residents were permitted and encouraged to use ecu for payments in shops and restaurants (see page 133).

B. Denmark

Denmark recognizes the ecu as a *de facto* foreign currency subject to its general foreign exchange regulations. The Danish central bank in Copenhagen first quoted the ecu on September 17, 1984. The fixing takes place at noon and the official rate is the average bid/offer rate. The Danish central bank intervenes in ecu at the foreign exchange markets.

There are no specific regulations for ecu-denominated instruments, ecu financing or capital movements in general. Denmark permits all types of ecu financial instruments. The government has used ecu in the past for some domestic and foreign public debt issuances and as denominator for Treasury bills. Beginning in 1992, the Danish government will issue short and long-term ecu bonds on the Copenhagen Stock Exchange. It appears to be reluctant, however, to introduce the ecu as single EC currency by the 1997 or 1999 deadlines and has reserved itself the right to hold a public referendum on this issue prior to the introduction.

C. France

France granted the ecu foreign currency status on May 21, 1982 and, since March 9, 1989, has treated it like any other major currency (see Appendix B). The latter decree abolished the remaining exchange controls regarding the ecu. Private French investors are now permitted to open bank accounts denominated in ecus without prior approval. The ecu also has preferential treatment as there is no obligation to sell received ecu within a three-month period as required for any other foreign currency. Ecu-denominated transfers valued at over FF50,000 require a justification.

The stock exchange in Paris has quoted the ecu daily at 1:30 pm since June 4, 1984. The official rate is the average bid/offer rate. The French central bank intervenes in ecu at the foreign exchange markets.

The French government has issued a significant amount of Treasury bills (OAT) in ecus (see page 104). It has committed itself to issue 15 percent of its public debt in ecus and is a very ardent supporter of the introduction of the ecu as the single EC currency. In addition, the French postal service introduced an ecu stamp in 1988.

France has also been rather active in ecu transactions outside its central government. The town of Bellême promoted the use of ecus last year when specially minted ecus were accepted by its businesses for payment. More recently, the government of the Picardy region in the north of France decided to denominate its 1992 budget in ecus as well as francs. Such steps, albeit limited in size, are very important for the success of the ecu because they involve entities and private parties outside of the more politically oriented central governments of the Member States. Only the Netherlands, Belgium and Luxembourg have presented similar ecu programs to acquaint their citizens with the ecu for daily use.

D. Greece

Greece has considered the ecu as a *de facto* currency since July 14, 1984. Non-resident banks have preferential access to the drachma for purposes of ecu basket transactions, for example, to create ecus from the appropriate amounts of the EMS currencies. The Athens Stock Market introduced ecu quotations on January 24, 1985. The fixing takes place at 1:00 pm and the official quotation is the average bid/offer rate. The Greek central bank intervenes in ecus. The Greek government has issued a substantial number of public bonds in drachma with special ecu clauses (see page 100).

E. Germany

Germany was the last EMS member to accept the private ecu and to permit residents of Germany to incur ecu liabilities and carry out other transactions in ecus in addition to ecu claims, which never had been subject to limitations. Initially, Germany regarded the ecu as an indexed currency which was not permitted under German law. Following the success of the private and commercial ecus and the attempts of the EC to liberalize capital movements, the Bundesbank (the German central bank) authorized the ecu and granted it quasi-foreign currency status on June 16, 1987 (see Appendix B). Germany's lifting of the prior absolute prohibition on ecu liabilities was an important step in the development of the ecu because the Bundesbank clearly stated that one of the reasons for the decision to treat the ecu like any other foreign currency was the fact of its growing importance in private money and capital transactions and in the foreign trade and payments of some partner countries. The acceptance of the private ecu by the largest and strongest economy in the EC, therefore, immediately increased the overall status of the ecu as a valid currency. The change followed outside pressures and outright refusals by the independent Bundesbank to authorize the private ecu. The Bundesbank, however, has explicitly and continuously stated that the ecu lacks the essential characteristics of a currency because it is not legal tender in any nation.

In a further move to lift exchange restrictions in early 1990, the Bundesbank now also allows the issuance of securities denominated in foreign currencies and ecus by residents of Germany. Formerly these entities had to issue foreign currency instruments through banks outside Germany.

The German government has been a strong supporter of the transformation of the ecu into the single EC currency. However, the Bundesbank strongly advocates a much slower approach and has publicly questioned the feasibility of the single currency. This caution is also reflected in the changing public attitude toward the single currency and the abolition of the status-symbol Deutsche Mark.

F. Ireland

Ireland treats the ecu as a *de facto* foreign currency. There is no official quotation of the ecu on the foreign exchange market. Instead, the Irish central bank publishes its daily value. Ireland has issued specific official regulations governing the ecu in addition to some preferential treatment of the ecu for banks in foreign trade transactions.

All types of financial instruments except futures are permitted in foreign currencies. There are no financing restrictions. The ecu is used in domestic and external debts such as the ecu debt instruments issued by the Irish government (see page 102).

G. Italy

The Italian Minister of Foreign Trade conveyed the status of a *valuta di conto valutario* - a currency - to the ecu per ministerial decree on July 27, 1981. The ecu may be used for all authorized financial and commercial transactions. The Rome and Milan Stock Exchanges have quoted the ecu since May 1984. Between October 1981 and May 1984, the official ecu rate was calculated and not determined on the foreign exchange markets. The rate is now the average of the fixed bid/offer values on the foreign exchange markets in Milan and Rome. The fixing takes place at 1:15 pm. The Banca d'Italia intervenes in the ecu fixing.

The Italian regulations only permit Floating Rate Notes, shares and bonds in ecu denomination. The Italian government has issued a substantial amount of medium-term notes, so called CTE (Treasury certificates) and short-term Treasury bills, so called BTE (Treasury bills) (see page 98). Approximately one third of the Italian public debt is in ecu. There is no transaction limit on the individual amount of ecu transactions but there are some restrictions on the transfer of ecus and ecu bonds.

H. The Netherlands

The Netherlands abolished practically all exchange control regulations and has treated the ecu as a *de facto* currency since May 1, 1981. The Amsterdam Stock Exchange has quoted the ecu since July 1, 1985. The fixing takes place at 1:30 pm and the official rate is the average bid/offer rate. The Dutch central bank intervenes in the ecu fixing.

The Netherlands permit all financial instruments in ecu denomination and there is no distinction between the ecu and any other foreign currency. There are no restrictions on ecu financing. The Dutch government has not issued any Treasury bills or public debt in ecus.

I. Portugal

Portugal treats the ecu as a *de facto* currency. There are no specific restrictions imposed by the exchange control authorities on ecu transactions except those generally related to capital movements. Over 10 percent of Portuguese public debt is in ecus. The central bank intervenes in the fixing of the official ecu rate.

J. Spain

Spain has treated the ecu as a *de facto* currency since May 27, 1987. It granted preferential treatment for ecu deposits on September 30, 1989. Since July 1, 1987, the Madrid Stock Exchange has provided a daily quotation of the ecu value.

Spain permits all types of financial instruments in ecus except Certificates of Deposits, Euro-Commercial Paper and shares. Borrowing in any foreign currency, including the ecu, requires special permission from the monetary authorities. There are no financing restrictions on ecu financing other than those permissions. There are some restrictions on investments in ecus and foreign currencies for insurance companies and social security and pension funds. The purchase of ecu bonds is unrestricted. Approximately 10 percent of the Spanish public debt and Treasury bonds issued by the Spanish government are denominated in ecus (see page 105).

K. United Kingdom

The United Kingdom accepts the ecu as a *de facto* currency. There are no exchange control, currency financing or investment restrictions on the ecu. All types of ecu financial instruments are permitted and ecu Treasury bills and notes can be held by any private, commercial or institutional investor. There are no specific stock exchange or currency regulations for ecus. The British government maintains a significant ecu Treasury bill program (see page 102).

The British government has been able to negotiate an "opt-out" clause into the Maastricht Treaty under which it Britain will not be required to introduce the ecu as its legal tender by the 1997 or 1999 deadlines. As the government has always been reluctant to agree to such drastic actions, it will introduce the single currency at its leisure and upon corresponding decision by the British Parliament.

L. Other Nations

The most important users of the ecu and ecu instruments are, of course, the EC institutions, the EC Member States and private parties mainly located in Europe. This applies to the official as well as private and commercial users. Despite this focus on the EC, a large number of other European and non-European countries have accepted the ecu as equal to other foreign currencies. Although the actual use of the ecu as a currency in those countries is generally limited or essentially non-existent, those countries thereby have already removed the bars to the future use of the ecu.

Depending on the individual degree of acceptance, the monetary authorities in those countries permit ecu-denomination for checks drawn on local banks, loans, acceptances, insurance policies, bank guaranties, documentary credits, book entries, spot and forward exchange transactions, transfers, current accounts, time deposits and import and export transactions with custom authorities.

According to a survey conducted by Générale Bank in April 1989 the ecu is accepted *de jure* or *de facto* in the following countries:

Argentina	Germany	Luxembourg	Spain
Australia	Great Britain	Mexico	Sweden
Austria	Greece	The Netherlands	Switzerland
Belgium	Hong Kong	New Zealand	Taiwan
Brazil	Hungary	Norway	Turkey
Canada	India	Oman	United States
Chile	Iraq	Pakistan	of America
Columbia	Ireland	PR China	Uruguay
Czechoslovakia	Israel	Poland	USSR*
Denmark	Italy	Portugal	Venezuela
Finland	Japan	Saudi Arabia	Yugoslavia
France	Lebanon	South Africa	Zaire

* The status of the ecu in the newly formed Commonwealth of Independent States is unclear but no obstacles should be expected as a result of the close ties with and support from the EC to these states.

The ecu has had a more specific impact in a number of non-EC countries. For example, bonds, loans, futures and options, denominated in ecus have been issued and traded in the United States since 1985. Although there have been some questions concerning the currency status of the ecu in general, the United States has been an important market for ecu-denominated instruments. Japan has also developed a taste for the ecu as a financing tool. The first Japanese ecu bonds were issued in 1985 and the share of Japanese investors and issuers of ecu instruments since has increased significantly. In 1984 the former Soviet Union accepted and began to use the ecu as a currency in foreign transactions (see page 155). Other countries with significant use of the ecu include the People's Republic of China, the Scandinavian countries, New Zealand and South Africa.

The status of the ecu as a currency in such countries is important for private and commercial users. A corporation, for example, interested in billing its customers, paying or expressing its balance sheet in ecus, must comply with domestic regulations. If such regulations did not accept the ecu as such, the corporation could not use it for these purposes.

With the transformation of the ecu into the single EC currency, presumably all countries will accept the ecu as foreign currency subject to their general regulations. Until such time, a party interested in using ecu-denomination in cross-border transactions outside the EC must ensure beforehand that such use is permitted under the local laws and regulations.

CONCLUSIONS

By the end of 1992, the EC will transform its 12 individual economies into the world's single largest economy, the Single Market. As early as five years later, it will complete this process with a single EC currency which will permit its citizens and businesses to take fullest advantage of the potential of the Single Market. This single EC currency entails the abolition of existing national currencies and a restructuring of the global currency system.

The ecu will be transformed into that single EC currency. With a market already approaching $300 billion, it has provided the international financial community with a reliable currency for over 10 years. Over the next few years, the ecu markets will show substantial growth and diversification so that, at the time of its transformation, it will rival the United States dollar and the Japanese yen in size and importance.

But the creation of the single currency will not be the end. Like the 1992 program, the EMU is but one step toward an even more complete integration and unification of the EC. The introduction of the ecu and the abolition of the national currencies will serve as a catalyst for the much higher goal declared in the Single European Act and the Maastricht Treaty of 1992:

the *European Union*

PART XVII.

BIBLIOGRAPHY AND REFERENCES

Abeele, Michel, 'L'ECU, une monnaie politique?', *Revue de la Banque*, 1979.

Abraham, J., Abraham, F. and Lacroix-Destrée, Y., 'EMS, ECU and Commercial Banking', *Revue de la Banque*, February 1984.

Aglietta, Michel, 'Un ECU ou deux?', *Economie Internationale*, 1986.

Aglietta, Michel, 'Union Monétaire et Banque Centrale', *Problémes économiques*, September 13, 1989.

Allen, Polly Reynolds, 'The ECU: Birth of a new Currency', *Occasional Papers No. 20*, Group of Thirty, New York, 1986.

Allen, Polly Reynolds, 'The ECU and Monetary Management in Europe', *The ECU and European Monetary Integration*, London, 1988.

Allen, Polly Reynolds, 'The Private ECU Markets, What They Are, Why They Exist, and Where They May Go', *Journal of Banking and Finance No. 14*, 1990.

Allen, Polly Reynolds, 'The ECU in the Transition to EMU', *Central Banking*, December/January 1990/91.

Alphandéry, Edmond und Fourcans André, 'L'ECU: Stratégie pour une Europe en crise', *Banque*, 1984.

Arendt, Georges *et al., The future of the ECU*, Luxembourg, 1983.

Artis, Michael and Brittan, Samuel, *Europe without currency barriers. The call of a common currency*, London, 1989.

Association Belge des Banques, *L'ECU et les Banques*, Brussels, 1985.

Association for the Monetary Union of Europe, *The Monetary Union for the Europe of 1992*, Paris/Strasbourg, 1989.

Association for the Monetary Union of Europe, *Comments on the Economic and Monetary Report submitted by the Delors-Committee*, May 1989.

Association for the Monetary Union of Europe, *A Single Currency for Europe*, Rome, February 21, 1989.

Association for the Monetary Union of Europe, 'The ECU for European Business', *The Quarterly Bulletin of the Association for the Monetary Union of Europe*.

BIBLIOGRAPHY AND REFERENCES

Association for the Monetary Union of Europe, *Europeans' Attitude to the Replacement of their National Currency by the ECU*, Paris, November 6, 1990.

Association Internationale pour L'Etude de L'Economie de L'Assurance, 'L'utilisation privée de l'ECU', *Etudes et Dossiers No. 136*, Geneva, 1989.

Bangemann, Martin, *Die Europäische Parallelwährung*, 1979.

Bank for International Settlements (BIS), 'Die ECU im internationalen Bankgeschäft', *Annual Report*, June 1985.

Bank for International Settlements, *Role of the BIS in a Private ECU Clearing System*, February, 1986.

Banking Federation of the European Community, *The Use of the ECU in Banking Transactions*, Brussels, 1980.

Banque Bruxelles Lambert, 'The EMS and the ECU After Their First Six Years', *BBL No. 122*, December, 1984.

Banque Nationale de Belgique, 'Le développement de l'ECU privé et la politique monétaire', *Bulletin No. 4*, April 1986.

Banque Paribas Capital Markets, *The ECU Bond Market - An Overview*, London, October 1988.

Barclays Bank, 'The ECU - Europe's new Currency', *Barclays Review No. 4*, November 1985.

Barrell, Ray, 'European Currency Union and the EMS', *National Institute Economic Review*, May 1990.

Bartha, Ferenc, 'A Hungarian View on the ECU and its Implications for East-West and Intra-Comecon Monetary Relations', Bank for International Settlements, *BIS Review No. 23*, February 2, 1989.

Basevi, Giorgio *et al.*, 'International Banking System and the Use of the ECU', *Economic and Financial Papers*, December 1980.

Baumann, Wolfgang, 'ECU im Widerstreit', *Zeitschrift für das gesamte Kreditwesen*, 1984.

Becker Mechthild *et al.*, 'Hat die ECU "Verwendungspotential"?', *Zeitschrift für das gesamte Kreditwesen*, January 1, 1989.

Beven, T., 'The ECU-Europe's New Currency', *Barclay's Review*, November 1985.

Blondel, Jean L., 'L'utilisation de l'ECU dans les marchés privés', *Eurépargne*, September 1984.

Bofinger, Peter, 'Die ECU als Währung', *Zeitschrift für das gesamte Kreditwesen*, 1984.

Bordo, Michael *et al.*, 'The ECU - An Imaginary or Embrionic Form of Money: What Can We Learn from History?', *The ECU and European Monetary Integration*, London, 1988.

Bresson, J.C., 'La BEI et le développement due marché de l'ecu', *European Investment Bank 1979-89, The ECU's Tenth Anniversary, EIB Papers, Special Issue*, December 1989.

British Treasury, '"Positive" Hard ECU Proposals', *Press Release*, November 12, 1990.

Britton, Andrew and Mayes, David, 'Obstacles to the Use of the ECU: Macroeconomic Aspects', *The Economic Journal*, September 1990.

Brown, Brendan, 'Valuing the ECU Alternative', *Philips & Drew Briefing*, June 25, 1984.

Brown, J.T., 'L'ECU devant les juges: monnaie ou unité de comte?', *Eurépargne*, 1985.

Bürger, Siegried, 'Zur Verwendung von ECU nach deutschem Währungsrecht', *Die Bank*, June 1984.

Camdessus, Michel, 'The ECU: Edging Closer to a Common Currency', *Euromoney*, September 1985.

Carpenter, F.A.W., 'The ECU as a Lending Instrument', *European Investment Bank 1979-89, The ECU's Tenth Anniversary, EIB Papers, Special Issue*, December 1989.

Chicago Mercantile Exchange, *ECU Futures: Composition and Application*, 1986.

Coffey, Peter, *The European Monetary System - past, present and future*, Dordrecht, Kluwer Academic Publishers, 2nd Edition, 1987.

Commission of the European Communities, *SCAD Dossier bibliographique, L'ECU*, Brussels, 1987.

Committee for the Monetary Union of Europe, *The European Currency, an Optional Currency*, Paris, 1990.

Committee of Governors of the Central Banks of the Member States of the EC, *Texts Concerning the European Monetary System and Related Documents*.

Committee of Governors of the Central Banks of the Member States of the EC, *Recent Developments in the Use of the Private ECU: Statistical Review*, Basel, February 1991.

Congdon, Tim, 'Would the Hard ECU be a Currency?', *Gerrard & National Monthly Economic Review No. 15*, London, September 1990.

Cooke, Stephanie, 'A new Era for the ECU', *Institutional Investor*, August 1989.

Corel de, Léo, 'L'usage privé de l'ECU', *Eurépargne*, 1983.

Deutsche Bundesbank, 'Die Märkte für private ECU', *Monatsbericht*, August 1987.

DeWolfs, J., 'The secondary market in ECU bonds', *ECU*, 1988.

Dini, Lamberto, 'A Single Currency for Europe. Economic Policy and Financial Choices', Bank for International Settlements, *BIS Review No. 58*, March 23, 1989.

Drayß, Ernst-Ludwig, 'ECU und ECU-Anleihen', *Deutsche Bank Group, Fixed Income Research*, February 1989.

Droulers, Frédéric, *A Short History of the European ECU and of Previous Monetary Unions*, Lagny-sur-Marne, 1991.

Drummond, Ian *et al.*, 'Der ECU-Markt im Jahre 1989', *Bank-Archiv*, September 1990.

ECU Banking Association, 'ECU Basket Revisions. Market Repercussions and Reform Proposals', *EBA-Newsletter, Special Issue No. 4*, May 1989.

Ehrenberg, Herbert, *Abstieg vom Währungsolymp. Zur Zukunft der Deutschen Bundesbank*, Frankfurt, 1991.

Eicke, Jürgen, 'Geschäfte unter Verwendung von ECU in der Bundesrepublik Deutschland', *Die Bank*, 1984.

Emerson, Michael and Huhne, Christopher, *The ECU-Report,* Brussels, 1991.

Ernst & Young, *A Strategy for the ECU*, London, 1991.

Eurépargne, *Chronique de l'ECU 1984/85*, May 1986.

Euromoney, The Ecu - *Currency for Europe*, London, 1991.

European Affairs, *Special Issue on the ECU*, Amsterdam/Brussels, March 1988.

European Community, Monetary Committee, *Compendium of Community Monetary Texts*, Brussels, 1986.

European Investment Bank, 'Das Clearingsystem für die private ECU', *EIB-Informations No. 50*, October 1986.

Eurostat, *ECU - EMS Information*, Luxemburg, monthly.

Evans, Gary, 'The Ups and Down of ECU-Bonds', *Euromoney*, 1986.

Evans, Richard, 'The ECU Bond Market Tries to Grow up', *Euromoney*, May 1985.

Fabra, Paul, 'L'ECU est-il une monnaie?', *Le Monde*, March 20, 1984.

Fairlamb, David, 'The Up-and-Coming ECU', *Banking World*, February 1984.

Faith, Nicholas, 'The ECU: It's all Things to all Men', *Euromoney*, Mai 1983.

Faits et Opinions, *European Business and the ECU*, Paris, October 25, 1988.

Foshag, Jörg, 'Frankreichs ECU-Werbung', *Börsenzeitung*, Frankfurt, March 30, 1985.

Frank, David, 'Second-guessing the ECU', *The Banker*, November 1988.

Franz, Otmar (Editor), *Europäische Währung - eine Utopie?*, Sindelfingen, 1988.

Franz, Otmar, *European Currency in the Making*, Sindelfingen 1989.

Froment, Eric, 'Chronique de l'ECU: Les paradoxes de la création d'écus', *Eurépargne*, July 1987.

Gabus, Eric, 'La Suisse et l'ECU', *Revue Economique et Sociale*, June 1989.

Ganaye, Renaud, 'Chronique de l'ECU - La compensation des réglements en ECU', *Eurépargne*, 1984.

Gillbert, Pier Luigi, 'The International ECU Primary Bond Market: Structure and Competition', *European Investment Bank 1979-89, The ECU's Tenth Anniversary, EIB Papers, Special Issue*, December 1989.

Girard, Jacques and Steinherr, Alfred, 'The ECU: A Currency Unlike Any Other?', *EIB-Papers No. 10*, June 1989.

Girard, Jacques, 'In What Sense is the ECU a Low Risk Currency', *European Investment Bank 1979-89. The ECU's Tenth Anniversary, EIB Papers, Special Issue*, December 1989.

Giscard d'Estaing, Valéry, 'Der ECU und das EWS', *Bulletin der Schweizerischen Kreditanstalt*, Zurich, February 1989.

Gleske, Leonhard, 'Die ECU - Eine zukünftige europäische Währung? Ihre derzeitige Rolle im EWS und ihre Zukunftsaussichten', *Deutsche Bundesbank, Auszüge aus Presseartikeln, No. 96*, December 4, 1989.

Godschalk, Hugo, 'Private und offizielle ECU: Ein Ordnungspolitisches Problem', *Österreichisches Bankarchiv*, April 1986.

Grauwe, Paul de, 'The EMS, Europe and the Dollar', *The Banker*, 1979.

Grauwe, Paul de, *The ECU and European Monetary Integration*, London, 1989.

Grisius, Henri, 'Une Bourse européene d'actions en écus?', *Eurépargne*, January 1988.

Gros, Rémi, 'Ce que pourrait être un clearing de l'ECU', *Eurépargne*, 1984.

Group of Thirty, 'Group of 30 Study Chronicles the Success of the 7-year-old European Currency Unit', *IMF-Survey No. 11*, June 2, 1986.

Groupement pour la coopération monétaire européene, *Le statut de l'ECU*, Paris, September 1984.

Guglielmotto, Enrica u. Passatore, Guiseppe, 'The Private ECU Market: A Case of International Financial Innovation', *Changing Money*, Florence 1987.

Guimbretiére, Pierre, 'L'estimation du marché de L'ECU', *Eurépargne*, 1984.

Hoffmeyer, Erik, 'The Probable Role of the ECU in the Process Towards Economic and Monetary Union', *BIS Review, No. 123*, June 28, 1991.

International Bond Manual, *European Currency Unit*, Salomon Brothers Inc, 1986.

Jager, Henk and Jong de, Elke, 'The Exchange-Rate Mechanism of the EMS and the ECU as a Reserve Asset', *European Economic Review*, 1987.

Jager, Henk and Jong de, Elke, 'The Private ECU's Potential Impact on Global and European Exchange Rate Stability', *Banca Nazionale del Lavoro, Quarterly Review No. 164*, Rome, March 1988.

Jeans, Alain, *L'écu, le SME et les marches financiers*, Paris, 1990.

Jozzo, Alfonso, 'ECU - Perspectives as Seen by a European Commercial Bank', *Geld und Währung Working Papers No. 10*, Frankfurt, November 1988.

Jozzo, Alfonso, 'The Use of the ECU as an Invoicing Currency', *The ECU and European Monetary Integration*, London, 1988.

Jurgensen, Philippe, 'Les rapports de l'ECU public et l'ECU privé', *Eurépargne*, 1984.

Keller, Paul, 'The Pursuit of the ECU', *Euromoney*, January 1990.

Kloten, Norbert, 'Die ECU: Perspektiven monetärer Integration in Europa', *Europa-Archiv*, 1985.

Kloten, Norbert, 'Towards European Monetary Union: The Role of ECU Coins and Bank Notes', *Deutsche Bundesbank, Auszüge aus Presseartikeln, No. 46*, June 23, 1988.

Kloten, Norbert and Kirelli, Sermin, 'Der ECU-Finanzmarkt - ein dynamischer Prozeß', *Markt und Wettbewerb*, Bern/Stuttgart.

Köhler, Heinz, 'Euro-Aktien-Index auf ECU-Basis', *Die Bank*, February 1987.

Lefévre, Thierry, *L'ECU: Un nouveau marché*, Paris, 1985.

Leigh-Pemberton, Robin, 'The Evolution of the ECU', *BIS Review, No. 246*, December 14, 1988.

Lelart, Michel, 'L'utilisation de DTS et de l'ECU par le secteur privé', *Banque*, November 1983.

Lelart, Michel, 'L'avenir de l'ECU', *Banque*, 1984.

Lelart, Michel, 'La création d'ECUs privés', *Eurépargne*, June 1986.

Levich, R. M., *Development of the ECU Markets: Perspectives on Financial Innovation*, 1987.

Lovich, R.M., *ECU: European Currency Unit*, London, Euromoney Publications, 1987.

Levich, Richard and Sommariva, Andrea (Edit.), *The ECU Market*, Lexington, 1988.

Lichter, Gilbert, 'The ECU clearing', *ECU*, 1988.

Lomax, David F., 'The ECU as Investment Currency', *The ECU and European Monetary Integration*, London, 1988.

Louw, André, 'The ECU and its Role on the European Monetary Scene', *International Monetary and Financial Integration - The European Dimension*, Dordrecht, 1988.

Louw, André, 'The ECU, the ECU Banking Association and European Monetary Intergration', *Financial Integration, International Trade and Finance Consultancy*, Philadelphia, 1990.

Major, John, *Economic and Monetary Union: Beyond Stage One*, London, June 20, 1990.

Marchat, Philippe, 'Le rôle de l'ECU et le financement des investissements', *Eurépargne*, 1984.

Marillia, Bernard, 'L'ECU ne doit pas être l'assignat de l'Europe', *Banque*, February 1988.

Masera, Rainer, 'An increasing role for the ECU: a character in search of a script', *Problems of European Monetary Co-Ordination and Integration*, Oxford, 1984.

Matthes, Heinrich, 'L'ECU et-il la monnaie européene de l'avenir?', *Eurépargne*, June 1986.

Maurus, H.J., 'Harter ECU - ein politisches Ablenkungsmanöver?', *Schweizer Bank*, Zurich, August 1990.

Mayer, Helmuth W., *Private ECUs potential macro-economic policy dimensions*, Basle, 1986.

Mayer, Helmuth W., 'Private ECUs. Potential Macro-Economic Policy Dimensions', *BIS Economic Papers No. 16*, April 1986.

Moltke von, Albrecht, *Die private Verwendung von ECU*, Institut für europäische Wirtschaftsstudien (IEWS), Reutlingen, 1986.

Morgan Grenfell, 'The ECU Treasury Bill Market', *Morgan Grenfell-Economics*, London, September 1988.

Moss, Frank, 'The Private Use of the ECU: Implications for National Monetary Authorities in EEC Member States', *Revue de la Banque*, February 1984.

Moss, Frank, 'Chronique de L'ECU - Quelqes conséquences pour les autorités monétaires d'une intensification de l'usage privé de L'ECU', *Eurépargne*, 4/84.

Muhlen, Ernest M., 'L'ECU comme devise', *Eurépargne*, 8,9/84.

Office for Official Publications of the European Community, *The ECU* (2nd edition), Luxemburg, 1987.

Osborn, Neil, 'European Currency Unit: Lawson's Initiative on the ECU', *Euromoney*, September 1988.

Pillet, Jacques, 'L'utilisation de l'ECU dans le groupe Saint Gobain', *Eurépargne,* 8,9/1984.

Rambure, Dominique, 'L'utilisation privée de l'écu', *Banque*, 1983.

Reuss, Conrad, 'Marges de fluctuation et stabilité de l'ECU', *Eurépargne*, March/April 1987.

Ribound, Jacques, *A stable external currency for Europe*, St. Martin's Press, 1991.

Ribound, Jacques, *The Case for a New ECU*, London, 1989.

Santer, Jacques, 'Europa und die ECU', *Zeitschrift für das gesamte Kreditwesen*, 1984.

Sarmet, Marcel, 'Le point de vue des emprunteurs', *Eurépargne*, 8,9/1984.

Sarmet, Marcel, 'Ist die ECU eine gute mittel- und langfristige Anlagewährung', *Banque*, 1984.

Schissel, Howard, 'ECU: Tell Me How it Works, Again...', *Euromoney*, September 1988.

Schlüter, Peter-Wilhelm, 'The Official ECU', Istituto Bancario San Paolo di Torino, *ECU-Newsletter Nr. 18*, October 1986.

Schmidhuber, Peter, 'Brauchen wir eine europäische Währung?', Deutsche Bundesbank, *Auszüge aus Presseartikeln, No. 48*, June 14, 1989.

Schmidt, Helmut, 'Wir schaffen ein Europäisches Währungssystem', *Die Deutschen und ihre Nachbarn*, Berlin, 1990.

Schmitt, Bernard, *L'Ecu et les souverainetés nationales en Europe,* Paris, 1988.

Schweizerischer Bankverein, *Die ECU als Anlagewährung*, 1985.

Schul, J.-J., 'The European Consumer and the ECU', *European Investment Bank 1979-89, The ECU's Tenth Anniversary, EIB Papers, Special Issue*, December 1989.

Steinherr, A., 'EMS and ECU: Proposals for Developing Their Synergy', *The ECU and European Monetary Integration*, London, 1988.

Steinherr, A., 'The ECU - To Be Or Not to Be A Basket - That Is the Question', ECU Banking Association, *EBA Newsletter, Special Issue*, June 1991.

Sunt, Chris, *Legal aspects of the ECU,* Butterworths, 1989.

Swings, André, 'Die private Verwendung der ECU, Entwicklungen, Anwendungsbereiche, Probleme und Aussichten', *Sparkasse*, 1985.

Swings, André, 'Currency: Has the European Currency Unit come into its own?', *Institutional Investor*, 07/1985.

Swings, André, 'Short and Medium Term Instruments and the ECU', *ECU Today*, Luxemburg, 1986.

Swings, André, 'Le marché secondaire des obligations en écu', *Eurépargne, June 1987.*

Swings, André, 'L'ECU dans l'entreprise', Eurépargne, June 1987.

Swings, André, 'Financial Integration in Europe Through Private Use of the ECU', *International Monetary and Financial Integration - The European Dimension*, Dordrecht, 1988.

Swiss Bank Corporation, *The ECU as an Investment Currency*, Basle, July 1985.

Thomas, Denis, '1989: la révolution de l'écu', *Eurépargne*, Februar 1989.

Thomaz, Bernard de, *Die ECU*, Banque Bruxelles Lambert, 1985.

Thygesen, Niels, *The Private Use of the ECU*, Brussels, 1980.

Thygesen, Niels, 'Problems for the European Currency Unit in the Private Sector', *World Economy*, 1980.

Triffin, Robert, 'The International Role and Fate of the Dollar (and the Role of the ECU as a European Parallel Currency)', *Foreign Affairs*, 1979.

Triffin, Robert, 'La réalité de l'ECU', *Eurépargne*, 8,9/1984.

Ungerer, Horst et al., 'The European Monetary System, The Experience 1979-82', *IMF Occasional Paper No. 19*, Washington, 1983.

Ungerer, Horst et al., 'The EMS: Recent Development', *IMF Occasional Paper No 48*, Washington, 1986.

Ungerer, Horst et al., 'THE EMS: Developments and Perspectives', *IMF Occasional Paper No. 73*, November 1990.

Vajda, Pierre, 'L'ECU et le marché financier', *Banque*, 1985.

Valenne, Pierre-Marie, *L'ECU et le rôle spécifique de la place financiére de Luxembourg*, Banque Internationale à Luxembourg, April 1985.

Wilson, Neil, 'A Life of its Own', *The Banker*, February 1990.

Winder, Robert, 'Hello America, Meet the ECU', *Euromoney*, May 1985.

Ypersele van, Jaques and Koeune, Jean-Claude, *The EMS*, Brussels 1985.

Zandano, Gianni, 'The Attractions of the ECU', *Euromoney*, February 1985.

Zandano, Gianni, 'How to Spur Wider Use of the ECU', *Lombard*, December 1988.

PART XVIII.

APPENDICES

APPENDIX A

ECU-RELATED EC DOCUMENTS

TABLE OF CONTENTS

TREATY OF ROME AS AMENDED BY THE SINGLE EUROPEAN ACT
(excerpts relating to monetary matters)

ECONOMIC AND MONETARY UNION)

Article 102a

1. In order to ensure the convergence of economic and monetary policies which is necessary for the further development of the Community, Member States shall cooperate in accordance with the objectives of Article 104. In so doing, they shall take account of the experience acquired in cooperation within the framework of the European Monetary System (EMS) and in developing the ecu, and shall respect existing powers in this field.

2. Insofar as further development in the field of economic and monetary policy necessitates institutional changes, the provisions of Article 236 shall be applicable. The Monetary Committee and the Committee of Governors of the Central Banks shall also be consulted regarding institutional changes in the monetary area.

BALANCE OF PAYMENTS

Article 104

Each Member State shall pursue the economic policy needed to ensure the equilibrium of its overall balance of payments and to maintain confidence in its currency, while taking care to ensure a high level of employment and a stable level of prices.

Article 105

1. In order to facilitate attainment of the objectives set out in Article 104, Member States shall coordinate their economic policies. They shall for this purpose provide for cooperation between their appropriate administrative departments and between their central banks.

The Commission shall submit to the Council recommendations on how to achieve such cooperation.

2. In order to promote coordination of the policies of Member States in the monetary field to the full extent needed for the functioning of the common market, a Monetary Committee with advisory status is hereby set up. It shall have the following tasks:

-- to keep under review the monetary and financial situation of the Member States and of the Community and the general payments system of the Member States and to report regularly thereon to the Council and to the Commission;

-- to deliver opinions at the request of the Council or of the Commission or on its own initiative, for submission to these institutions.

The Member States and the Commission shall each appoint two members of the Monetary Committee.

Article 106

1. Each Member State undertakes to authorize, in the currency of the Member State in which the creditor of the beneficiary resides, any payments connected with the movement of goods, service or capital, and any transfers of capital and earnings, to the extent that the movement of goods, services, capital and persons between Member States has been liberalized pursuant to this Treaty.

The Member States declare their readiness to undertake the liberalization of payments beyond the extent provided in the preceding subparagraph, in so far as their economic situation in general and the state of their balance of payments in particular so permit.

2. In so far as movements of goods, services, and capital are limited only by restrictions on payments connected therewith, these restrictions shall be progressively abolished by applying, mutatis mutandis, the provisions of the Chapters relating to the abolition of quantitative restrictions, to the liberalization of services and to the free movement of capital.

3. Member States undertake not to introduce between themselves any new restrictions on transfers connected with the invisible transactions listed in Annex III to this Treaty.

The progressive abolition of existing restrictions shall be effected in accordance with the provisions of Articles 63 to 65, in so far as such abolition is not governed by the provisions contained in paragraphs 1 and 2 or by the Chapter relating to the free movement of capital.

4. If need be, Member States shall consult each other on the measures to be taken to enable the payments and transfers mentioned in this Article

to be effected; such measures shall not prejudice the attainment of the objectives set out in this Chapter.

Article 107

1. Each Member State shall treat its policy with regard to rates of exchange as a matter of common concern.

2. If a Member State makes an alteration in its rate of exchange which is inconsistent with the objectives set out in Article 104 and which seriously distorts conditions of competition, the Commission may, after consulting the Monetary Committee, authorize other Member States to take for a strictly limited period the necessary measures, the conditions and details of which it shall determine, in order to counter the consequences of such alteration.

Article 108

1. Where a Member State is in difficulties or is seriously threatened with difficulties as regards its balance of payments either as a result of an overall disequilibrium in its balance of payments, or as a result of the type of currency at its disposal, and where such difficulties are liable in particular to jeopardize the functioning of the common market or the progressive implementation of the common commercial policy, the Commission shall immediately investigate the position of the State in question and the action which, making use of all the means at its disposal, that State has taken or may take in accordance with the provisions of Article 104. The Commission shall state what measures it recommends the State concerned to take.

If the action taken by a Member State and the measures suggested by the Commission do not prove sufficient to overcome the difficulties which have arisen or which threaten, the Commission shall, after consulting the Monetary Committee, recommend to the Council the granting of mutual assistance and appropriate methods therefor.

The Commission shall keep the Council regularly informed of the situation and of how it is developing.

2. The Council, acting by a qualified majority, shall grant such mutual assistance; it shall adopt directives or decisions laying down the conditions and details of such assistance, which may take such forms as:

(a) a concerted approach to or within any other international organizations to which Member States may have recourse;

(b) measures needed to avoid deflection of trade where the State which is in difficulties maintains or reintroduces quantitative restrictions against third countries;
(c) the granting of limited credits by other Member States, subject to their agreement.

During the transitional period, mutual assistance may also take the form of special reductions in customs duties or enlargements of quotas in order to facilitate an increase in imports from the State which is in difficulties, subject to the agreement of the States by which such measures would have to be taken.

3. If the mutual assistance recommended by the Commission is not granted by the Council or if the mutual assistance granted and the measures taken are insufficient, the Commission shall authorize the State which is in difficulties to take protective measures, the conditions and details of which the Commission shall determine.

Such authorization may be revoked and such conditions and details may be changed by the Council acting by a qualified majority.

Article 109

1. Where a sudden crisis in the balance of payments occurs and a decision within the meaning of Article 108(2) is not immediately taken, the Member State concerned may, as a precaution, take the necessary protective measures. Such measures must cause the least possible disturbance in the functioning of the common market and must not be wider in scope than is strictly necessary to remedy the sudden difficulties which have arisen.

2. The Commission and the other Member States shall be informed of such protective measures not later than when they enter into force. The Commission may recommend to the Council the granting of mutual assistance under Article 108.

3. After the Commission has delivered an opinion and the Monetary Committee has been consulted, the Council may, acting by a qualified majority, decide that the State concerned shall amend, suspend or abolish the protective measures referred to above.

TREATY ON EUROPEAN UNION ("MAASTRICHT TREATY")
(excerpts relating to the EMU and the ecu)

TITLE II
PROVISIONS AMENDING THE TREATY ESTABLISHING THE EUROPEAN ECONOMIC COMMUNITY WITH A VIEW TO ESTABLISHING THE EUROPEAN COMMUNITY

ARTICLE 3a

1. For the purposes set out in Article 2, the activities of the Member States and the Community shall include, as provided in this Treaty and in accordance with the timetable set out therein, the adoption of an economic policy which is based on the close coordination of Member States' economic policies, on the internal market and on the definition of common objectives, and conducted in accordance with the principle of an open market economy with free competition.

2. Concurrently with the foregoing, and as provided in this Treaty and in accordance with the timetable and the procedures set out therein, **these activities shall include the irrevocable fixing of exchange rates leading to the introduction of a single currency, the ECU, and the definition and conduct of a single monetary policy and exchange rate policy the primary objective of both of which shall be to maintain price stability** and, without prejudice to this objective, to support the general economic policies in the Community, in accordance with the principle of an open market economy with free competition.

3. These activities of the Member States and the Community shall entail compliance with the following guiding principles: stable prices, sound public finances and monetary conditions and a sustainable balance of payments.

TITLE VI
ECONOMIC AND MONETARY POLICY

CHAPTER 2
MONETARY POLICY

ARTICLE 105

1. The primary objective of the ESCB shall be to maintain price stability. Without prejudice to the objective of price stability, the ESCB shall support the general economic policies in the Community with a view to contributing to the achievement of the objectives of the Community as laid down in Article 2.

   The ESCB shall act in accordance with the principle of an open market economy with free competition, favoring an efficient allocation of resources, and in compliance with the principles set out in Article 3a.

2. The basic tasks to be carried out through the ESCB shall be:

   - to define and implement the monetary policy of the Community;
   - to conduct foreign exchange operations consistent with the provisions of Article 109;
   - to hold and manage the official foreign reserves of the Member States;
   - to promote the smooth operation of payment systems.

3. The third indent of paragraph 2 shall be without prejudice to the holding and management by the governments of Member States of foreign exchange working balances.

4. The ECB shall be consulted:

   - on any proposed Community act in its fields of competence;
   - by national authorities regarding any draft legislative provision in its fields of competence, but within the limits and under the conditions set out by the Council in accordance with the procedure laid down in Article 106(6).

   The ECB may submit opinions to the appropriate Community institutions or bodies or to national authorities on matters within its fields of competence.

5. The ESCB shall contribute to the smooth conduct of policies pursued by the competent authorities relating to the prudential supervision of credit institutions and the stability of the financial system.

6. The Council may, acting unanimously on a proposal from the Commission and after consulting the ECB and after receiving the assent of the European Parliament, confer upon the ECB specific tasks concerning policies relating to the prudential supervision of credit institutions and other financial institutions with the exception of insurance undertakings.

ARTICLE 105a

1. **The ECB shall have the exclusive right to authorize the issue of bank notes within the Community. The ECB and the national central banks may issue such notes.**

   The bank notes issued by the ECB and the national central banks shall be the only such notes to have the status of legal tender within the Community.

2. **Member States may issue coins subject to approval by the ECB of the volume of the issue. The Council may, acting in accordance with the procedure referred to in Article 189c and after consulting the ECB, adopt measures to harmonize the denominations and technical specifications of all coins intended for circulation to the extent necessary to permit their smooth circulation within the Community.**

ARTICLE 106

1. The ESCB shall be composed of the ECB and of the national central banks.

2. The ECB shall have legal personality.

3. The ESCB shall be governed by the decision-making bodies of the ECB which shall be the Governing Council and the Executive Board.

4. The Statute of the ESCB is laid down in a Protocol annexed to this Treaty.

5. Articles 5.1, 5.2, 5.3, 17, 18, 19.1, 22, 23, 24, 26, 32.2, 32.3, 32.4, 32.6, 33.1(a) and 36 of the Statute of the ESCB may be

amended by the Council, acting either by a qualified majority on a recommendation from the ECB and after consulting the Commission or unanimously on a proposal form the Commission and after consulting the ECB. In either case, the assent of the European Parliament shall be required.

6. The Council, acting by a qualified majority either on a proposal form the Commission and after consulting the European Parliament and the ECB or on a recommendation from the ECB and after consulting the European Parliament and the Commission, shall adopt the provisions referred to in Articles 4, 5.4, 19.2, 20, 28.1, 29.2, 30.4 and 34.3 of the Statute of the ESCB.

ARTICLE 107

When exercising the powers and carrying out the tasks and duties conferred upon them by this Treaty and the Statute of the ESCB, neither the ECB, nor a national central bank, nor any Member of their decision-making bodies shall seek or take instructions from Community institutions or bodies, from any government of a Member State or from any other body.

The Community institutions and bodies and the governments of the Member States undertake to respect this principle and not to seek to influence the Members of the decision-making bodies of the ECB or of the national central banks in the performance of their tasks.

ARTICLE 108

Each Member State shall ensure, at the latest at the date of the establishment of the ESCB, that its national legislation including the statutes of its national central bank is compatible with this Treaty and the Statute of the ESCB.

ARTICLE 108a

1. In order to carry out the tasks entrusted to the ESCB, the ECB shall, in accordance with the provisions of this Treaty and under the conditions laid down in the Statute of the ESCB:

   - make regulations to the extent necessary to implement the task defined in Article 3.1, first indent, Articles 19.1, 22 and 25.2 of the Statute of the ESCB and in cases which shall be laid down in the acts of the Council referred to in Article 106(6);

- take decisions necessary for carrying out the tasks entrusted to the ESCB under this Treaty and the Statute of the ESCB;

- make recommendations and deliver opinions.

2. A regulation shall have general application. It shall be binding in its entirety and directly applicable in all Member States. Recommendations and opinions shall have no binding force. A decision shall be binding in its entirety upon those to whom it is addressed.

   Articles 190 to 192 shall apply to regulations and decisions adopted by the ECB.

   The ECB may decide to publish its decisions, recommendations and opinions.

3. Within the limits and under the conditions adopted by the Council under the procedure laid down in Article 106(6), the ECB shall be entitled to impose fines or periodic penalty payments on undertakings for failure to comply with obligations under its regulations and decisions.

ARTICLE 109

1. **By way of derogation from Article 228, the Council may, acting unanimously on a recommendation from the ECB or from the Commission, and after consulting the ECB in an endeavor to reach a consensus consistent with the objective of price stability, after consulting the European Parliament, in accordance with the procure in paragraph 3 for determining the arrangements, conclude formal agreements on an exchange rate system for the ECU in relation to non-Community currencies.**

   The Council may, acting by a qualified majority on a recommendation from the ECB or from the Commission, and after consulting the ECB in an endeavor to reach a consensus consistent with the objective of price stability, adopt, adjust or abandon the central rates of the ECU within the exchange rate system.

   The President of the Council shall inform the European Parliament of the adoption, adjustment or abandonment of the ECU central rates.

2. In the absence of an exchange rate system in relation to one or more non-Community currencies as referred to in paragraph 1, the Council, acting by a qualified majority either on a recommendation from the Commission and after consulting the ECB or on a recommendation from the ECB, may formulate general orientations for exchange rate policy in relation to these currencies.

   These general orientations shall be without prejudice to the primary objective of the ESCB to maintain price stability.

3. By way of derogation from Article 228, where agreements concerning monetary or foreign exchange regime matters need to be negotiated by the Community with one or more States or international organizations, the Council, acting by a qualified majority on a recommendation from the Commission and after consulting the ECB, shall decide the arrangements for the negotiation and for the conclusion of such agreements.

   These arrangements shall ensure that the Community expresses a single position. The Commission shall be fully associated with the negotiations.

   Agreements concluded in accordance with this paragraph shall be binding on the institutions of the Community, on the ECB and on Member States.

4. Subject to paragraph 1, the Council shall, on a proposal from the Commission and after consulting the ECB, acting by a qualified majority decide on the position of the Community at international level as regards issues of particular relevance to economic and monetary union and, acting unanimously, decide its representation in compliance with the allocation of powers laid down in Articles 103 and 105.

5. Without prejudice to Community competence and Community agreements as regards economic and monetary union, Member States may negotiate in international bodies and conclude international agreements.

CHAPTER 3
INSTITUTIONAL PROVISIONS

ARTICLE 109a

1. The Governing Council of the ECB shall comprise the Members of the Executive Board of the ECB and the Governors of the national central banks.

2.(a) The Executive Board shall comprise the President, the Vice-President and four other Members.

(b) The President, the Vice-President and the other Members of the Executive Board shall be appointed from among persons of recognized standing and professional experience in monetary or banking matters by common accord of the Governments of the Member States at the level of Heads of State or of Government, on a recommendation from the Council, after it has consulted the European Parliament and the Governing Council of the ECB.

Their term of office shall be eight years and shall not be renewable. Only nationals of Member States may be Members of the Executive Board.

ARTICLE 109b

1. The President of the Council and a Member of the Commission may participate, without having the right to vote, in meetings of the Governing Council of the ECB.

   The President of the Council may submit a motion for deliberation to the Governing Council of the ECB.

2. The President of the ECB shall be invited to participate in Council meetings when the Council is discussing matters relating to the objectives and tasks of the ESCB.

3. The ECB shall address an annual report on the activities of the ESCB and on the monetary policy of both the previous and current year to the European Parliament, the Council and the Commission, and also to the European Council.

The President of the ECB shall present this report to the Council and to the European Parliament, which may hold a general debate on that basis.

The President of the ECB and the other Members of the Executive Board may, at the request of the European Parliament or on their own initiative, be heard by the competent Committees of the European Parliament.

ARTICLE 109c

1. In order to promote coordination of the policies of Member States to the full extent needed for the functioning of the internal market, a Monetary Committee with advisory status is hereby set up.

   It shall have the following tasks:

   - to keep under review the monetary and financial situation of the Member States and of the Community and the general payments system of the Member States and to report regularly thereon to the Council and to the Commission;
   - to deliver opinions at the request of the Council or of the Commission, or on its own initiative for submission to those institutions;
   - without prejudice to Article 151, to contribute to the preparation of the work of the Council referred to in Articles 73f, 73g, 103(2), (3), (4) and (5), 103a, 104a, 104b, 104c, 109e(2), 109f(6), 109h, 109i, 109j(2) and 109k(1);
   - to examine, at least once a year, the situation regarding the movement of capital and the freedom of payments, as they result from the application of this Treaty and of measures adopted by the Council, the examination shall cover all measures relating to capital movements and payments; the Committee shall report to the Commission and to the Council on the outcome of this examination. The Member States and the Commission shall each appoint two Members of the Monetary Committee.

2. At the start of the third stage, an Economic and Financial Committee shall be set up. The Monetary Committee provided for in paragraph 1 shall be dissolved.

   The Economic and Financial Committee shall have the following task:

- to deliver opinions at the request of the Council or of the Commission, or on its own initiative for submission to those institutions;
- to keep under review the economic and financial situation of the Member States and of the Community and to report regularly thereon to the Council and to the Commission, in particular on financial relations with third countries and international institutions;
- without prejudice to Article 151, to contribute to the preparation of the work of the Council referred to in Articles 73f, 73g, 103(2), (3), (4) and (5), 103a, 104a, 104b, 104c, 105(6), 105a(2), 106(5) and (6), 109, 109h, 109i(2) and (3), 109k(2), 109l(4) and (5), and to carry out other advisory and preparatory tasks assigned to it by the Council;
- to examine, at least once a year, the situation regarding the movement of capital and the freedom of payments, as they result from the application of this Treaty and of measures adopted by the Council; the examination shall cover all measures relating to capital movements and payments; the Committee shall report to the Commission and to the Council on the outcome of this examination.

The Member States, the Commission and the ECB shall each appoint no more than two Members of the Committee.

3. The Council shall, acting by a qualified majority on a proposal from the Commission and after consulting the ECB and the Committee referred to in this Article, lay down detailed provisions concerning the composition of the Economic and Financial Committee. The President of the Council shall inform the European Parliament of such a decision.

4. In addition to the tasks set out in paragraph 2, if and as long as there are Member States with a derogation as referred to in Articles 109k and 109l, the Committee shall keep under review the monetary and financial situation and the general payments system of those Member States and report regularly thereon to the Council and to the Commission.

ARTICLE 109d

For matters within the scope of Articles 103(4), 104c with the exception of paragraph 14, 109, 109j, 109k and 109l(4) and (5), the Council or a Member State may request the Commission to make a recommendation or a proposal, as appropriate. The Commission shall examine this request and submit its conclusions to the Council without delay.

CHAPTER 4
TRANSITIONAL PROVISIONS

ARTICLE 109e

1. **The second stage for achieving economic and monetary union shall begin on 1 January 1994.**

2. Before that date

(a) each Member State shall :

- adopt, where necessary, appropriate measures to comply with the prohibitions laid down in Article 73b, without prejudice to Article 73e, and in Articles 104 and 104a(1);

- adopt, if necessary, with a view to permitting the assessment provided for in subparagraph (b), multiannual programmes intended to ensure the lasting convergence necessary for the achievement of economic and monetary union, in particular with regard to price stability and sound public finances;

(b) the Council shall, on the basis of a report from the Commission, assess the progress made with regard to economic and monetary convergence, in particular with regard to price stability and sound public finances, and the progress made with the implementation of Community law concerning the internal market.

3. The provisions of Articles 104, 104a(1), 104b(1) and 104c with the exception of paragraphs 1, 9, 11 and 14 shall apply from the beginning of the second stage.

   The provisions of Articles 103a(2), 104c(1), (9) and (11), 105, 105a, 107, 109, 109a, 109b and 109c(2) and (4) shall apply from the beginning of the third stage.

4. In the second stage, Member States shall endeavor to avoid excessive government deficits.

5. During the second stage, each Member State shall, as appropriate, start the process leading to the independence of its central bank, in accordance with Article 108.

ARTICLE 109f

1. At the start of the second stage, a European Monetary Institute (hereinafter referred to as "EMI") shall be established and take up its duties; it shall have legal personality and be directed and managed by a Council, consisting of a President and the governors of the national central banks, one of whom shall be Vice-President.

   The President shall be appointed by common accord of the Governments of the Member States at the level of Heads of State or of Government, on a recommendation from, as the case may be, the Committee of Governors of the central banks of the Member States (hereinafter referred to as "Committee of Governors") or the Council of the EMI, and after consulting the European Parliament and the Council. The President shall be selected from among persons of recognized standing and professional experience in monetary or banking matters. Only nationals of Member States may be President of the EMI. The Council of the EMI shall appoint the Vice-President.

   The Statute of the EMI is laid down in a protocol annexed to this Treaty.

   The Committee of Governors shall be dissolved at the start of the second stage.

2. The EMI shall :

   - strengthen cooperation between the national central banks;
   - strengthen the coordination of the monetary policies of the Member States, with the aim of ensuring price stability;
   - monitor the functioning of the European Monetary System;
   - hold consultations concerning issues falling within the competence of the national central banks and affecting the stability of financial institutions and markets;
   - take over the tasks of the European Monetary Cooperation Fund, which shall be dissolved; the modalities of dissolution are laid down in the Statute of the EMI;

- **facilitate the use of the ECU and oversee its development, including the smooth functioning of the ECU clearing system.**

3. For the preparation of the third stage, the EMI shall:

   - prepare the instruments and the procedures necessary for carrying out a single monetary policy in the third stage;
   - promote the harmonization, where necessary, of the rules and practices governing the collection, compilation and distribution of statistics in the areas within its field of competence;
   - prepare the rules for operations to be undertaken by the national central banks within the framework of the ESCB;
   - promote the efficiency of cross-border payments;
   - **supervise the technical preparation of ECU bank notes.**

   At the latest by 31 December 1996, the EMI shall specify the regulatory, organizational and logistical framework necessary for the ESCB to perform its tasks in the third stage. This framework shall be submitted for decision to the ECB at the date of its establishment.

4. The EMI, acting by a majority of two thirds of the Members of its Council, may:

   - formulate opinions or recommendations on the overall orientation of monetary policy and exchange rate policy as well as on related measures introduced in each Member State;
   - submit opinions or recommendations to Governments and to the Council on policies which might affect the internal or external monetary situation in the Community and, in particular, the functioning of the European Monetary System;
   - make recommendations to the monetary authorities of the Member States concerning the conduct of their monetary policy.

5. The EMI, acting unanimously, may decide to publish its opinions and its recommendations.

6. The EMI shall be consulted by the Council regarding any proposed Community act within its field of competence.

   Within the limits and under the conditions set out by the Council, acting by a qualified majority on a proposal from the Commission and after consulting the European Parliament and the EMI, the EMI shall be consulted by the authorities of the Member States on any draft legislative provision within its field of competence.

7. The Council may, acting unanimously on a proposal from the Commission and after consulting the European Parliament and the EMI, confer upon the EMI other tasks for the preparation of the third stage.

8. Where this Treaty provides for a consultative role for the ECB, references to the ECB shall be read as referring to the EMI before the establishment of the ECB.

Where this Treaty provides for a consultative role for the EMI, references to the EMI shall be read, before 1 January 1994, as referring to the Committee of Governors.

9. During the second stage, the term "ECB" used in Articles 173, 175, 176, 177, 180 and 215 shall be read as referring to the EMI.

ARTICLE 109g

The currency composition of the ECU basket shall not be changed. From the start of the third stage, the value of the ECU shall be irrevocably fixed in accordance with Article 109l(4).

ARTICLE 109h

1. Where a Member State is in difficulties or is seriously threatened with difficulties as regards its balance of payments either as a result of an overall disequilibrium in its balance of payments, or as a result of the type of currency at its disposal, and where such difficulties are liable in particular to jeopardize the functioning of the common market or the progressive implementation of the common commercial policy, the Commission shall immediately investigate the position of the State in question and the action which, making use of all the means at its disposal, that State has taken or may take in accordance with the provisions of this Treaty.

The Commission shall state what measures it recommends the State concerned to take.

If the action taken by a Member State and the measures suggested by the Commission do not prove sufficient to overcome the difficulties which have arisen or which threaten, the Commission shall, after consulting the Committee referred to in Article 109c, recommend to the Council the granting of mutual assistance and appropriate methods therefor.

The Commission shall keep the Council regularly informed of the situation and of how it is developing.

2. The Council, acting by a qualified majority, shall grant such mutual assistance; it shall adopt directives or decisions laying down the conditions and details of such assistance, which may take such forms as:

(a) a concerted approach to or within any other international organizations to which Member States may have recourse;
(b) measures needed to avoid deflection of trade where the State which is in difficulties maintains or reintroduces quantitative restrictions against third countries;
(c) the granting of limited credits by other Member States, subject to their agreement.

3. If the mutual assistance recommended by the Commission is not granted by the Council or if the mutual assistance granted and the measures taken are insufficient, the Commission shall authorize the State which is in difficulties to take protective measures, the conditions and details of which the Commission shall determine.

Such authorization may be revoked and such conditions and details may be changed by the Council acting by a qualified majority.

4. Subject to Article 109k(6), this Article shall cease to apply from the beginning of the third stage.

ARTICLE 109i

1. Where a sudden crisis in the balance of payments occurs and a decision within the meaning of Article 109h(2) is not immediately taken, the Member State concerned may, as a precaution, take the necessary protective measures. Such measures must cause the least possible disturbance in the functioning of the common market and must not be wider in scope than is strictly necessary to remedy the sudden difficulties which have arisen.

2. The Commission and the other Member States shall be informed of such protective measures not later than when they enter into force. The Commission may recommend to the Council the granting of mutual assistance under Article 109h.

3. After the Commission has delivered an opinion and the Committee referred to in Article 109c has been consulted, the Council may, acting by a qualified majority, decide that the State concerned shall amend, suspend or abolish the protective measures referred to above.

4. Subject to Article 109k(6), this Article shall cease to apply from the beginning of the third stage.

ARTICLE 109j

1. The Commission and the EMI shall report to the Council on the progress made in the fulfillment by the Member States of their obligations regarding the achievement of economic and monetary union.

These reports shall include an examination of the compatibility between each Member State's national legislation, including the statutes of its national central bank, and Articles 107 and 108 of this Treaty and the Statute of the ESCB. The reports shall also examine the achievement of a high degree of sustainable convergence by reference to the fulfillment by each Member State of the following criteria:

- the achievement of a high degree of price stability; this will be apparent from a rate of inflation which is close to that of, at most, the three best performing Member States in terms of price stability;
- the sustainability of the government financial position; this will be apparent from having achieved a government budgetary position without a deficit that is excessive as determined in accordance with Article 104c(6);
- the observance of the normal fluctuation margins provided for by the Exchange Rate Mechanism of the European Monetary System, for at least two years, without devaluing against the currency of any other Member State;
- the durability of convergence achieved by the Member State and of its participation in the Exchange Rate Mechanism of the

European Monetary System being reflected in the long-term interest rate levels.

The four criteria mentioned in this paragraph and the relevant periods over which they are to be respected are developed further in a Protocol annexed to this Treaty.

The reports of the Commission and the EMI shall also take account of the development of the ECU, the results of the integration of markets, the situation and development of the balances of payments on current account and an examination of the development of unit labour costs and other price indices.

2. On the basis of these reports, the Council, acting by a qualified majority on a recommendation from the Commission, shall assess:

- **for each Member State, whether it fulfills the necessary conditions for the adoption of a single currency;**
- **whether a majority of the Member States fulfil the necessary conditions for the adoption of a single currency, and recommend its findings to the Council, meeting in the composition of the Heads of State or of Government. The European Parliament shall be consulted and forward its opinion to the Council, meeting in the composition of the Heads of State or of Government.**

3. Taking due account of the reports referred to in paragraph 1 and the opinion of the European Parliament referred to in paragraph 2, the Council, meeting in the composition of Heads of State or of Government, shall, acting by a qualified majority, not later than 31 December 1996;

- **decide, on the basis of the recommendations of the Council referred to in paragraph 2, whether a majority of the Member States fulfil the necessary conditions for the adoption of a single currency;**
- **decide whether it is appropriate for the Community to enter the third stage,**

and if so

- **set the date for the beginning of the third stage.**

4. If by the end of 1997 the date for the beginning of the third stage has not been set, the third stage shall start on 1 January 1999. Before 1

July 1998, the Council, meeting in the composition of Heads of State or of Government, after a repetition of the procedure provided for in paragraphs 1 and 2, with the exception of the second indent of paragraph 2, taking into account the reports referred to in paragraph 1 and the opinion of the European Parliament, shall, acting by a qualified majority and on the basis of the recommendations of the Council referred to in paragraph 2, confirm which Member States fulfil the necessary conditions for the adoption of a single currency.

ARTICLE 109k

1. **If the decision has been taken to set the date in accordance with Article 109j(3), the Council shall, on the basis of its recommendations referred to in Article 109j(2), acting by a qualified majority on a recommendation from the Commission, decide whether any, and if so which, Member States shall have a derogation as defined in paragraph 3 of this Article. Such Member States shall in this Treaty be referred to as "Member States with a derogation". If the Council has confirmed which Member States fulfil the necessary conditions for the adoption of a single currency, in accordance with Article 109j(4), those Member States which do not fulfil the conditions shall have a derogation as defined in paragraph 3 of this Article. Such Member States shall in this Treaty be referred to as "Member States with a derogation".**

2. **At least once every two years, or at the request of a Member State with a derogation, the Commission and the ECB shall report to the Council in accordance with the procedure laid down in Article 109j(1). After consulting the European Parliament and after discussion in the Council, meeting in the composition of the Heads of State or of Government, the Council shall, acting by a qualified majority on a proposal from the Commission, decide which Member States with a derogation fulfil the necessary conditions on the basis of the criteria set out in Article 109j(1), and abrogate the derogations of the Member States concerned.**

3. **A derogation referred to in paragraph 1 shall entail that the following Articles do not apply to the Member State concerned: Articles 104c(9) and (11), 105(1), (2), (3) and (5), 105a, 108a, 109, and 109a(2)(b). The exclusion of such a Member State and its national central bank from rights and obligations within the ESCB is laid down in Chapter IX of the Statute of the ESCB.**

4. **In Articles 105(1), (2) and (3), 105a, 108a, 109 and 109a(2)(b), "Member States" shall be read as "Member States without a derogation".**

5. **The voting rights of Member States with a derogation shall be suspended for the Council decisions referred to in the Articles of this Treaty mentioned in paragraph 3. In that case, by way of derogation from Articles 148 and 189a(1), a qualified majority shall be defined as two thirds of the votes of the representatives of the Member States without a derogation weighted in accordance with Article 148(2), and unanimity of those Member States shall be required for an act requiring unanimity.**

6. **Articles 109h and 109i shall continue to apply to a Member State with a derogation.**

ARTICLE 109l

1. Immediately after the decision on the date for the beginning of the third stage has been taken in accordance with Article 109j(3), or, as the case may be, immediately after 1 July 1998:

   - the Council shall adopt the provisions referred to in Article 106(6);
   - the governments of the Member States without a derogation shall appoint, in accordance with the procedure set out in Article 50 of the Statute of the ESCB, the President, the Vice-President and the other Members of the Executive Board of the ECB.

   If there are Member States with a derogation, the number of Members of the Executive Board may be smaller than provided for in Article 11.1 of the Statute of the ESCB, but in no circumstances shall it be less than four.

   As soon as the Executive Board is appointed, the ESCB and the ECB shall be established and shall prepare for their full operation as described in this Treaty and the Statute of the ESCB. The full exercise of their powers shall start from the first day of the third stage.

2. As soon as the ECB is established, it shall, if necessary, take over functions of the EMI. The EMI shall go into liquidation upon the establishment of the ECB; the modalities of liquidation are laid down in the Statute of the EMI.

3. If and as long as there are Member States with a derogation, and without prejudice to Article 106(3) of this Treaty, the General Council of the ECB referred to in Article 45 of the Statute of the ESCB shall be constituted as a third decision-making body of the ECB.

4. **At the starting date of the third stage, the Council shall, acting with the unanimity of the Member States without a derogation, on a proposal from the Commission and after consulting the ECB, adopt the conversion rates at which their currencies shall be irrevocably fixed and at which irrevocably fixed rate the ECU will become a currency in its own right. This measure shall by itself not modify the external value of the ECU. The Council shall, acting according to the same procedure, also take the other measures necessary for the rapid introduction of the ECU as the single currency of those Member States.**

5. **If it is decided, according to the procedure set out in Article 109k(2), to abrogate a derogation, the Council shall, acting with the unanimity of the Member States without a derogation and the Member State concerned, on a proposal from the Commission and after consulting the ECB, adopt the rate at which the ECU shall be substituted for the currency of the Member State concerned, and take the other measures necessary for the introduction of the ECU as the single currency in the Member State concerned.**

ARTICLE 109m

1. Until the beginning of the third stage, each Member State shall treat its exchange rate policy as a matter of common interest. In so doing, Member States shall take account of the experience acquired in cooperation within the framework of the European Monetary System (EMS) and in developing the ECU, and shall respect existing powers in this field.

2. From the beginning of the third stage and for as long as a Member State has a derogation, paragraph 1 shall apply by analogy to the exchange rate policy of that Member State.

TREATY ON EUROPEAN UNION PROTOCOL ON THE STATUTE OF THE EUROPEAN SYSTEM OF CENTRAL BANKS AND THE EUROPEAN CENTRAL BANK

(excerpts relating to the ecu)

ARTICLE 16

Bank Notes

In accordance with Article 105a(1) of this Treaty, the Governing Council shall have the exclusive right to authorize the issue of bank notes within the Community.
The ECB and the national central banks may issue such notes. The bank notes issued by the ECB and the national central banks shall be the only such notes to have the status of legal tender within the Community.
The ECB shall respect as far as possible existing practices regarding the issuing and design of bank notes.

ARTICLE 52

Exchange of bank notes in Community currencies

Following the irrevocable fixing of exchange rates, the Governing Council shall take the necessary measures to ensure that bank notes denominated in currencies with irrevocable fixed exchange rates are exchanged by the national central banks at their respective par values.

TREATY ON EUROPEAN UNION PROTOCOL ON THE STATUTE OF THE EUROPEAN MONETARY INSTITUTE

(excerpts relating to the ecu)

ARTICLE 2

The EMI shall contribute to the realization of the conditions necessary for the transition to the third stage of EMU, in particular by:

- ...
- overseeing the development of the ECU.

ARTICLE 4

4.1 In accordance with Article 109f(2) of this Treaty, the EMI shall:

- strengthen co-operation between the national central banks of the Member States;
- Strengthen the co-ordination of the monetary policies of the Member States with the aim of ensuring price stability;
- monitor the functioning of the European Monetary System (EMS);
- hold consultations concerning issues falling within the competence of the national central banks and affecting the stability of financial institutions and markets;
- take over the tasks of the ESCB; in particular it shall perform the functions referred to in Articles 6.1, 6.2 and 6.3;
- facilitate the use of the ECU and oversee its development, including, the smooth functioning of the ECU Clearing System;
- hold regular consultations concerning the course of monetary policies and the use of monetary policy instruments;
- normally be consulted by the national monetary authorities before they take decisions on the course of monetary policy in the context of the common framework for ex ante coordination.

4.2 At the latest by 31 December 1996, the EMI shall specify the regulatory, organization framework necessary for the ESCB to perform its tasks in the third stage, in accordance with the principle of open economy with free competition. This framework shall be submitted by the Council of the EMI for decision to the ECB at the date of its establishment.

In accordance with Article 109f(3) of this Treaty, the EMI shall in particular:

- ...
- supervise the technical preparation of ECU bank notes.

ARTICLE 6

...

6.2 The EMI may receive monetary reserves from the national central banks and issue ECUs against such assets for the purpose of implementing the EMS Agreement. These ECUs may be used by the EMI and the national central banks as a means of settlement and for transactions between them and the EMI. The EMI shall take the necessary administrative measures for the implementation of this paragraph.

63. The EMI may grant to the monetary authorities of third countries and to international monetary institutions the status of "Other Holders" of ECUs and fix the terms and conditions under which such ECUs may be acquired, held and used by Other Holders."

...

ARTICLE 12

Currency denomination.

The operations of the EMI shall be expressed in ECU.

TREATY ON EUROPEAN UNION PROTOCOL ON THE CONVERGENCE CRITERIA REFERRED TO IN ARTICLE 109j OF THE TREATY

THE HIGH CONTRACTING PARTIES,

DESIRING to lay down the details of the convergence criteria which shall guide the Community in the decision making on the passage to the third stage of economic and monetary union referred to in Article 109j(1) of this Treaty,

HAVE AGREED upon the following provisions, which shall be annexed to the Treaty establishing the European Community:

ARTICLE 1

The criterion on price stability as mentioned in Article 109j(1) of this Treaty shall mean that a Member State has a price performance that is sustainable and an average rate of inflation, observed over a period of one year before the examination, that does not exceed by more than 1 1/2 percentage points that of, at most, the three best performing Member States in terms of price stability. Inflation shall be measured by means of the consumer price index (CPI) on a comparable basis, taking into account differences in national definitions.

ARTICLE 2

The criterion on the government budgetary position referred to in second indent of Article 109j(1) of this Treaty shall mean that at the time of the examination the Member State is not the subject of a Council decision under Article 104c(6) of this Treaty that an excessive deficit exists.

ARTICLE 3

The criterion on participation in the Exchange Rate Mechanism of the European Monetary System referred to in the third indent of Article 109j(1) of this Treaty shall mean that a Member State has respected the normal fluctuation margins provided for by the Exchange Rate Mechanism of the European Monetary System without severe tensions for at least the last two years before the examination. In particular the Member State shall not have devalued its currency's bilateral central rate against any other Member State's currency on its own initiative for the same period.

ARTICLE 4

The criterion on the convergence of interest rates referred to in the fourth indent of Article 109j(1) of this Treaty shall mean that, observed over a period of one year before the examination, a Member State has an average nominal long-term interest rate that does not exceed by more than 2 percentage points that of, at most, the three best performing Member States in terms of price stability. Interest rates shall be measured on the basis of long term government bonds or comparable securities, taking into account differences in national definitions.

ARTICLE 5

The statistical data to be used for the application of this Protocol shall be provided by the Commission.

ARTICLE 6

The Council shall, acting unanimously on a proposal from the Commission and after consulting the European Parliament, the EMI or ECB as the case may be, and the Committee referred to in Article 109c, adopt the appropriate provisions to lay down the details of the convergence criteria referred to inn Article 109j of this Treaty, which shall then replace this Protocol.

TREATY ON EUROPEAN UNION PROTOCOL ON THE TRANSITION TO THE THIRD STAGE OF ECONOMIC AND MONETARY UNION

THE HIGH CONTRACTING PARTIES,

Declare the irreversible character of the Community's movement to the third stage of Economic and Monetary Union by signing the new Treaty provisions on Economic and Monetary Union.

Therefore all Member States shall, whether they fulfil the necessary conditions for the adoption of a single currency or not, respect the will for the Community to enter swiftly into the third stage, and therefore no Member State shall prevent the entering into the third stage.

If by the end of 1997 the date of the beginning of the third stage has not been set, the Member States concerned, the Community Institutions and other bodies involved, shall expedite all preparatory work during 1998, in order to enable the Community to enter the third stage irrevocably on 1 January 1999 and to enable the ECB and the ESCB to start their full functioning from this date on.

This Protocol shall be annexed to the Treaty establishing the European Community.

TREATY ON EUROPEAN UNION PROTOCOL ON CERTAIN PROVISIONS RELATING TO THE UNITED KINGDOM AND NORTHERN IRELAND

THE HIGH CONTRACTING PARTIES,

RECOGNIZING that the United Kingdom shall not be obliged or committed to move to the third stage of Economic and Monetary Union without a separate decision to do so by its government and Parliament,

NOTING the practice of the government of the United Kingdom to fund its borrowing requirement by the sale of debt to the private sector,

HAVE AGREED the following provisions, which shall be annexed to the Treaty establishing the European Community:

1. The United Kingdom shall notify the Council whether it intends to move to the third stage before the Council makes its assessment under Article 109j(2) of this Treaty.
Unless the United Kingdom notifies the Council that it intends to move to the third stage, it shall be under no obligation to do so.
If no date is set for the beginning of the third stage under Article 109j(3) of this Treaty, the United Kingdom may notify its intention to move to the third stage before 1 January 1998.

2. Paragraphs 3 to 9 shall have effect if the United Kingdom notifies the Council that it does not intend to move to the third stage.

3. The United Kingdom shall not be included among the majority of Member States which fulfill the necessary conditions referred to in the second indent of Article 109j(2) and the first indent of Article 109j(3) of this Treaty.

4. The United Kingdom shall retain its powers in the field of monetary policy according to national law.

5. Articles 3(a), 104c(1), (9) and (11), 105(1) to (5), 105a, 107, 108, 108a, 109, 109a(1) and (2)(b) and 109l(4) and (5) of this Treaty shall not apply to the United Kingdom. In these provisions references to the Community or the Member States shall not include the United Kingdom and references to national central banks shall not include the Bank of England.

6. Articles 109e(4) and 109h and i of this Treaty shall continue to apply to the United Kingdom. Articles 109c(4) and 109m shall apply to the United Kingdom as if it has a derogation.

7. The voting rights of the United Kingdom shall be suspended in respect to act of the Council referred to in the Articles listed in paragraph 5. For this purposes the weighted votes of the United Kingdom shall be excluded from any calculation of a qualified majority under Article 109k(5) of this Treaty.
The United Kingdom shall also have no right to participate in the appointment of the President, the Vice-President and the other members of the Executive Board of the ECB under Articles 109a(2)(b) and 109l(1) of this Treaty.

8. Articles 3, 4, 6, 7, 9.2, 10.2, 10.3, 11.2, 12.1, 14, 16, 18 to 20, 22, 23, 26, 27, 30 to 34, 50 and 52 of the Protocol on the Statute of the

European System of Central Banks and of the European Central Bank (the "Statute") shall not apply to the United Kingdom.
In those Articles, references to the Community of the Member States shall not include the United Kingdom and references to the national central banks of shareholders shall not include the Bank of England. References in Articles 10.3 and 30.2 of the Statute to "subscribe capital of the ECB" shall not include capital subscribed by the Bank of England.

9. Article 109l(3) of this Treaty and Articles 44 to 48 of the Statute shall have effect, whether or not there is any Member State with a derogation, subject to the following amendments:
(a) References in Article 44 to the tasks of the ECB and the EMI shall include those tasks that still need to be performed in the third stage owing to any decision of the United Kingdom not to move to that stage.
(b) In addition to the tasks referred to in Article 47 the ECB shall also give advice in relation to and contribute to the preparation of any decision of the Council with regard to the United Kingdom taken in accordance with paragraphs 10(a) and 10(c).
(c) The Bank of England shall pay up its subscription to the capital of the ECB as a contribution to its operational costs on the same basis as national central banks of member states with a derogation.

10. If the United Kingdom does not move to the third stage, it may change its notification at any time after the beginning of that stage. In that event:
(a) The United Kingdom shall have the right to move to the third stage provided only that it satisfies the necessary conditions. The Council, acting at the request of the United Kingdom and under the conditions and in accordance with the procedure laid down in Article 109k(2) of this Treaty, shall decide whether it fulfills the necessary conditions.
(b) The Bank of England shall pay up its subscribed capital, transfer to the ECB foreign reserve assets and contribute to its reserves on the same basis as the national bank of a Member State whose derogation has been abrogated.
(c) The Council, acting under the conditions and in accordance with the procedure laid down in Article 109l(5) of this Treaty, shall take all other necessary decisions to enable the United Kingdom to move to the third stage.
If the United Kingdom moves to the third stage pursuant to the provisions of this protocol, paragraphs 3 to 9 shall cease to have effect.

11. Notwithstanding Articles 104 and 109e(3) of this Treaty and Article 21.1 of the Statute, the government of the United Kingdom may maintain its Ways and Means facility with the Bank of England if and so long as the United Kingdom does not move to the third stage.

TREATY ON EUROPEAN UNION PROTOCOL ON CERTAIN PROVISIONS RELATING TO DENMARK

THE HIGH CONTRACTING PARTIES,

DESIRING to settle, in accordance with the general objectives of the Treaty establishing the European Community, certain particular problems existing at the present time,

TAKING INTO ACCOUNT that the Danish Constitution contains provisions which may imply a referendum in Denmark prior to Danish participation in the third stage of Economic and Monetary Union,

HAVE AGREED on the following provisions, which shall be annexed to the Treaty establishing the European Community:

1. The Danish Government shall notify the Council of its position concerning participation in the third stage before the Council makes its assessment under Article 109j(2) of this Treaty.

2. In the event of a notification that Denmark will not participate in the third stage, Denmark shall have an exemption. The effect of the exemption shall be that all Articles and provisions of this Treaty and the Statute of the ESCB referring to a derogation shall be applicable to Denmark.

3. In such case, Denmark shall not be included among the majority of Member States which fulfil the necessary conditions referred to in the second indent of Article 109jj(2) and the first indent of Article 109j(3) of this Treaty.

4. As for the abrogation of the exemption, the procedure referred to in Article 109k(2) shall only be initiated at the request of Denmark.

5. In the event of abrogation of the exemption status, the provisions of this Protocol shall no longer be applicable.

TREATY ON EUROPEAN UNION PROTOCOL ON FRANCE

THE HIGH CONTRACTING PARTIES,

DESIRING to take into account a particular point relating to France,

HAVE AGREED upon the following provisions, which shall be annexed to the Treaty establishing the European Community:

France will keep the privilege of monetary emission in its overseas territories under the terms established by its national laws, and will be solely entitled to determine the parity of the CFP franc.

DECLARATION ON MONETARY RELATIONS WITH THE REPUBLIC OF SAN MARINO, THE VATICAN CITY AND THE PRINCIPALITY OF MONACO

The conference agrees that the existing monetary relations between Italy and San Marino and Vatican City and between France and Monaco remain unaffected by this Treaty until the introduction of the ECU as the single currency of the Community.

The Community undertakes to facilitate such renegotiations of existing arrangements as might become necessary as result of the introduction of the ECU as a single currency.

EXTRACTS FROM THE FINAL COMMUNIQUE OF THE CONFERENCE OF HEADS OF STATE OR GOVERNMENT OF MEMBER STATES AND FUTURE MEMBERS OF THE EC
Paris, 19 to 21 October 1972

Economic and monetary policy

1. The Heads of State or Government reaffirm the resolve of the Member States of the enlarged Community to move irrevocably to Economic and Monetary Union, by confirming all the details of the Acts passed by the Council and by the Member States' representatives on 22 March 1971 and 21 March 1972.

The required decisions will have to be taken during 1973 to allow transition to the second stage of the economic and monetary union on 1 January 1974 and in view of its complete realization by 31 December 1980 at the latest.

The Heads of State or Government reaffirmed the principle of parallel progress in the various fields of the economic and monetary union.

2. They declared that fixed but adjustable parities between their currencies are an essential basis for achieving the union and expressed their resolve to set up mutual defence and support mechanisms within the Community, which will allow the Member States to ensure that they are honored.

They decided to set up officially a European Monetary Cooperation Fund before 1 April 1973. Based on the EEC Treaty, the Fund will be run by the Governors' Committee of the Central Banks within the overall guidelines of economic policy adopted by the Council of Ministers. In its early stage the Fund will function on the following basis:

(i) concertation between the central banks over the required shrinkage of fluctuation margins between their currencies;
(ii) multilateralizing of positions arising from interventions in Community currencies and multilateralizing intra-Community rules;
(iii) utilization for the above of a European monetary unit of account;
(iv) administration of short-term monetary support between the central banks;
(v) the very short-term financing of the Agreement on shrinking the margins and short-term monetary support, will be regrouped within the Fund through an updated mechanism. For this, the short-term monetary support will be adjusted technically without changing its basic character or the consultation procedures involved.

The competent Community agencies will have to submit reports:

(i) on short-term aid dealings by 30 September at the latest;
(ii) on terms for progressive pooling of reserves by 31 December 1973.

3. The Heads of State or Government insisted on the need for closer coordination of Community economic policies and adopting more effective procedures for same.

In the present economic situation, they consider that the anti-inflation campaign and stabilization of prices must get priority. They officially briefed their authorized Ministers, when the enlarged Council meets on 30 and 31 October 1972, to take specific measures in the various areas ripe for effective and realistic short-term moves to attain these objectives allowing for the different conditions in the countries of the enlarged Community.

4. The Heads of State or Government express their resolve that the Member States of the enlarged Community will contribute through a joint outlook in guiding the reform of the international monetary system towards the adoption of a lasting equitable order.

They consider that the system should be based on the following principles:

(i) fixed but adjustable parities;
(ii) an overall convertibility of currencies;
(iii) an effective international regulation of world liquidity supply;
(iv) curtailing the role of national currencies as reserve resources;
(v) an equitable and effective adjustment process;
(vi) equality of rights and obligations for all under the system;
(vii) the need to reduce the unbalancing effects of short-term capital movements;
(viii) consideration of the developing countries' interests.

Such a system would be completely suitable for achieving economic and monetary union.

ANNEX TO THE CONCLUSIONS OF THE PRESIDENCY OF THE EUROPEAN COUNCIL
Bremen, 6 and 7 July 1978

1. In terms of exchange rate management the European Monetary System (EMS) will be at least as strict as the 'snake'. In the initial stages of its operation and for a limited period of time Member countries currently not participating in the snake may opt for somewhat wider margins around central rates. In principle, interventions will be in the currencies of participating countries. Changes in central rates will be subject to mutual consent. Non-Member countries with particularly strong economic and financial ties with the Community may become associate Members of the

system. The European currency unit (ecu)[1] will be at the center of the system; in particular, it will be used as a means of settlement between EEC monetary authorities.

2. An initial supply of ecus (for use among Community central banks) will be created against deposits of US dollars and gold on the one hand (e.g. 20% of the stock currently held by Member central banks) and Member currencies on the other hand in an amount of a comparable order of magnitude.

The use of ecus created against Member currencies will be subject to conditions varying with the amount and the maturity; due account will be given to the need for substantial short-term facilities (up to one year).

3. Participating countries will coordinate their exchange rate policies vis-à-vis third countries. To this end they will intensify the consultations in the appropriate bodies and between central banks participating in the scheme. Ways to coordinate dollar interventions should be sought which avoid simultaneous reverse interventions. Central banks buying dollars will deposit a fraction (say 20%) and receive ecus in return; likewise, central banks selling dollars will receive a fraction (say 20%) against ecus.

4. Not later than two years after the start of the scheme, the existing arrangements and institutions will be consolidated in a European Monetary Fund.[2]

5. A system of closer monetary cooperation will only be successful if participating countries pursue policies conducive to greater stability at home and abroad; this applies to deficit and surplus countries alike.

EXTRACTS FROM THE CONCLUSIONS OF THE PRESIDENCYOF THE EUROPEAN COUNCIL
Brussels, 4 and 5 December 1978

The European Council agreed, on the basis of the preparatory work of the Council (Economics and Finance Ministers) and of the Monetary Committee and the Committee of the Governors of the Central Banks to set up a

1. The ecu has the same definition as the European unit of account.

2. The EMF will take the place of the EMCF.

European Monetary System as from 1 January 1979. This agreement is enclosed as an Annex.

The purpose of the European Monetary System is to establish a greater measure of monetary stability in the Community. It should be seen as a fundamental component of a more comprehensive strategy aimed at lasting growth with stability, a progressive return to full employment, the harmonization of living standards and the lessening of regional disparities in the Community. The Monetary System will facilitate the convergence of economic development and give fresh impetus to the process of European Union. The Council expects the European Monetary System to have a stabilizing effect on international economic and monetary relations. It will therefore certainly be in the interests of the industrial and the developing countries alike.

EXTRACTS FROM THE CONCLUSIONS OF THE PRESIDENCY OF THE EUROPEAN COUNCIL
Madrid, June 26-27, 1989

B. ECONOMIC AND MONETARY UNION

1. The European Council restated its determination progressively to achieve Economic and Monetary Union as provided for in Single Act and confirmed that the European Council meeting in Hannover. Economic and Monetary Union must be seen in the perspective of the completion of the Internal Market and in the context of economic and social cohesion.

2. The European Council considered that the report by the committee chaired by Jacques DELORS, which defines a process designed to lead by stages to Economic and Monetary Union, fulfilled the mandate given in Hannover. The European Council felt that its realization would have to take account of the parallelism between economic and monetary aspects, respect the principle of "subsidiary" and allow for the diversity of specific situations.

3. The European Council decided that the first stage of the realization of Economic and Monetary Union would begin on July 1, 1990.

EXTRACTS FROM THE CONCLUSIONS OF THE PRESIDENCY OF THE EUROPEAN COUNCIL
Strasbourg, December 8-9, 1989

III. ECONOMIC AND MONETARY UNION (EMU)

1. The European Council examined the work carried out since the European Council meeting in Madrid with a view to a meeting of the Intergovernmental Conference. It noted the agreement reached in the ECOFIN Council and the initiatives of the Governors of the Central Banks with a view to strengthen the coordination of economic policies and improve thc collaboration between Central Banks. It notes that these decisions will enable the first stage of EMU as defined in the report from the DELORS Committee to begin on July 1, 1990.

2. It took note of the report from the High Level Working Party, which identified the main technical, institutional and political issues to be discussed with a view to a Treaty on Economic and Monetary Union.

On this basis, and following a discussion of the calling of an Intergovernmental Conference charged with preparing an amendment to the Treaty with a view to the final stages of EMU, the President of the European Council noted that the necessary majority existed for convening such a conference under Article 236 of the E.C. Treaty. That conference will meet, under the auspices of the Italian authorities, before the end of 1990. It will draw up its own agenda and set the timetable for its proceedings.

3. The European Council emphasized, in this context, the need to insure the proper observance of democratic control in each of the Member States.

With a view to the new term of the European Parliament which will begin in 1994, it calls for the Economic and Monetary Union to comply fully with this democratic requirement.

4. The European Council also took note of the Commission's intention to submit before April 1 a composite paper on all aspects of the achievements of the Economic and Monetary Union which will take into account all of available analyses and contributions.

EXTRACTS FROM THE CONCLUSIONS OF THE PRESIDENCY OF THE EUROPEAN COUNCIL
Dublin, April 28, 1990

6(ii) The Community will establish in stages an Economic Monetary Union (EMU) in accordance with the principles of economic and social cohesion and in accordance with the conclusions of the European Council in Madrid and Strasbourg. The preparations for the Intergovernmental Conference on EMU, which are already well-advanced, will be further intensive with a view to permitting that Conference, which will open in December 1990, to conclude its work rapidly with the objective of ratification by Member States before the end of 1992.

EXTRACTS FROM THE CONCLUSIONS OF THE PRESIDENCY OF THE EUROPEAN COUNCIL
Dublin, June 25-26, 1990

2. Economic and Monetary Union

The first stage of Economic and Monetary Union will come into effect on July 1, 1990. The European Council considered that this stage should be used to used to conversions in the economic performance of the Member States, to advance cohesion and to further the use of the ecu, all of which are for importance for the further progressive towards EMU.

The European Council reviewed the preparation for the forthcoming Intergovernmental Conference. It noted that all the relevant issues are now being fully and thoroughly clarified, with constructive contribution of all Member States, and that common group is emerging in a number of fields. In these circumstances, the European Council decided that the Intergovernmental Conference will open on December 13, 1990 with a view to establishing the final stages of Economic and Monetary Union and the prospective of the completion of Internal Market and in the context of the economic and social cohesion. The Conference should conclude its work rapidly with the objective of ratification of the results by Member States before the end of 1992.

EXTRACTS FROM THE CONCLUSIONS OF THE PRESIDENCY OF THE EUROPEAN COUNCIL
Rome, 27 and 28 October, 1990

I.5. Conference on Economic and Monetary Union

The European Council in Madrid fixed the date for the start of the first phase of economic and monetary union; in Strasbourg and Dublin it set the timetable for the Intergovernmental Conference and the ratification of its results. It now notes with satisfaction the important developments that have occurred in the wake of these decisions.

The European Council takes note of the results of the preparatory work that constitutes the basis for the Intergovernmental Conference.

For the final phase of the economic and monetary union 11 Member States consider that the work on the amendment of the Treaty will be directed to the following points:

(i) for economic union, an open market system that combines price stability with growth, employment and environmental protection and is dedicated to sound and sustainable financial and budgetary conditions and to economic and social cohesion. To this end, the ability to act of the Community institutions will be strengthened;
(ii) for monetary union, the creation of a new monetary institution comprising Member States' central banks and a central organ, exercising full responsibility for monetary policy. The monetary institution's prime task will be to maintain price stability; without prejudice to this objective, it will support the general economic policy of the Community. The institution as such, as well as the Members of its Council, will be independent of instructions. It will report to the institutions which are politically responsible.

With the achievement of the final phase of economic and monetary union, exchange rates will be irrevocably fixed. The Community will have a single currency -a strong and stable ecu - which will be an expression of its identity and unity. During the transitional phase, the ecu will be further strengthened and developed.

The second phase will start on 1 January 1994 after:
(i) the single market programme has been achieved:
(ii) the Treaty has been ratified; and, by its provisions:

(iii) a process has been set in train designed to ensure the independence of the Members of the new monetary institution at the latest when monetary powers have been transferred,
(iv) the monetary financing of budget deficits has been prohibited and any responsibility on the part of the Community or its Member States for one Member State's debt precluded;
(v) the greatest possible number of Member States have adhered to the exchange-rate mechanism.

The European Council recalls that, in order to move on to the second phase, further satisfactory and lasting progress towards the real and monetary convergence will have to be achieved, especially as regards price stability and the restoration of sound public finances.

At the start of the second phase, the new Community institution will be established. This will make it possible, in particular, to:
(i) strengthen the coordination of monetary policies;
(ii) develop the instruments and procedures needed for the future conduct of a single monetary policy;
(iii) oversee the development of the ecu.

At the latest within three years of the start of the second phase, the Commission and the Council of the monetary institution will report to the Economic and Financial Council and to the General Affairs Council on the functioning of the second phase and in particular on the progress made in real convergence, in order to prepare the decision concerning the passage to the third phase, which will occur within a reasonable time. The General Affairs Council will submit the dossier to the European Council.

The Treaty may lay down transitional provisions for the successive stages of economic and monetary union according to the circumstances of the various countries.

The United Kingdom is unable to accept the approach set out above. It agrees, however, that the overriding objective of monetary policy should be price stability, that the Community's development should be based on an open market system, that excessive budget deficits should be avoided, and that there should be no monetary financing of deficits nor the assumption of responsibility on the part of the Community or its Member States for one Member State's debt. The United Kingdom, while ready to move beyond Stage I through the creation of a new monetary institution and a common Community currency, believes that decisions on the substance of that move should precede decisions on its timing. It would, however, be prepared to see the approach it advocates come into effect as soon as possible after ratification of the necessary Treaty provision.

EXTRACTS FROM THE CONCLUSIONS OF THE PRESIDENCY OF THE EUROPEAN COUNCIL
Rome, 14 and 15 December, 1990

I.10. Economic and Monetary Union.

The European Council takes note of the Report by the Committee of Governors of the Central Banks, of the draft statute and of the draft Treaty on Economic and Monetary Union submitted by the Commission.

The European Council notes that the Intergovernmental Conferences on Political Union and Economic and Monetary Union will open in Rome on 15 December 1990. The Conferences will take due account of the opinions given by the European Parliament and by the Commission under Article 236 of the Treaty.

The European Council confirms that the work of the two Conferences will proceed in parallel and should be concluded rapidly and at the same time. The results will be submitted for ratification simultaneously with the objective of ratification before the end of 1992.

The European Council takes note of the President's report on his discussions with the European Parliament concerning, inter alia, the contacts between the Conferences and the European Parliament.

The European Council decides to take the fullest account of the European Parliament's views during the Intergovernmental Conferences and at the time of their conclusion.

EXTRACTS FROM THE CONCLUSIONS OF THE PRESIDENCY OF THE EUROPEAN COUNCIL
Luxembourg, 28 and 29 June, 1991

I.12. Economic and Monetary Union.

The Intergovernmental Conference has revealed, with its draft Treaty and the draft statute of the ESCB annexed thereto, that there are broad areas of agreement on the basic components of EMU. At the next European Council these draft texts should be finalized according to the guidelines worked out there and in keeping with the European Council's conclusions of 27 and 28 October 1990, recalling the United Kingdom reserve attached thereto.

The European Council emphasizes the need to make satisfactory and lasting progress with economic and monetary convergence as of now, and as part of the first stage of economic and monetary union, with particular reference to price stability and sound public finance.

In this context, the European Council notes that, in the near future, several governments intend to submit specific multiannual programmes designed to secure the requisite progress on convergence, which will quantify the objectives and the means of securing them. The European Council would encourage other governments to submit such programmes and calls upon the Commission and the Council (economic and financial affairs) to report regularly on the implementation of these programmes and on progress with convergence.

RESOLUTION OF THE EUROPEAN COUNCIL
on the establishment of the European Monetary System (EMS)
Brussels, 5 December 1978

A. THE EUROPEAN MONETARY SYSTEM

1. Introduction

1.1 In Bremen we discussed a 'scheme for the creation of closer monetary cooperation leading to a zone of monetary stability in Europe'. We regarded such a zone 'as a highly desirable objective' and envisaged 'a durable and effective scheme'.

1.2 Today, after careful examination of the preparatory work done by the Council and other Community bodies, we are agreed as follows:

A EUROPEAN MONETARY SYSTEM (EMS) WILL BE SET UP ON 1 JANUARY 1979.

1.3 We are firmly resolved to ensure the lasting success of the EMS by policies conducive to greater stability at home and abroad for both deficit and surplus countries.

1.4 The following chapters deal primarily with the initial phase of the EMS.

We remain firmly resolved to consolidate, not later than two years after the start of the scheme, into a final system the provisions and procedures thus created. This system will entail the creation of the European Monetary Fund as announced in the conclusions of the European Council meeting at Bremen on 6 and 7 July 1978, as well as the full utilization of the ecu as a reserve asset and a means of settlement. It will be based on adequate legislation at the Community as well as the national level.

2. The ecu and its functions

2.1 A European Currency Unit (ecu) will be at the center of the EMS. The value and the composition of the ecu will be identical with the value of the EUA at the outset of the system.

2.2 The ecu will be used:
(a) as the denominator (numéraire) for the exchange rate mechanism;
(b) as the basis for a divergence indicator;

(c) as the denominator for operations in both the intervention and the credit mechanism;

(d) as a means of settlement between monetary authorities of the European Community.

2.3 The weights of currencies in the ecu will be re-examined and if necessary revised within six months of the entry into force of the system and thereafter every five years or, on request, if the weight of any currency has changed by 25% [repealed by Art. 109E of Maastricht Treaty].

Revisions have to be mutually accepted; they will, by themselves, not modify the external value of the ecu. They will be made in line with underlying economic criteria.

3. The exchange rate and intervention mechanism

3.1 Each currency will have an ecu-related central rate. These central rates will be used to establish a grid of bilateral exchange rates.

Around these exchange rates fluctuation margins of ± 2.25% will be established. EC countries with presently floating currencies may opt for wider margins up to ± 6% at the outset of EMS; these margins should be gradually reduced as soon as economic conditions permit to do so.

A Member State which does not participate in the exchange rate mechanism at the outset may participate at a later date.

3.2 Adjustments of central rates will be subject to mutual agreement by a common procedure which will comprise all countries participating in the exchange rate mechanism and the Commission. There will be reciprocal consultation in the Community framework about important decisions concerning exchange rate policy between countries participating and any country not participating in the system.

3.3 In principle, interventions will be made in participating currencies.

3.4 Intervention in participating currencies is compulsory when the intervention points defined by the fluctuation margins are reached.

3.5 An ecu basket formula will be used as an indicator to detect divergences between Community currencies. A 'threshold of divergence' will be fixed at 75% of the maximum spread of divergence for each currency. It will be calculated in such a way as to eliminate the influence of weight on the probability of reaching the threshold.

3.6 When a currency crosses its 'threshold of divergence', this results in a presumption that the authorities concerned will correct this situation by adequate measures, namely:
(a) diversified intervention;
(b) measures of domestic monetary policy;
(c) changes in central rates;
(d) other measures of economic policy.

In case such measures, on account of special circumstances, are not taken, the reasons for this shall be given to the other authorities, especially in the 'concertation between central banks'.

Consultations will, if necessary, then take place in the appropriate Community bodies, including the Council of Ministers.

After six months these provisions shall be reviewed in the light of experience. At that date the questions regarding imbalances accumulated by divergent creditor or debtor countries will be studied as well.

3.7 A very short-term facility of an unlimited amount will be established. Settlements will be made 45 days after the end of the month of intervention with the possibility of prolongation for another three months for amounts limited to the size of debtor quotas in the short-term monetary support.

3.8 To serve as a means of settlement, an initial supply of ecus will be provided by the EMCF against the deposit of 20% of gold and 20% of dollar reserves currently held by central banks.

This operation will take the form of specified, revolving swap arrangements. By periodical review and by an appropriate procedure it will be ensured that each central bank will maintain a deposit of at least 20% of these reserves with the EMCF. A Member State not participating in the exchange rate mechanism may participate in this initial operation on the basis described above.

4. The credit mechanisms

4.1 The existing credit mechanisms with their present rules of application will be maintained for the initial phase of the EMS. They will be consolidated into a single fund in the final phase of the EMS.

4.2 The credit mechanisms will be extend to an amount of ECU 25,000 million of effectively available credit. The distribution of this amount will be as follows:

Short-term monetary support = ECU 14,000 million
Medium-term financial assistance = ECU 11,000 million

4.3 The duration of the short-term monetary support will be extended for another three months on the same conditions as the first extension.

4.4 The increase of the medium-term financial assistance will be completed by 30 June 1979. In the meantime, countries which still need national legislation are expected to make their extended medium-term quotas available by an interim financing agreement of the central banks concerned.

5. Third countries and international organizations

5.1 The durability of the EMS and its international implications require coordination of exchange rate policies vis-à-vis third countries and, as far as possible, a concertation with the monetary authorities of those countries.

5.2 European countries with particularly close economic and financial ties with the European Communities may participate in the exchange rate and intervention mechanism.

Participation will be based upon agreements between central banks; these agreements will be communicated to the Council and the Commission of the European Communities.

5.3 The EMS is and will remain fully compatible with the relevant articles of the IMF agreement.

6. Further procedure

6.1 To implement the decisions taken under A., the European Council requests the Council to consider and to take a decision on 18 December 1978 on the following proposals of the Commission:

(a) Council Regulation modifying the unit of account used by the European Fund of Monetary Cooperation, which introduces the ecu in the operations of the EMCF and defines its composition;
(b) Council Regulation permitting the EMCF to receive monetary reserves and to issue ecus to the monetary authorities of the Member States which may use them as a means of settlement;
(c) Council Regulation on the impact of the European Monetary System on the common agricultural policy. The European Council considers that the introduction of the EMS should not of itself result in any change in the situation obtaining prior to 1 January 1979 regarding the expression in national currencies of agricultural prices, monetary compensatory amounts and all other amounts fixed for the purposes of the common agricultural policy.

The European Council stresses the importance of henceforth avoiding the creation of permanent MCAs and progressively reducing present MCAs in order to re-establish the unity of prices of the common agricultural policy, giving also due consideration to price policy.

6.2 It requests the Commission to submit in good time a proposal to amend the Council Decision of 22 March 1971 on setting up machinery for medium-term financial assistance to enable the Council (Economics and Finance Ministers) to take a decision on such a proposal at their session of 18 December 1978.

6.3 It requests the central banks of Member States to modify their Agreement of 10 April 1972 on the narrowing of margins of fluctuation between the currencies of Member States in accordance with the rules set forth above (see paragraph 3).

6.4 It requests the central banks of Member States to modify as follows the rules on short-term monetary support by 1 January 1979 at the latest:
(a) the total of debtor quotas available for drawings by the central banks of Member States shall be increased to an aggregate amount of ECU 7,900 million;

(b) the total of creditor quotas made available by the central banks of Member States for financing the debtor quotas shall be increased to an aggregate amount of ECU 15,800 million;
(c) the total of the additional creditor amounts as well as the total of the additional debtor amount may not exceed ECU 8,800 million;
(d) the duration of credit under the extended short-term monetary support may be prolonged twice for a period of three months.

B. MEASURES DESIGNED TO STRENGTHEN THE ECONOMIES OF THE LESS PROSPEROUS MEMBER STATES OF THE EUROPEAN MONETARY SYSTEM

1. We stress that, within the context of a broadly-based strategy aimed at improving the prospects of economic development and based on symmetrical rights and obligations of all participants, the most important concern should be to enhance the convergence of economic policies towards greater stability. We request the Council (Economic and Finance Ministers) to strengthen its procedures for coordination in order to improve that convergence.

2. We are aware that the convergence of economic policies and of economic performance will not be easy to achieve. Therefore, steps must be taken to strengthen the economic potential of the less prosperous countries of the Community. This is primarily the responsibility of the Member States concerned. Community measures can and should serve a supporting role.

3. The European Council agrees that in the context of the European Monetary System, the following measures in favor of the less prosperous Member States effectively and fully participating in the exchange rate and intervention mechanism will be taken.

3.1 The European Council requests the Community Institutions by the utilization of the new financial instrument and the European Investment Bank to make available for a period of five years loans of up to 1,000 million EUA per year to these countries on special conditions.

3.2 The European Council requests the Commission to submit a proposal to provide interest rate subsidies of 3% for these loans, with the following elements: The total cost of this measure, divided into annual tranches of 200 million EUA each over a period of five years shall not exceed 1,000 million EUA.

3.3 Any less prosperous Member country which subsequently effectively and fully participates in the mechanisms would have the right of access to this facility within the financial limits mentioned above. Member States not participating effectively and fully in the mechanisms will not contribute to the financing of the scheme.

3.4 The funds thus provided are to be concentrated on the financing of selected infrastructure projects and programs, with the understanding that any direct or indirect distortion of the competitive position of specific industries within Member States will have to be avoided.

3.5 The European Council requests the Council (Economics and Finance Ministers) to take a decision on the above mentioned proposals in time so that the relevant measures can become effective on a April 1979 at the latest. There should be a review at the end of the initial phase of the EMS.

4. The European Council requests the Commission to study the relationship between greater convergence in economic performance of the Member States and the utilization of Community instruments, in particular the funds which aim at reducing structural imbalances. The results of these studies will be discussed at the next European Council.

AGREEMENT BETWEEN THE CENTRAL BANKS OF THE MEMBER STATES OF THE EUROPEAN ECONOMIC COMMUNITY LAYING DOWN THE OPERATING PROCEDURES FOR THE EUROPEAN MONETARY SYSTEM

The central banks of the Member States of the European Economic Community.

Having regard to the Resolution of the European Council of 5 December 1978 on the establishment of the European Monetary System (EMS) and related matters:

Having regard to Regulation (EEC) No. 907/73 of the Council of the European Communities of 3 April 1973 establishing a European Monetary Cooperation Fund;

Having regard to Regulation (EEC) No. 3180/78 of the Council of the European Communities of 18 December 1978 changing the value of the unit of account used by the European Monetary Cooperation Fund;

Having regard to Regulation (EEC) No. 3181/78 of the Council of the European Communities of 18 December 1978 concerning the European Monetary System;

Whereas the European Council has agreed to set up a scheme for the creation of closer monetary cooperation leading to a zone of monetary stability in Europe;

Whereas the said Resolution provides that a European currency unit, the ECU, shall be at the center of the European Monetary System and that the value and composition of the ECU shall, initially, be identical with the value and composition of the European unit of account (EUA):

Whereas under the terms of the said Resolution:

(i) each currency will have an ECU-related central rate and the central rates will be used to establish a grid of bilateral parities or central rates;

(ii) fluctuation margins of 2.25% will be fixed around these bilateral central rates, although Member States not at present participating in the narrower margins mechanism may in the initial stage of the European Monetary system opt for wider margins of up to 6% which must be progressively reduced as soon as economic conditions permit;

Whereas the said Resolution further provides that a formula for an ECU-based basket shall be used as an indicator to detect divergences between Community currencies, and sets out the principles governing the operation of this Indicator, which will be re-examined at the end of a period of six months;

Whereas this re-examination will also cover questions regarding imbalances accumulated by divergent creditor or debtor countries;

Whereas a Member State that does not initially participate in the exchange rate mechanism can do so at a later date and whereas it is therefore advisable to ensure cooperation between the central bank of such a State and the central banks of the participating States;

Whereas very short-term credit facilities of unlimited amount will be created;

Whereas the European Council has asked the central banks of the Member States of the Community to amend their Agreement of 10 April 1972 on the narrowing of the margins of fluctuation between the currencies of the Member States so as to embody the rules set forth in the said Resolution;

Whereas in order to make provision for means of settlement the central banks have been asked initially to transfer to the European Monetary Cooperation Fund, the form of revolving swaps against ECUs, 20% of their gold holdings and 20% of their US dollar reserves, and thereafter to keep at least 20% of the said reserves on deposit with the European Monetary Cooperation Fund;

Have agreed as follows:

I. Exchange rate mechanism

Article 1 - Central rates in terms of the ECU

Each participating central bank shall notify the Secretariat of the Committee of Governors of the Central Banks of the Member States of the European Economic Community of a central rate in terms of the ECU for its currency. The Secretariat shall pass on this information to the other central banks and the European Communities.

Article 2 - Intervention rules

2.1 Each participating central bank shall notify the Secretariat of the Committee of Governors of the rates for compulsory intervention expressed in its currency, and the Secretariat shall pass on this information to the other central banks. These rates shall be fixed in relation to the bilateral central rates derived from the central rates in terms of the ECU referred to in Article 1 of the present Agreement. The market shall be notified of them.

2.2 Interventions shall in principle be effected in currencies of the participating central banks. These interventions shall be unlimited at the compulsory intervention rates. Other interventions in the foreign exchange market shall be conducted in accordance with the relevant guidelines that were adopted by the Committee of Governors in its Report of 9 December 1975 or that may be adopted in the future, or shall be subject to concertation among all the participating central banks.

Article 3 - Operation of the indicator of divergence

3.1 On either side of the central rate for its currency in terms of the ECU each participating central bank shall establish rates for its currency in terms of the ECU that will constitute thresholds of divergence. These thresholds of divergence shall be calculated in such a way as to neutralize the influence of the differences in weights on the probability of their being reached; they shall be set at 75% of the maximum divergence spread, this being measured by the percentage difference between the daily rate and the central rate of a currency against the ECU when that currency is standing at the opposite pole from all the other currencies at the compulsory intervention rates referred to in Article 2.1 of the present Agreement. The necessary steps shall be taken to take account of the effects of the adoption of different maximum margins of fluctuation for the participating currencies and of the possible nonparticipation of a currency in the exchange rate mechanism.

3.2 If a currency crosses a divergence threshold, this shall entail the consequences set out in paragraph 3.6 of the Resolution of the European Council of 5 December 1978.

Article 4 - Method of calculating the values of the ECU in each currency.

For the purposes of the operation of the indicator of divergence provided for under Article 3 of the present Agreement, the market value of the ECU in each currency shall be calculated by a uniform method as frequently as necessary and at least on the occasion of each daily concertation session among central banks.

Article 5 - Non-participation

Any central bank that is not participating in the exchange rate mechanism shall cooperate with the other central banks in the concertation and the other exchanges of information necessary for the proper functioning of the exchange rate mechanism.

II. Very short-term financing

Article 6 - Basic principles

6.1 To enable interventions to be made in Community currencies, the participating central banks shall open for each other very short-term credit facilities, unlimited in amount, in accordance with the conditions set out in Articles 7 to 16 of the present Agreement.

6.2 The financing operations concluded in this connection shall take the form of spot sales and purchases of Community currencies against the crediting or debiting of accounts denominated in ECUs with the European Monetary Cooperation Fund (hereinafter referred to as "EMCF").

Article 7 - Accounting procedures

7.1 The accounts opened for the central banks in the books of the EMCF shall be denominated in ECUs. The conversion of currencies into ECUs shall be effected at the daily rates of the ECU as established by the Commission's staff on the basis of the method adopted. The relevant rates shall be those ruling on the day on which the interventions were made.

7.2 The value date of the financing operations shall be identical with the value date of the interventions in the market.

Article 8 - Remuneration

8.1 The debtor and creditor interest rates applying to very short-term financing operations shall be the average of the official discount rates of all

EEC central banks, weighted in accordance with their respective currencies' weights as derived from the ruling ECU central rates. This average shall be calculated once a month on the basis of the discount rates ruling on the last working day of the month and shall apply during the following month to all outstanding amounts in respect of very short-term financing operations.

8.2 Accrued interest shall be paid in ECUs at each monthly settlement date or, between settlement dates, at the same time as advance liquidation of a debtor balance is effected.

Article 9 - Initial Settlement Date

The initial settlement date for a very short-term financing operation shall be the last working day preceding the sixteenth day of the second month following that in which the value date of the intervention fell.

Article 10 - Automatic renewal

At the request of the debtor central bank, the initial settlement date for a financing operation may be extended for a period of three months.

However:

(a) any initial settlement date may only be automatically extended once for a maximum of three months;

(b) recourse may only be had to the renewal facility referred to above if the relevant debt does not thereby remain continuously outstanding for more than six consecutive months;

(c) the total amount of indebtedness resulting from application of the present Article may at no time exceed a ceiling equal to the debtor quota of the central bank concerned under the short-term monetary support arrangement;

(d) if a central bank has recourse to the additional automatic borrowing facility for six consecutive months, the Committee of Governors shall take steps to ascertain whether the payments deficit of the country concerned is such that recourse to other means of financing, in particular Short-Term Monetary Support or Medium-Term Financial Assistance within the EEC, would be more appropriate.

Article 11 - Renewal by mutual agreement

11.1 Any debt exceeding the ceiling laid down in Article 10(c) of this Agreement may be renewed once for three months subject to the agreement of the creditor or creditors in the EMCF.

11.2 Any debt already renewed automatically for three months may be renewed a second time for a further three months subject to the agreement of the creditor or creditors in the EMCF.

11.3 Debts and claims thus extended by mutual agreement shall be settled separately outside the provisions of Articles 12, 13 and 14 of this Agreement without prejudice, however, to the priority accorded to settlements carried out under those Articles. Offsetting or advance settlement of debts and claims of the kind for which provision is made in the present Article shall be subject to the agreement of all creditors and debtors in the EMCF, whatever their status.

Article 12 - Order of repayment of claims

12.1 Claims arising from financing operations carried out in accordance with Articles 9 and 10 above shall be settled on order of seniority; however, if a central bank's claim exceeds the amount of its creditor quota under the Short-Term Monetary Support arrangement, that central bank may request that the excess be treated for purposes of the next settlement as equal in seniority to the most senior claims of other creditor central banks.

12.2 All claims arising within the same monthly accounting periods shall be regarded as of equal seniority. When a settlement covers a number of claims regarded as of equal seniority, each of the components of the settlement shall be distributed in proportion to the respective amounts of the claims.

12.3 The rules governing the order or distribution of settlements may be departed from subject to the agreement of all the parties to the financing operations carried out in accordance with Articles 9 and 10 of the present Agreement.

Article 13 - Automatic offsetting

13.1 All the debts and claims of a single central bank arising from the operations provided for under Articles 9 and 10 of the present Agreement shall, where appropriate, be automatically offset against each other.

13.2 Any new liability shall be offset against the most senior claim of the same central bank. Any new claim shall be offset against the most senior debt of the same central bank.

Article 14 - Advance repayment

14.1 Any debtor balance recorded in accordance with Articles 9 and 10 of the present Agreement may be settled in advance at the request of the debtor central bank;

(i) at any time in the currency of a creditor in the EMCF under Articles 9 and 10 of the present Agreement;

(ii) on the monthly settlement date by transfer of the means of settlement provided for in Article 16 of the present Agreement.

14.2 Any advance repayment shall be applied first to the most senior liabilities contracted under Article 10 of the present Agreement.

Article 15 - Working balances

The central banks may hold working balances in Community currencies within the limits laid down by t he Committee of Governors. These limits may be exceeded only with the consent of the central bank concerned.

Article 16 - Means of settlement

16.1 When a financing operation falls due, settlement shall be carried out--insofar as it has not been settled in the first instance by means of holdings in the creditor's currency--entirely or in part by transferring ECUs, with the proviso that a creditor central bank shall not be obliged to accept settlement by means of ECUs of an amount more than 50% of its claim which is being settled. The balance shall be settled by transferring other reserve components in accordance with the composition of the debtor central bank's reserves as at the end of the month preceding the settlement.

These provisions shall be without prejudice to other forms of settlement agreed between creditor and debtor central banks.

Debtor balances in ECUs settled by means of assets denominated in currencies and in SDRs shall be converted into such assets on the basis of the daily rates for the ECU established by the Commission's staff.

16.2 For the purposes of the preceding paragraph the composition of the debtor's reserves shall be determined on the basis of assets denominated in SDRs and in currencies. Nevertheless, gold holdings may also be taken into account if the price proposed by the debtor central bank is accepted by the creditor central bank. As far as assets denominated in SDRs and in currencies are concerned, the debtor central bank may choose which assets it will deliver in settlement.

16.3 If the debtor central bank no longer possesses ECUs and wishes to acquire some, it shall apply in the first instance to central banks that are net accumulators of ECUs or possibly to the EMCF. In the latter case, the ECUs shall be acquired against the contribution of an equal percentage of the gold and dollar assets held by that central bank.

III. Creation, utilization and remuneration of ECUs

Article 17 - Creation of ECUs against contributions of gold and dollars.

17.1 Each central bank participating in the exchange rate mechanism outlined in Chapter 1 of the present Agreement shall contribute to the EMCF 20% of its gold holdings and 20% of its gross dollar reserves as at the last working day of the month preceding the month in which the present Agreement takes effect, it shall be credited by the EMCF with an amount of ECUs corresponding to these contributions.

Central banks that are not participating in the exchange rate mechanism referred to above may likewise make contributions in accordance with the terms of the preceding subparagraph.

17.2 The contributions referred to in Article 17.1 of the present Agreement shall be made available in the case of the participating central banks at the latest ten working days after the implementation of the present Agreement or in the case of the non-participating central banks at the time of exercising the option referred to above.

17.3 The contributions of gold and dollars shall take the form of three-month revolving swaps against ECUs which may be unwound at two working days notice. These operations shall be concluded at flat rates.

17.4 For the purposes of the swap operations referred to in the present Article the value of the reserve components transferred to the EMCF shall be established as follows:

(i) for the gold portion, the average of the prices, converted into ECUs, recorded daily at the two London fixings during the previous six calendar months, but not exceeding the average price of the two fixings on the penultimate working day of the period;

(ii) for the dollar portion, the market rate two working days prior to the value date.

17.5 Contracts shall be concluded between each central bank and the EMCF detailing the arrangements for the delivery of the gold and dollars to the EMCF and for their management insofar as this is entrusted to the central banks.

17.6 At the beginning of each quarter, when the swaps referred to in the present Article are renewed, the central banks and the EMCF shall make the necessary adjustments to these swaps, firstly, to ensure that each central bank's contribution to the EMCF continues to represent at least 20% of its gold and dollar reserves on the basis of its gross reserve position recorded on the last working day of the preceding quarter and secondly, to take account of any price or rate changes that may have occurred since the initial contribution or previous adjustment.

Article 18 - Utilization of ECUs

18.1 ECU assets shall be used in intra-Community settlements within the limits and on the terms set out in Article 16 of the present Agreement.

18.2 The central banks may transfer ECUs to one another against dollars. EEC currencies, Special Drawing Rights or gold.

18.3 For the purposes of meeting a decline in its dollar reserves a central bank may acquire dollars against ECUs from the EMCF between two periodic adjustments, initially by unwinding a swap transaction.

18.4 The operations referred to in Articles 18.2 and 18.3 of the present Agreement shall not be carried out for the sole purpose of altering the composition of a central bank's reserves.

Article 19 - Remuneration

19.1 Central banks whose ECU assets are less than their forward sales of ECUs shall pay interest to the EMCF on the difference between these two aggregates. The EMCF shall pay central banks whose ECU assets exceed their forward sales interest on the difference between these two aggregates. The amount of interest due shall be calculated in proportion to the average daily balances.

19.2 The rate of interest provided for in Article 19.1 of the present Agreement shall be determined in accordance with the provisions of Article 8 of the present Agreement. Such interest shall be paid monthly.

Article 20 - Liquidation

20.1 Save in the event of a unanimous decision to the contrary, the swaps of gold and dollars against ECUs referred to in Article 17.3 of the present Agreement, shall be unwound at the end of the two-year transitional period.

20.2 For this purpose central banks that are net users of ECU assets shall bring these back up to a level equal to that of their forward sales and central banks that are net accumulators shall transfer to the net users the excess of their ECU assets over their forward sales either directly or through the intermediary of the EMCF.

20.3 The transfers of ECUs provided for in the preceding paragraph shall be effected in exchange for the currency of the central banks that are net accumulators, or in accordance with any other arrangements agreed between the parties, or against the transfer of reserve components in proportion to the composition of the reserves of the central bank repurchasing ECUs, this composition being determined in accordance with the provisions of Article 16.2 of the present Agreement.

Article 21 - Institutional provisions

The Committee of Governors shall periodically review the operation of the present Agreement in the light of experience gained.

Article 22 - Termination of the Agreement of 10 April 1972

22.1 The present Agreement terminates and replaces, with effect from 13 March 1979, the Agreement of 10 April 1972, as amended by the Agreement of 8 July 1975, establishing a system for the narrowing of the margins of fluctuation between the currencies of the European Economic Community.

22.2 The present Agreement shall be drawn up in duly signed versions in English, French and German. A certified copy of the original in each language shall be sent to each central bank by the Secretariat of the Committee of Governors, which is required to retain the originals.

COMMUNICATION FROM THE COMMISSION
on the calculation of the equivalent of the ecu

1. Definition of the ecu

The ecu, as most recently defined in Council Regulation (EEC) No. 2626/84 of 17 September 1984 is composed of the following amounts of national currencies:

German mark	0.719
Pound sterling	0.0878
French franc	1.31
Italian lire	140
Dutch guilder	0.256
Belgian franc	3.71
Luxembourg franc	0.14
Danish krone	0.219
Irish pound	0.00871
Greek drachma	1.15

The equivalent of the ecu in any currency is equal to the sum of the equivalents of these amounts in that currency.

2. Exchange rates used for calculating the ecu

The central bank in each Member State communicates a representative market exchange rate for its currency against the United States dollar. The dollar has been chosen as giving the most representative rate in all financial centers. The rates are taken from the exchange markets at 2:15 p.m. They are communicated by the National Bank of Belgium to the Commission, which uses them to calculate an ecu equivalent first in dollars and then in currencies of the Member States. If an exchange market is closed, the central banks agree on a representative exchange rate for the currency against the dollar which is communicated to the Commission.

The Commission also calculates an equivalent of the ecu for other currencies using for each its market rate against the dollar at 2:15 p.m.

Example: Calculation of equivalents for 27 October 1988

National currency amount of the ecu of total USD		27 October 1988 exchange rate against the USD	Equivalent in USD of national currency amount	Equivalent in national currency amount
(a)		(b)	(c) = (a):(b)	(d) = USD total x (b)
0.719	DM	1.7705	0.406100	2.07091
1.31	FF	6.044	0.216744	7.06951
0.0878	UKL	1.773	0.155669	2.07383
140	Lit	1319.5	0.106101	1543.39
0.256	Hfl	1.9962	0.128244	2.3349
3.71	FB	37.1175	0.099953	43.4154
0.14	FLux	37.1175	0.003772	43.4154
0.219	Dkr	6.8305	0.032062	7.98946
0.00871	IrL	1.5101	0.013153	1.76632
1.15	Dr	146	0.007877	170.772
		Total of USD amounts:	1.169674	

3. Publication of the currency equivalents of the ecu

The daily equivalents in the different currencies calculated by the Commission are published correct to six significant figures in the 'C' edition of the Official Journal of the European Communities.

COUNCIL REGULATION (EEC) NO. 907/73
of 3 April 1973
establishing a European Monetary Cooperation Fund

THE COUNCIL OF THE EUROPEAN COMMUNITIES,

Having regard to the Treaty establishing the European Economic Community, and in particular Article 235 thereof,

Having regard to the proposal from the Commission,

Having regard to the Opinion of the European Parliament,

Having regard to the Opinion of the Economic and Social Committee,

Whereas the Resolution of the Council and of the Representatives of the Governments of the Member States of 22 March 1971 on the progressive establishment of economic and monetary union in the Community provided for the establishment of a European Monetary Cooperation Fund to be integrated at a later stage into a Community organization of central banks;

Whereas the Heads of State or Government meeting in Paris on 19 and 20 October 1972 envisaged that the Fund should be established before 1 April 1973;

Whereas the Council has been informed of the Opinions requested on this subject, in the Resolution of the Council and of the Representatives of the Member States of 21 March 1972, from the Monetary Committee and from the Committee of Governors of the Central Banks;

Whereas the purpose of the Fund must be to contribute to the progressive establishment of an Economic and Monetary Union between the Member States of the European Economic Community, which, in its final stage as regards its monetary aspects will have the following characteristics:

(i) either the total and irreversible convertibility, at irrevocable parities, of Community currencies against each other,

(ii) or the introduction of a common currency;

Whereas it is necessary to confer immediately on the Fund the responsibility for facilitating both the concertation necessary for the smooth operation of the exchange arrangements introduced in the Community and the settlement of the position resulting from intervention in Community currencies, for assuring thereby the multilateralization of intra-Community settlements, and for administering a financing mechanism which combines the mechanism for short-term monetary support contained in the Agreement of 9 February 1970 between the central banks of the Community with the mechanism for very short-term financing which was contained in the Agreement of 10 April 1972 between those same central banks;

Whereas the conferment of these responsibilities constitutes merely a first stage in the progressive development of the Fund; whereas it is therefore important that the Statutes of the Fund should be drawn up in such a way as to permit the scope of its activities to be gradually extended;

Whereas it is necessary to establish the Fund if Community objectives are to be attained, in particular as regards the progressive harmonization of the

Member States' economic policies, the proper functioning of the common mark and the establishment of economic and monetary union; whereas the Treaty made no provision for the powers essential to the establishment of the Fund;

Whereas it is appropriate to specify that the general provisions of the Treaties concerning the European Communities as regards privileges and immunities, non-contractual liability and the obligation of professional secrecy are applicable to the Fund,

HAS ADOPTED THIS REGULATION:

Article 1

A European Monetary Cooperation Fund, hereinafter referred to as 'the Fund', is hereby established; it shall have legal personality.

Article 2

Within the limits of its powers the Fund shall promote:

(i) the proper functioning of the progressive narrowing of the margins of fluctuation of the Community currencies against each other;

(ii) interventions in Community currencies on the exchange markets;

(iii) settlements between central banks leading to a concerted policy on reserves.

Article 3

In the first stage of its function the Fund shall be responsible for:

(i) the concerted action necessary for the proper functioning of the Community exchange system;

(ii) the multilateralization of positions resulting from interventions by central banks in Community currencies and the multilateralization of intra-Community settlements;

(iii) the administration of the very short-term financing provided for by the Agreement between the central banks of the enlarged Community of 10 April 1972 and of the short-term monetary support provided for in the Agreement between the central banks of the Community of 9 February 1970, to which the central banks of Denmark, Ireland and the United Kingdom acceded with effect from 8 January 1973, and the regroupment of these mechanisms in a renewed mechanism.

Article 4

The provisions contained in the Agreements referred to in the third indent of Article 3 shall become the administrative rules of the Fund. The necessary technical adaptation to those provisions shall be made by the Board of Governors of the Fund without however changing the basic nature of those provisions and in particular the consultation procedures contained therein.

Article 5

The Statues of the Fund are set out in the Annex to this Regulation and form an integral part thereof.

Article 6

This Regulation shall enter into force on 6 April 1973.

This Regulation shall be binding in its entirety and directly applicable in all Member States.

Done at Luxembourg, 3 April 1973.

For the Council
The President
R. VAN ELSLANDE

COUNCIL REGULATION (EEC) No. 3180/78
of 18 December 1978
changing the value of the unit of account used by the European Monetary Cooperation Fund

THE COUNCIL OF THE EUROPEAN COMMUNITIES,

Having regard to the Treaty establishing the European Economic Community,

Having regard to Council Regulation (EEC) No. 907/73 of 3 April 1973 establishing a European Monetary Cooperation Fund, and in particular the last paragraph of Article 5 of the Statutes of the Fund,

Having regard to the proposal from the Commission,

Having regard to the opinion of the Monetary Committee,

Having regard to the opinion of the Board of Governors of the European Monetary Cooperation Fund,

Whereas Regulation (EEC) No. 907/73, in Article 5 of the Statutes of the Fund, requires the latter's operations in the currencies of the Member States to be expressed in a European monetary unit of account of a value of 0.88867088 gram of fine gold;

Whereas this definition no longer conforms with the rules in force in the international monetary system;

Whereas, apart from cases in which the value of the European monetary unit of account is changed automatically, the last paragraph of the said Article 5 provides that any other changes shall be decided on by the Council, acting unanimously on a proposal from the Commission, after consulting the Monetary Committee and the Board of Governors of the Fund;

Whereas the establishment of a new European monetary system, which was the subject of the resolution of the European Council meeting in Brussels on 4 and 5 December 1978, provides for the use of an 'ecu' defined as a basket of Member States' currencies,

HAS ADOPTED THIS REGULATION:

Article

With effect from 1 January 1979, the Fund's operations shall be expressed in a unit of account known as the ecu which is defined as the sum of the following amounts of the currencies of the Member States:

[Amended last by Regulation (EEC) No. 1971/89]

Article 2

The Council, acting unanimously on a proposal from the Commission after consulting the Monetary Committee and the Board of Governors of the Fund, shall determine the conditions under which the composition of the ecu may be changed.

Article 3

This Regulation shall enter into force on 1 January 1979.

This Regulation shall be binding in its entirety and directly applicable in all Member States.

Done at Brussels, 18 December 1978.

For the Council
The President
H. MATTHÖFER

COUNCIL REGULATION (EEC) No. 3181/78
of 18 December 1978
relating to the European Monetary System

THE COUNCIL OF THE EUROPEAN COMMUNITIES,

Having regard to the Treaty establishing the European Economic Community, and in particular Article 235 thereof,

Having regard to the proposal from the Commission,

Having regard to the opinion of the European Parliament,

Having regard to the opinion of the Economic and Social Committee,

Whereas, the European Council meeting in Brussels adopted, on 5 December 1978, a resolution setting out the arrangements related to the establishment of the European Monetary System which will come into effect from 1 January 1979;

Whereas, in this context, and not later than two years after the start of the system, the existing arrangements and institutions would be merged into a European Monetary Fund; whereas, in the mean time, responsibility for administering the new monetary system should be entrusted initially to the European Monetary Cooperation Fund, set up by Regulation (EEC) No. 907/73;

Whereas, by Regulation (EEC) No. 3180/78, the Council adopted the ecu as the unit of account used by the European Monetary Cooperation Fund;

Whereas, for the system to begin functioning, it is necessary to provide immediately for the creation of a supply of ecus against part of the central banks' reserves placed with the system, and for those ecus to be used as a means of settlement within the system;

Whereas, in this context, the introduction of the ecu into the operations of the European Monetary Cooperation Fund and its utilization as a means of settlement are necessary if the objectives pursued by the Community are to be achieved, notably the gradual convergence of Member States' economic policies, the smooth functioning of the common market and the attainment of economic and monetary union; whereas the powers needed to set up the system are not provided for in the Treaty,

HAS ADOPTED THIS REGULATION:

Article 1

The European Monetary Cooperation Fund is hereby empowered to receive monetary reserves from the monetary authorities of the Member States and to issue ecus against such assets.

Article 2

The Fund and the monetary authorities of the Member States are hereby empowered to use ecus as a means of settlement and for transactions between those authorities and the Fund.

The Fund is also empowered to grant to the monetary authorities of non-Member countries and international monetary institutions the status of 'Other Holders' of ecus as referred to in Article 1 and to fix the terms and conditions under which such ecus may be acquired, held and used.

Article 3

The Board of Governors of the Fund shall take the administrative measures necessary for the implementation of Articles 1 and 2.

Article 4

This Regulation shall enter into force on 1 January 1979.

This Regulation shall be binding in its entirety and directly applicable in all Member States.

Done at Brussels, 18 December 1978.

For the Council
The President
H. MATTHÖFER

COUNCIL REGULATION (EEC) NO. 2626/84
of 15 September 1984
amending Article 1 of Council Regulation (EEC) No. 3180/78 changing the value of the unit of account used by the EMCF

THE COUNCIL OF THE EUROPEAN COMMUNITIES,

Having regard to the Treaty establishing the European Economic Community,

Having regard to the Act concerning the conditions of accession of the Hellenic Republic and to the adjustments to the Treaties of 28 May 1979, and in particular Annex VIII thereof,

Having regard to the proposal from the Commission,

Having regard to the opinion of the Monetary Committee,

Having regard to the opinion of the Board of Governors of the European Monetary Cooperation Fund,

Whereas Article 1 of Council Regulation (EEC) No. 3180/78 of 18 December 1978 defines the ECU as the sum of amounts of currencies of the Member States;

Whereas Article 2.3 of the resolution of the European Council of 5 December 1978 on the establishment of the European Monetary System stipulates that the weights of the currencies in the ECU shall be re-examined and if necessary revised within six months of the entry into force of the system and thereafter every five years or, on request, if the weight of any currency has changed by 25%;

Whereas a re-examination has been carried out and the results indicate that a revision is appropriate;

Whereas in accordance with Article 2.3 of the resolution of the European Council of 5 December 1978, the revision should be made in line with underlying economic criteria and should not, by itself, modify the external value of the ECU;

Whereas Annex VIII of the Act annexed to the Treaty of Accession of the Hellenic Republic to the European Communities specifies that the drachma shall be included in the ECU before 31 December 1985 if, before that date, a revision of the ECU is undertaken;

Whereas the Greek authorities have taken the necessary measures to ensure that the inclusion of the drachma in the ECU will take place in conditions which ensure the smooth functioning of the ECU market,

HAS ADOPTED THIS REGULATION:

Article 1

With effect from 17 September 1984 the composition of the ECU as laid down in Article 1 of Council Regulation (EEC) No. 3180/78 of 18 December 1978 is amended as follows:

0,719 German mark,
0,0878 Pound sterling,
1,31 French francs,
140 Italian lire,
0,256 Dutch guilder,
3,71 Belgian francs,
0,14 Luxcmbourg franc,
0,219 Danish krone,
0,00871 Irish pound,
1,15 Greek drachmas.

Article 2

This Regulation shall enter into force on 17 September 1984.

This Regulation shall be binding in its entirety and directly applicable in all Member States.

Done at Dromoland Castle, 15 September 1984

For the Council
The President
A. DUKES

COUNCIL REGULATION (EEC) No. 3066/85
of 28 October 1985
amending Article 2 of Council Regulation (EEC) No. 3181/78
as regards the use of ECU by 'other holders'

THE COUNCIL OF THE EUROPEAN COMMUNITIES,

Having regard to the Treaty establishing the European Economic Community, and in particular Article 235 thereof,

Having regard to the proposal from the Commission,

Having regard to the opinion of the European Parliament,

Having regard to the opinion of the Economic and Social Committee,

Whereas Council Regulation (EEC) No. 3181/78 of 18 December 1978 relating to the European monetary system provides for the issue of ECU by the European Monetary Cooperation Fund and for their use by the Fund and the monetary authorities of the Member States;

Whereas provision should be made for such ECU to be acquired and used by holders other than those referred to in Article 2 of Regulation (EEC) No. 3181/78,

HAS ADOPTED THIS REGULATION:

Article 1

The following paragraph is hereby added to Article 2 of Regulation (EEC) No. 3181/78:

> 'The Fund is also empowered to grant to the monetary authorities of non-Member countries and international monetary institutions the status of "other holders" of ECU as referred to in Article 1 and to fix the terms and conditions under which such ECU may be acquired, held and use.'

Article 2

This Regulation shall enter into force on the third day following its publication in the Official Journal of the European Communities.

This Regulation shall be binding in its entirety and directly applicable in all Member States.

Done at Luxembourg, 28 October 1985.

For the Council
The President
J. SANTER

COUNCIL REGULATION (EEC) No. 1971/89
of 19 June 1989
amending Article 1 of Regulation (EEC) No. 3180/78 amending the value of the unit of account used by the European Monetary Cooperation Fund

THE COUNCIL OF THE EUROPEAN COMMUNITIES,

Having regard to the Treaty establishing the European Economic Community,

Having regard to Council Regulation (EEC) No. 3180/78 and in particular Article 2 thereof,

Having regard to the proposal from the Commission,

Having regard to the opinion of the Monetary Committee,

Having regard to the opinion of the Board of Governors of the European Monetary Cooperation Fund,

Whereas Article 1 of Regulation (EEC) No. 3180/78, as amended by Regulation (EEC) No. 2626/84, defines the ecu as the sum of amounts of currencies of the Member States;

Whereas Article 2(3) of the resolution of the European Council of 5 December 1978 on the establishment of the European Monetary System stipulates that the weights of the currencies in the ecu shall be re-examined and if necessary revised within six months of the entry into force of the system and thereafter every five years or, on request, if the weight of any currency has changed by 25%;

Whereas a re-examination has been carried out and indicates that a revision is appropriate;

Whereas, in accordance with Article 2(3) of the said resolution, the revision should be made in line with underlying economic criteria and will not, by itself, modify the external value of the ecu;

Whereas the Joint Declaration on the inclusion of the peseta and the escudo in the ecu, annexed to the Treaty of Accession of Spain and Portugal, states that the decisions to include the peseta and the escudo must take into account the necessity of ensuring a stable development of the functions and uses of the ecu and that either of these decisions could be made at the request of the new Member State concerned, after consultation with the Monetary Committee, on the occasion of the first five-year review of the weighting of the currencies within the ecu;

Whereas the Spanish and Portuguese authorities have requested that their respective currencies be included in the ecu;

Whereas the inclusion of the peseta and the escudo, in particular following the steps taken by the issuing authorities for these currencies, is compatible with the need to ensure a stable development of the functions and uses of the ecu;

Whereas it is desirable that an interval of time should elapse between the decision on the new weights of the currencies in the ecu and the date on which this decision takes effect,

HAS ADOPTED THIS REGULATION:

Article 1

With effect from 21 September 1989, the composition of the ecu as laid down in Article 1 of Regulation (EEC) No. 3180/78 will be determined by:

--- firstly, the following weights:

	%
German mark	30.1
Pound sterling	13.0
French franc	19.0
Italian lira	10.15
Dutch guilder	9.4

Belgian franc	7.6
Luxembourg franc	0.3
Danish krone	2.45
Irish pound	1.1
Greek drachma	0.8
Spanish peseta	5.3
Portuguese escudo	0.8

--- secondly, the rates for the ecu derived by the Commission from the rates of the dollar recorded by the central banks of the Member States on their respective exchange market, on Wednesday 20 September 1989 at 14·15.

The Commission shall be responsible for carrying out, on 20 September 1989, the calculations required to determine the new national currency amounts corresponding to the weights set out in this Regulation. It shall ensure that the new composition is communicated to the monetary authorities and published in the Official Journal of the European Communities.

Article 2

This Regulation shall enter into force on 20 June 1989.

This Regulation shall be binding in its entirety and directly applicable in all Member States.

Done at Luxembourg, 19 June 1989.

For the Council
The President
C. SOLCHAGA CATALAN

APPENDIX B

ECU-RELATED NATIONAL DOCUMENTS

TABLE OF CONTENTS

Notice of the Deutsche Bundesbank No. 1010/87 of June 16, 1987 (expanded in Notice No. 1002/90 of January 5, 1990)

(Source: Deutsche Bundesbank)

Re: Incurrence of liabilities denominated in the European Currency Unit ECU

The incurrence of liabilities denominated in the European Currency Unit ECU is subject to authorization in accordance with section 3 sentence 1 or sentence 2 of the Currency Act (Währungsgesetz)(No. 2(c) sentence 1 or sentence 2 of the Currency Ordinance for Berlin), depending on the currency of payment which has been or can be chosen. In this context, the Deutsche Bundesbank announces the following:

1. To the extent that the incurrence of money debt in foreign currency between residents has been permitted heretofore (Notice No. 1009/61), this shall also apply in future to the same degree to liabilities denominated in the European Currency Unit ECU. Accordingly, residents are hereby permitted pursuant to section 3 of the Currency Act (No. 2(c) of the Currency Ordinance for Berlin) to incur liabilities denominated in the European currency Unit ECU

(a) by maintaining ECU accounts at banks,

(b) by raising ECU loans with a period to maturity not exceeding 12 months from banks,

(c) to purchase precious metals (gold, silver, platinum) or gold and silver coins,

(d) to purchase ECU claims and securities denominated in ECUs,

(e) by assuming guarantees and warranties on behalf of non-residents or for liabilities denominated in ECUs,

(f) by concluding life insurance contracts (capital and annuity insurance) and reinsurance contracts in respect of them, as well as by lending against the collateral of such insurance contracts, provided that the insurance enterprise only has the right to set off the claim arising from such lending if the event insured against occurs or if the insurance is surrendered,

(g) by concluding insurance contracts (including reinsurance contracts in respect of them) on account of risks connected with foreign trade and payments, the international transportation of removal goods, passenger baggage, exhibition goods and assets located in foreign economic territories.

Paragraph 1(a) of the principles governing decisions on applications for authorizations pursuant to section 3 of the Currency Act (No. 2 (c) of the Currency Ordinance for Berlin) - Notice of the Deutsche Bundesbank No. 1015/78 - remains unaffected.

2. Furthermore, in the case of

   (a) contracts concerning international transactions in goods or services,

   (b) follow-up import contracts between importers and first customers, export subcontracting agreements between exporters and their immediate suppliers or sales contracts in "broken" merchanting trade, provided that the goods are resold unchanged by the importers, the exporters or the transit agents,

   the granting of an authorization pursuant to section 3 of the Currency Act (No. 2(c) of the Currency Ordinance for Berlin) for the incurrence of liabilities denominated in the European Currency Unit ECU can in the future generally be expected. Applications for authorizations must be submitted to the appropriate Land Central Bank.

3. The authorization under paragraph 1 above does not include the incurrence of liabilities denominated in the European Currency Unit ECU if the amount there of is in turn to be determined by the future exchange rate of a currency, by the future gold price or by the future price or value of other goods or services.

4. The right to amend this Notice is reserved.

DEUTSCHE BUNDESBANK

Pöhl Prof. Dr. Gleske

BANK OF GREECE
Circular 16: Government Bonds with ECU Clause Issue of 6th Series of September 9, 1989

A. Terms

According to the common decisions 97767/3613/17.9.86 and 2069515/3037 7.9.89 signed by the Minister of National Economy and the Minister of Finance, the terms of the new bonds are as follow:

1. The bonds are Bearer Certificates with a European Currency Unit (ECU) clause and their disposition is effected through Public Announcement. The European Currency Unit (ECU) is defined as a basket of Currencies of the member countries of the European Economic Community (EEC), according to the rules of the Community.

2. The amount of the bond will be determined in the amount that will result from the total of the relevant documents of purchase of bonds.

3. The duration of the bond will be three years. On the bonds, three coupons are attached, one for each year of the duration of the issue.

4. The rate of interest has been fixed at 9.5% per annum and is fixed for the whole duration of the bond. This rate of interest is in line with the corresponding interest rate of the ECU in the Euromarket for equivalent maturities. The interest is calculated in ECU and is accrued and payable at the Payment day, being the date written on the coupon.

5. Date of issue of the bonds has been decided to be September 15th 1989.

6. The registrations for the purchase of bonds will take place from September 11th to 21st 1989.

The purchases who register after the date of issue (15.9.1989), i.e. from 18.9.1989 to 21.9.1989 will be charged the interest of the days which pass from the date of issue to the date of registration and payment of the price of Bonds. This interest is calculated according to the interest rate in drachmas applied by Banks.

7. The nominal value of the Bonds which are issued in five Series of different colours each is as follows:

A (brown) ECU	1,000 or Drs 178,700
B (violet) ECU	2,000 or Drs 357,400
C (blue) ECU	5,000 or Drs 893,500
D (Red) ECU	10,000 or Drs 1,787,000
E (Green) ECU	20,000 or Drs 3,574,000

B. General characteristics of the bonds

The characteristics of the new issue of the bonds are as follows:

1. The Bonds have the signature of the Minister of Finance typed mechanically.

2. The interests of the bonds are exempted from any income tax. The disposition and the repayment of bonds, their transfer or the repayment of interest as well as the possible plus value of bonds, have no tax burden.

3. The Bonds are negotiable in the Athens Stock Exchange, a fact which allows their liquidation in a time of need.

Also, the Banks are allowed to prepay Government bonds.

4. The Government Bonds will be sold to persons, legal entities of private law, legal entities of public law, Banks, State Organisations, insurance companies and insurance funds.

5. The holders of bonds purchased in foreign currency not necessarily assignable, have the right to convert the proceeds of repayment or prepayment of the bonds and the interest coupons into any one of the currencies traded in the Athens interbanking market as well as to transfer it abroad without any limitation. Also, it is allowed the transfer of the titles abroad.

6. The constitution of guarantee or the granting of a loan by Banks on the security of Government Bonds is allowed.

CERTIFICATI DI CREDITO DEL TESORO DENOMINATI IN ECU -- CTE
Treasury certificates denominated in Ecu

(Source: Banca d'Italia)

1. General features:
The Finance Law authorizes the Treasury Minister to issue securities denominated either in Ecu or Italian lire indexed to the Ecu, having maturities of not up to 10 years.

The Treasury Minister is empowered to fix the maturity and other features of the securities as well as the issue price, the interest rate and all the other conditions regarding the issue and placement of these securities.

In practice the interest rate on Treasury certificates denominated in Ecu has been fixed in line with those provided by long-term securities in the Ecu bond market.

The certificates denominated in Ecu earn an interest which is paid annually. CTEs may be transferred abroad by non resident holders; in this case, the certificates must be stamped "payable abroad" by the Bank of Italy and are considered foreign bonds. "Payable abroad" certificates enjoy all payments in Ecu. The unstamped certificates, circulating in Italy, are paid in Italian lire.

The issue price is fixed in Ecu at par.

2. Denomination:
CTEs are available in denomination with face values of 1,000, 10,000, 100,000, 500,000 and 1 million Ecu.

3. Final maturity:
The maturity of the CTEs issued has been in line with those prevailing on Ecu bond market, maturities of 7-8 years have been adopted; the last issue (November 1987) had a maturity of 4 years.

4. Redemption features:
CTEs are redeemable at face valuable at maturity.

Unstamped certificates will be reimbursed in Italian lire at the average of the daily lira-Ecu exchange rate on the first twenty days of the month preceding the payment month (the same for coupon payment).

Stamped certificates are reimbursed in Ecu by credit or transfer to an Ecu account

In the event that the Ecu is no longer the EMS monetary unit, the interest and the principal will be calculated in one of the component currencies of the Ecu, at the choice of the holder of the security and in accordance with the special procedures laid down.

The value of the Ecu is defined as the sum of the amounts of the component currencies established in EEC regulation No. 3180/78 of 18 December 1978. This composition can be changed with regard both to the number of component currencies and to the unification or division of any component currency or currencies.

Issue and distribution techniques:
The certificates may be placed, either in the domestic market or abroad. All the certificates for the domestic market are underwritten by a syndicate of banks organized and coordinated by the Bank of Italy. The banks offer the certificates for public subscription at the price indicated in the issue decree and in the period of time and in the way laid down by the Bank of Italy. The Treasury pays the syndicate a placement commission of 1% and a guarantee commission of 0.25% on the amount of certificates underwritten. All the certificates to be placed abroad are underwritten by a foreign bank appointed by the Bank of Italy. The foreign bank leads an international syndicate of banks.

5. Cost to the borrower:
In addition to the commissions indicated above, the Treasury pays the Bank of Italy a 0.05% commission on the full nominal amount of the loan to cover all the expenses connected with the placement, delivery, administration and advertising of the issue. The cost of the loan, in lira terms, can only be established at its maturity when all the lira/Ecu rates used for the payments of interest and principal can be known.

6. Comments on issue volumes:
The Treasury has not fixed regular intervals for the issue of CTEs; the volume largely depends on domestic and international market conditions.

7. Liquidity and marketability:
CTEs are eligible by law for official quotation on all Italian Stock Exchanges. The CTEs placed directly abroad and those transferred

abroad (stamped "payable abroad") are listed at the Luxembourg Stock Exchange.

8. Regulations for holders:
CTEs can be either bearer or registered instruments.
Bearer certificates may be combined, split up and changed into registered securities. There are no restrictions on the purchase of unstamped certificates by non-residents.

9. Taxation:
Only one issue of CTEs, launched in September 1987, is submitted to the withholding tax (12.50%); the other ones are tax exempt.

10. Purpose of the instrument:
By introducing certificates denominated in Ecu the Italian Treasury had three objectives:
a) to enlarge the range of available borrowing instruments;
b) to increase its scope for raising funds in foreign market; and
c) to lengthen the average maturity of the public debt.

11. Competing instruments:
In Italy CTEs compete directly with Treasury credit certificates with variable rates linked to Treasury bill rates.

BUONI DEL TESORO DENOMINATI IN EUROSCUDI -- BTE
Treasury bonds denominated in Ecu
(Source Banca d'Italia)

1. General features:
The Finance Law gives authorization to the Treasury Minister to issue securities denominated in Ecu having maturities of twelve months (or about).

Treasury bonds in Ecu are short-term instruments and offer a yield which is in lien with those provided by similar securities in the Ecu market.

The BTE earns an interest which is paid at maturity: the interest is determined through the auction technique, but the Treasury establishes a rate ceiling for each issue.

The issue price is fixed -- in Ecu terms -- at par; the price in Italian lira will be established on the basis of the lira/Ecu exchange rate which prevails two working days before the day of the issue.

2. Denomination:
The BTE has a unitary value of 1,000 Ecu. A global certificate will represent the whole amount issued. The BTEs allotted must be lodged with the Bank of Italy in book-entry system.

3. Final maturity:
The standard maturity will be of about one year; for instance, a final maturity of 373 days has been chosen for the latest BTE issue, launched in January 1988.

4. Redemption features:
Treasury bonds in Ecu are redeemed at par at maturity; the reimbursement in Italian lira will be calculated on the basis of the lira/Ecu rate prevailing two working days before the maturity date.

5. Issue and distribution techniques:
BTEs are issued with the technique of uniform yield auction (i.e. every participant has to declare the yield he wishes to obtain for the amount demanded). Tenders are therefore ranked in ascending order of yield, from the lowest to the highest yield that allots the entire issue; the latter yield -- stock out yield -- cannot be superior to the one previously fixed by the Treasury. The marginal yield is then applied to the whole issue. Auction participation is open to banks, medium and long-term credit institutions, insurance companies, financial companies and stockbrokers; practically, the same range of participants accepted for the T-bills auction.

6. Cost to the borrower:
The total cost of a BTE issue can be calculated in lira terms only at maturity, since the cost also depends on the difference between the lira/Ecu exchange rate prevailing on the issue day and the one prevailing on the maturity day.

7. Comments on issue volume:
The first BTE issue (October 1987) amounted to 500 million Ecu; the latest (January 1988) amounted to 750 million Ecu.

8. Liquidity and marketability:
BTEs are not quoted on the Stock Exchange; therefore dealings take place on the over-the-counter market. BTEs in that secondary market are traded in terms of simple yield.

9. Regulation for holders:
Treasury bonds in Ecu are registered in book-entry system controlled by the Bank of Italy and can be purchased without restrictions by non residents.

10. Taxation:
Interest on Treasury bonds in Ecu is taxed at a rate of 12.50%, withheld at the source.

11. Purpose of the instrument:
By introducing short-term securities denominated in Ecu the Italian Treasury has intended not only to enlarge the range of its debt instruments but also to offer investors the opportunity to diversify the currency composition of their bond portfolios.

12. Competing instruments:
The main competing financial instruments are the twelve months Treasury Bills.

INFORMATION MEMORANDUM
Irish £ -- Ecu floating rate stock, 1993
Issue of Ecu 100 million fully subscribed for by Allied Irish Banks plc
price of issue 100 per cent

(Source: Irish Department of Finance)

1. For the purpose of this Memorandum, Allied Irish Banks plc shall hereinafter be described as "The Bank."

2. Rate of Interest: The rate of interest payable on the stock shall be determined as follow:

(i) On the Interest Determination Date, that is, two business days prior to each interest payment date described in paragraph 4 below ("Interest Payment Dates"), but subject to the proviso hereunder, The Bank will request the specified offices of each of the Reference Banks referred to in paragraph 3 below (the "Reference Banks") to provide The Bank with its offered quotations to leading banks in the international market for Ecu deposits for the relevant Interest Period described in paragraph 4 below ("Interest Payment Dates and Interest Period") as at 10.00 a.m. (Dublin time) on the Interest Determination Date in question, provided that in the case of the first Interest Period commencing 25 September, 1987, the Interest Determination Date for the purpose of this paragraph shall be 23 September, 1987. The Rate of Interest for such Interest Period shall be equal to 1/8 per cent per annum above the arithmetic mean (rounded upwards if necessary to the nearest 1/16 per cent) of such offered quotations as determined by The Bank.

As used in this paragraph, or in any paragraph below, "business day" means a day on which banks and foreign exchange markets are open for business in the principal financial centres for component currencies of the Ecu, described in paragraph 9(a) below.

(ii) If on any Interest Determination Date two only of the Reference Banks provide such offered quotations, the Rate of Interest for the next Interest Period shall be determined on the basis of the offered quotations of those Reference Banks providing such quotations and in the manner prescribed at (i) above.

(iii) If on any Interest Determination Date fewer than two of the Reference Banks provide such offered quotations, The Bank will request each of the Reference Banks to provide The Bank with the quotations offered to them by leading banks in each relevant inter-bank market for deposits in each of the then component currencies of the Ecu specified in paragraph 9(a) below and hereinafter described as the "Relevant Currencies" for the Interest Period concerned as at 10.00 am (Dublin time) on the Interest Determination Date in question (provided that, if the EC Ecu is then neither used in the European Monetary System nor for the settlement of transactions by the public institutions of or within the EC, the component currencies of the Ecu shall be those provided for in paragraph 9(b)). The Rate of Interest for such Interest Period shall be equal to 1/8 per cent, per annum above the arithmetic mean as determined by The Bank (rounded upwards if necessary to the nearest 1/16 per cent) of the respective offered rates so communicated by the Reference Banks or any two or more of them (if only such provide quotations), weighted in the manner provided below, provided that, if on any Interest Determination Date the Reference

Banks or any two or more of them (if only such provide quotations) do not provide offered quotations for all the Relevant Currencies but do provide such quotations for relevant currencies representing in aggregate 95 per cent or more of one Ecu on such Interest Determination Date, then the Rate of Interest for such Interest Period shall nevertheless be calculated pursuant to this sub-paragraph (iii) on the basis of the quotations so provided and ignoring the Relevant Currencies for which such quotations are not provided.

(iv) If The Bank is unable to determine the Rate of Interest for an Interest Period in accordance with subparagraph (i), (ii) or (iii) above, the Rate of Interest for such Interest Period shall be the Rate of Interest in effect for the last preceding Interest Period to which subparagraph (i), (ii) or (iii) above shall have applied.

(v) The interest rate so determined will be announced by the Minister for Finance on the business day immediately preceding the commencement of each Interest Period.

For the purposes (iii) of this paragraph, the weighting to be given to a Relevant Currency or the percentage which it bears to one Ecu shall be determined by The Bank by reference to the proportion that the amount of such Relevant Currency included in one Ecu bears to one Ecu and calculated on the basis of the US dollar equivalent of each of the Relevant Currencies as at the Interest Determination Date in question.

Interest will be calculated on the actual number of days elapsed on a year of 360 days.

3. Reference Banks: The Reference Banks shall be Allied Irish Banks plc, Bankcentre, Ballsbridge, Dublin 4; Banca Commerciale Italiana S.P.A., Piazza Della Scala 6, 20121 Milan; Kredietbank N.V., Arenbergstraat 7, B-1000 Brussels; Generale Bank (Générale de Banque), Rue Montagne du Parc 3, B-1000 Brussels and Banque Générale du Luxembourg S.A., 14 Rue Aldringen / 27 Avenue Monterey, 2951 Luxembourg.

4. Interest Payment Dates and Interest Period: Interest on the stock will be payable half-yearly in arrear on 31 March and 30 September ("Interest Payment Date"). If any Interest Payment Date would otherwise fall on a day which is not a business day, the Interest Payment Date in question shall be postponed to the next business day.

The period beginning 25 September, 1987, and ending 31 March, 1988, and each successive period beginning on an Interest Payment Date and ending on the next Interest Payment Date following is herein referred to as an "Interest Period."

5. **Payment in IR£:** Payments of interest and repayment of principal will be made in IR£ and Ecu (as described at paragraph 9 below) and quoted by the Central Bank of Ireland (which will be the official market rate for Ecu against IR£), for the twenty-eighth day (the "Quotation Date") preceding the due payment date of interest or principal, as the case may be. The Quotation Date shall constitute the ex-dividend date for the purpose of calculating interest due.

6. **Principal repayment:** The stock will be redeemed at its principal amount on 31 March, 1993.

7. **Purchase of Stock:** The Bank shall pay in IR£ to the account of the Minister for Finance at the Central Bank of Ireland before the close of business on 25 September, 1987, an amount which shall be determined by converting the Ecu 100m stock subscribed for by Allied Irish Banks from Ecu to IR£ at the conversion rate between the Ecu and IR£ quoted by the Central Bank of Ireland on 23 September, 1987, which will be the official market rate for Ecu against IR£.

8. **Market-making:** The Bank shall during trading hours of the Irish Stock Exchange offer to sell and to buy the stock of this issue.

9. **Value of the Ecu:**

(a) Subject to the provisions hereof, the value of the Ecu in which the Bonds are denominated ("Ecu") is equal to the value of the Ecu that is from time to time used in the European Monetary System (the "EC Ecu") and which is at the date of issue hereof valued on the basis of specified amounts of the currencies of the member countries of the European Communities ("EC") as shown below.

Pursuant to Council Regulation (EEC) No. 3180/78 of 18 December, 1978, as amended by Council Regulation (EEC) No. 2626/84 of 15 September, 1984, the EC Ecu is at the date of issue hereof defined as the sum of the following components:

0.719	German mark
0.0878	Pound sterling
1.31	French francs

140.00	Italian lire
0.256	Dutch guilder
3.71	Belgian francs
0.14	Luxembourg franc
0.219	Danish krone
0.00871	Irish pound
1.15	Greek drachmas

This basis may be changed by the EC, including changes in the components, in which event the basis of valuation of the Ecu will change accordingly.

(b) For the purpose of paying interest or repaying principal hereunder if the EC Ecu is used neither in the European Monetary System nor for the settlement of transactions by the public institutions of or within the EC, the equivalent of the Ecu as of any date (the "day of valuation") shall be chosen as set out hereunder.

The component currencies of the Ecu for this purpose shall be the currency amounts which were components of the EC Ecu when the EC Ecu was most recently used in the European Monetary System or for the settlement of transactions by public institutions of or within the EC. The equivalent of the Ecu in IR£ shall be on the valuation day the sum of each component currency converted into IR£. The conversion rate in IR£ of each component currency shall be the official quotation of such currency as recorded by the Central Bank of Ireland. In the event that such official quotation of one or more component currencies is not available for any reason on the valuation day, the most recent official quotation of such currency or currencies recorded by the Central Bank of Ireland shall be used to calculate the value of the Ecu in IR£.

10. Authority: The Principal and interest of the stock, which is issued under the authority of the Finance Act, 1970, and other statutes, will be a charge on the Central Fund.

11. Purpose of Issue: The proceeds of the issue will be used for general financing purposes of the Exchequer.

12. Trustee Status: The stock is an authorised trustee investment and trustees may invest therein even if the price at the time of investment exceeds the redemption value of 100 per cent.

13. Tax Privileges: Interest on the stock will be paid without deduction of income tax but will be assessable to income tax in the hands of recipient(s). Gains arising on the disposal of the stock are exempt from Capital Gains Tax.

The stock and the interest payable thereon will be exempt from all Irish taxation, present or future, if the beneficial ownership of the stock at the relevant time by a person not ordinarily resident in the Sate is established in the manner prescribed by the Minister for Finance, provided that where the stock is the subject of a gift or inheritance, the donee or successor is on the relevant date neither domiciled nor ordinarily resident in the State.

14. Registration: The Register of the issue will be kept at the Department of Finance.

15. Transfers: The stock will be transferable in any sums which are multiples of an Ecu. Instruments for the transfer of the stock will be free of stamp duty.

16. Stock Exchange Quotation: The stock will be listed on The Irish Stock Exchange and be quoted thereon in IR£ per 100 Ecu.

17. Exchange Control: For exchange control purposes the stock shall rank as a domestic security.

18. Brokers: Allied Irish Securities and Butler and Briscoe, Government Stockbroker, are the brokers to the issue.

Department of Finance, Dublin 2.
23 September 1987.

Bank of England
Press Notice
UK Government ECU Treasury Bills

The Bank of England has today issued a revised Information Memorandum for the UK Government ECU Treasury Bill programme. The Chancellor of the Exchequer announced in his Budget speech on 14 March that the programme would continue and the new Memorandum incorporates changes being made as a result of a review of the programme following the initial series of six tenders.

Experience with the programme so far has been very positive and the changes are therefore minor and technical in nature.

Summary of Main Details

UK Government ECU Treasury Bills will continue to be issued in a regular series of monthly tenders to be held on the second Tuesday of each month. The next tender will be held on Tuesday 11 April; the amounts and maturities of the Bills to be offered at that tender will be announced on Tuesday, 4 April.

The changes incorporated in the new Memorandum are all minor and technical in nature, as follows:

(i) The new Memorandum brings forward the time set for announcement of the result of the monthly tender to around 1.00 pm on the day of the tender. The previous Memorandum set a time of 3.00 pm, though in practice the announcement was made earlier.

(ii) From 11 April, definitive (ie, bearer) Bills will be available in smaller denominations of ECU 10,000 and ECU 50,000 as well as the denominations of ECU 100,000, ECU 500,000, ECU 1,000,000, ECU 5,000,000 and ECU 10,000,000 already provided for in the previous Memorandum.

(iii) In addition to Bills offered at the monthly tenders, the new Memorandum contains provision for Bills to be allotted to the Bank of England to be made available to the market makers (listed in the Memorandum) through sale and repurchase transactions in order to alleviate settlement problems.

In other respects the programme continues unchanged on the basis of the arrangements set out in full in the new Information Memorandum. Copies of the Memorandum are available at the Bank of England. The arrangements will be kept under review in the light of experience and a further Information Memorandum (or supplements to today's Information Memorandum) will be issued if material changes are made.

Bank of England, 28 March 1989.

EXCERPT OF A LETTER FROM THE FRENCH MINISTRY OF ECONOMICS TO THE PRESIDENT OF THE FRENCH BANKING ASSOCIATION
Paris, May 21, 1982

(Source: French Ministry of Economics)

...

Par lettre du 24 juillet 1981, je vous avais indiqué qu'afin de permettre aux banques françaises de développer leur participation dans les opérations financières internationales libellées en écus, je n'avais pas, nonobstant la règle générale d'interdiction des prêts de francs à des non-résidents, d'objections à ce que des banques françises accordent des prêts de francs à des non-résidents lorsque ces prêts constituent la part en francs de prêts libellés en écus. Chaque banque devrait cependant veiller à ce que le total des prêts de francs qu'elle accordait à ce titre à des non-résidents n'excède pas le total des dépôts de francs de non-résidents figurant à son passif.

Afin de poursuivre cette évolution et de placer les banques françaises en position d'exercer un rôle majeur sur le marché international des opérations libellées en écus, j'ai décidé de modifier cette position et d'assimiler désormais ces opérations du point de vue de la règlementation des changes à des opérations en devises étrangères. Cette décision comporte en particulier les conséquences suivantes:

- Les banques françaises gèrent leurs avoirs et engagements libellés en écus dans les mêmes conditions que leurs avoirs et engagements en devises étrangères, à l'intérieur de leur position de change globale. Lorsque pour se constituer des avoirs en écus, elles sont amenées à emprunter des francs, ces emprunts doivent être effectués auprès de non-résidents; lorsque leurs dépôts en écus excèdent leur capacité de placement en écus et qu'elles doivent éclater en ses diverses composantes leurs excédents d'écus, les francs dont elles disposent ainsi peuvent être prêtés à des non-résidents.

- Les banques françaises peuvent accorder à des résidents des prêts et advances en écus dans les mêmes conditions que les prêts et advances libellés en devises étrangères. Paralellément les résidents peuvent contracter des emprunts libellés en écus directement auprès de banques étrangères dans les mêmes conditions que des emprunts en devises étrangères.

...

Décret n° 89-154 du 9 mars 1989
réglementant les relations financières avec l'étranger
(Source: Official Journal of the French Republic)

Le Premier ministre,

Sur le rapport du ministre d'Etat, ministre de l'économie, des finances et du budget,

Vu la loi n° 66-1008 du 28 décembre 1966 relative aux relations financières avec l'étranger, et notamment son article 3;

Vu le décret n° 67-78 du 27 janvier 1967 fixant les modalités d'application de la loi n° 66-1008 du 28 décembre 1966, modifié;

Vu le décret n° 68-1021 du 24 novembre 1968 règlementant les relations financières avec l'étranger, modifié,

Décrète:

Art. 1er. - Pour l'application du présent décret, il faut entendre par:

1° France:

La France métropolitaine, les départements d'outre-mer, les territoires d'outre-mer et les collectivités territoriales à statut particulier de Mayotte et de Saint-Pierre-et-Miquelon. La Principauté de Monaco est assimilée à la France.

Les Etats dont l'institut d'émission est lié au Trésor français par une convention de compte d'opérations sont également assimilés à la France. Toutefois, pour les besoins statistiques liés à l'établissement de la balance des paiements et pour les obligations déclaratives relatives à l'importation et à l'exportation de moyens de paiement, lesdits Etats sont considérés comme l'étranger.

2° Etanger:

Les pays autres que ceux compris dans la France telle que définie au 1° ci-dessus.

3° Résidents:

Les personnes physiques ayant leur résidence habituelle en France et les personnes morales françaises ou étrangères pour leurs établissements en France. Les personnes physiques de nationalité étrangère, à l'exception des fonctionnaires étrangers en poste en France, acquièrent la qualité de résident lorsqu'elles sont établies en France depuis deux ans.

Toutefois, le ministre chargé de l'économie peut accorder aux personnes physiques de nationalité étrangère établies en France depuis moins de deux ans l'autorisation d'opter pour la qualité de résident avant l'expiration de ce délai.

Cette option est ouverte de droit aux ressortissants des pays membres de la communauté économique européenne au moment de leur installation en France.

4° Non-résidents:

Les personnes physiques ayant leur résidence habituelle à l'étranger et les personnes morales françaises ou étrangères pour leurs établissements à l'étranger. Les personnes physiques, à l'exception des fonctionnaires et coopérants français en poste à l'étranger, acquièrent la qualité de non-résident dès leur installation à l'étranger.

Art. 2. - Les résidents n'ayant pas la qualité d'intermédiaire agréé et n'exerçant pas à titre habituel et professionnel une activité d'exportation, d'importation ou de négoce international de biens ou services ne peuvent constituer d'avoirs à l'étranger sous forme monétaire ou détenir en France des comptes en devises autres que l'ECU qu'avec l'autorisation préalable du ministre chargé de l'économie.

Les avoirs qu'ils détiennent à l'étranger sous forme de titres placés sous le contrôle d'intermédiaires agréés.

Art. 3. - Les mouvements de fonds réalisés par transferts entre la France et l'étranger ou en France entre résidents et non-résidents s'effectuent par l'entremise d'intermédiaires agréés.

Sont intermédiaires agréés les établissements relevant de la loi n° 84-46 du 24 janvier 1984 relative à l'activité et au contrôle des établissements de crédit ainsi que les institutions et services énumérés à l'article 8 de cette loi.

Art. 4. - Tous les mouvements de fonds entre la France et l'étranger, entre résidents et non-résidents, et toutes les opérations financières réalisées directement à l'étranger, et notamment les règlements et encaissements effectués à partir de comptes à l'étranger ou par compensation de créances et dettes, les opérations de mise en place et de remboursement relatives aux emprunts réalisés directement à l'étranger et les échanges de devises ou d'intérêts font l'objet de déclarations statistiques adressées mensuellement à la Banque de France directement ou sous couvert d'un intermédiaire agréé.

Les comptes rendus relatifs aux paiements effectués par l'entremise d'intermédiaires agréés sont établis par ces derniers, qui se font communiquer les éléments d'identification statistique des opérations.

Art. 5. - En application des dispositions de l'article 4:

- la Banque de France peut convenir avec tout résident des modalités de déclaration directe par celui-ci de ses opérations réalisées avec l'étranger ou en France avec des non-résidents;
- les entreprises ou groupes d'entreprises dont le montant des règlements avec l'étranger au titre des biens et services excède au cours d'une année civile un montant fixé par arrêté du ministre chargé de l'économie doivent déclarer directement à la Banque de France l'ensemble de leurs opérations avec l'étranger ou en France avec des non-résidents;
- les résidents rendent compte à la Banque de France des opérations de mise en place et de remboursement relatives aux emprunts réalisés directement à l'étranger ainsi qu'aux emprunts en devises réalisés auprès d'intermédiaires agréés lorsque l'encours total de leurs engagements excède un montant fixé par arrêté;
- les ouvertures de comptes à l'étranger font l'objet d'une déclaration à la Banque de France par leurs titulaires dans le délai d'un mois.

Art. 6. - Les voyageurs résidents et non-résidents déclarent à l'administration des douanes les moyens de paiement exportés ou importés en devises, lorsqu'ils excèdent un montant fixé par arrêté.

Art. 7. - Les exportations et importations matérielles de titres s'effectuent par l'entremise d'intermédiaires agréés.

Art. 8. - Les résidents sont autorisés à facturer et à régler en devises d'autres résidents dans le cadre de contrats internationaux de négoce, d'importation ou d'exportation de biens et services facturés en devises.

Art. 9. - Sont soumises à l'autorisation préalable du ministre chargé de l'économie prévue, en ce qui concerne les titres de collectivités publiques et de sociétés françaises, par l'article 82 de la loi du 23 décembre 1946, l'émission avec appel public à l'épargne et l'intoduction sur le marché en France de titres de quelque nature que ce soit d'Etats étrangers, de collectivités publiques ou de sociétés étrangères et d'institutions internationales.

Sont toutefois dispensées d'autorisation les opérations visées ci-dessus et portant:

1° Sur des valeurs mobilières émises par des ressortissants des pays membres de la Communauté économique européenne ou par les institutions de la Communauté économique européenne et des autres organisations internationales dont la France est membre;

2° Sur des emprunts bénéficiant de la garantie de la République française;

3° Sur des actions assimilables, ou de nature à se substituer à la suite de division, de regroupement, d'élévation ou de cote officielle d'une bourse de valeurs en France ou bien dont l'émission ou l'introduction sur le marché en France a été précédemment autorisée.

Est également dispensée d'autorisation l'introduction sur le marché de valeurs mobilières émises par des ressortissants de pays membres de l'Organisation de coopération et de développement économique et l'introduction sur le marché de valeurs mobilières étrangères dont l'émission en France a été précédemment autorisée.

Art. 10. - Le ministre chargé de l'économie peut déléguer les pouvoirs d'autorisation qui lui sont confiés par le présent texte à la Banque de France et, pour les départements et territoires d'outre-mer, à la Caisse centrale de coopération économique.

Art. 11. - Les modalités d'application du présent décret sont précisées par arrêtés du ministre chargé de l'économie et, en tant que de besoin, du ministre chargé des départements et territoires d'outre-mer.

Art. 12. - Les dispositions du décret n° 68-1022 du 24 novembre 1968 relatif au contrôle de la position en francs ou en devises des établissements bancaires et financiers vis-à-vis de l'étranger sont abrogées à compter du 1er juin 1989.

Art. 13. - Le décret n° 67-78 du 27 janvier 1967 susvisé est ainsi modifié:

Les articles 5 et 6 et les intitulés des sections III et IV du titre III ainsi que l'article 8 et l'intitulé du titre IV sont abrogés.

Le 1° de l'article 2 est abrogé et remplacé par les dispositions suivantes:

> "1° France: La France métropoloitaine, les départements d'outre-mer, les territoires d'outre-mer et les collectivités territoriales à statut particulier de Mayotte et Saint-Pierre-et-Miquelon. La Principauté de Monaco est assimilée à la France;"

Au 2° de l'article 2, la dernière phrase est abrogée.

L'article 3 est abrogé et remplacé par les dispositions suivantes:

"Art. 3. - La constitution d'investissements directs français en Afrique du Sud est soumise à l'autorisation préalable du ministre chargé de l'économie."

A l'article 9, les mots "les relations financières avec l'étranger" sont remplacés par les mosts "des investissements directs".

<u>Art. 14.</u> - Les articles 1er, 2 et 3, le premier alinéa de l'article 4, les mots "d'autre part" au deuxième alinéa de cet article ainsi que la référence à l'article 3 aux deuxième et quatrième alinéas du même article, le dernier alinéa de l'article 4 bis, les articles 5, 6 et 7, la référence aux articles 3 et 5 à l'article 8, et l'article 9 du décret n° 68-1021 susvisé sont abrogés.

<u>Art. 15.</u> - Le ministre d'Etat, ministre de l'économie, des finances et du budget, et le ministre des départements et territoires d'outre-mer, porte-parole du Gouvernement, sont chargés, chacun en ce qui le concerne, de l'exécution du présent décret, qui sera publié au **Journal officiel** de la République française.

Fait à Paris, le 9 mars 1989.

MICHEL ROCARD

Par le premier ministre:
Le ministre d'Etat, ministre de l'économie, des finances et du budget,
PIERRE BEREGOVOY

Le ministre des départements et territoires d'outre-mer, porte-parole du Gouvernement,
LOUIS LE PENSEC

Arrêté du 9 mars 1989 portant fixation de certaines modalités d'application du décret n° 89-154 du 9 mars 1989 réglementant les relations financières avec l'étranger
NOR: ECOT8970002A

Le ministre d'Etat, ministre de l'économie, des finances et du budget,
Vu la loi n° 66-1008 du 28 décembre 1966 relative aux relations financières avec l'étranger;
Vu le décret n° 89-154 du 9 mars 1989 réglementant les relations financières avec l'étranger, et notamment son article 2.

Arrête:

<u>Art. 1er.</u> - Les résidents frontaliers exerçant une activité professionnelle à l'étranger sont autorisés à conserver dans le pays d'exercice de cette activité la part de leur rémunération qui est nécessaire au règlement de leurs dépenses courantes dans ce pays sans que celle-ci puisse excéder 50.000 F.

Les fonctionnaires français ainsi que les coopérants en poste à l'étranger peuvent détenir en France ou à l'étranger des comptes en devises alimentés du montant de leur traitement et de ses accessoires. Ils doivent conserver les justificatifs correspondants. Les règlements excédant leurs disponibilités sur ces comptes relèvent de la procédure de droit commun des transferts à l'étranger applicable aux résidents.

Les résidents de nationalité étrangère sont autorisés à transférer à l'étranger l'ensemble de leurs revenus ou à les verser sur des comptes spéciaux en devises de résidents ouverts en France.

<u>Art. 2.</u> - Les résidents qui ne sont pas autorisés à détenir des comptes à l'étranger et qui effectuent des paiements à l'étranger d'un montant supérieur à 50.000 F, par virement bancaire ou par chèque, présentent à l'intermédiaire agréé une pièce attestant l'exigibilité du paiement et, pour les transferts unilatéraux, tout document ou déclaration attestant que lesdits transferts n'ont pas pour objet la constitution irrégulière d'avoirs à l'étranger.

Ils conservent à la disposition de l'administration des douanes les documents justifiant l'exigibilité des paiements ou la régularité des transferts de montant supérieur à 50.000 F effectués au profit de non-résidents.

Ils sont tenus de rapatrier dans un délai de trois mois à compter de leur encaissement, et pour les devises autres que l'ECU, de céder sur le marché des changes, l'intégralité des recettes perçues à l'étranger et non affectées dans ce même délai à un paiement en devises exigible.

<u>Art. 3.</u> - Le montant visé au deuxième alinéa du décret n° 89-154 du 9 mars 1989 est fixé à cinq milliards de francs.

Les entreprises qui ont franchi ce seuil au cours de l'exercice 1988 devront avoir convenu avec la Banque de France avant le 1er janvier 1990 des modalités de déclaration directe à celle-ci de l'ensemble de leurs opérations avec l'étranger ou en France avec des non-résidents pour l'établissement de la balance des paiements. Celles qui franchiront ce seuil au cours des exercices suivants disposeront d'un délai maximum d'un an à compter de la clôture de l'exercice correspondant pour convenir avec la Banque de France des modalités d'application de cette disposition.

<u>Art. 4.</u> - Le montant visé au troisième alinéa de l'article 5 du décret du 9 mars 1989 susvisé est fixé à 500 millions de francs.

Art. 5. - En application de l'article 6 du décret du 9 mars 1989 susvisé, les moyens de paiement doivent être délcarés au bureau de douane à la frontière lorsqu'ils excèdent 50.000 F.

Art. 6. - L'arrêté du 9 août 1973 relatif à l'exportation matérielle de moyens de paiement et de valeurs mobilières par colis postaux ou envois par la poste, l'arrêté du 3 août 1987 fixant la liste des intermédiaires agréés et l'arrêté du 1er juin 1988 portant fixation de certaines modalités d'application du décret n° 68-021 du 24 novembre 1968 réglementant les relations financières avec l'étranger sont abrogés et remplacés par le présent arrêté.

Art. 7. - Le directeur du Trésor et le directeur général des douanes et droits indirects sont chargés, chacun en ce qui le concerne, de l'exécution du présent arrêté, qui sera publié au **Journal officiel** de la République française.

Fait à Paris, le 9 mars 1989.

PIERRE BEREGOVOY

Circulaire du 9 mars 1989 relative aux opérations commerciales et financières avec l'étranger réalisées par les résidents

NOR: ECOT8970003C

Paris, le 9 mars 1989.

Le ministre d'Etat, ministre de l'économie, des finances et du budget, aux intermédiaires agréés

La présente circulaire a pour objet d'abroger les circulaires rendues caduques par le décret n° 89-154 du 9 mars 1989 réglementant les relations financières avec l'étranger et par l'arrêté du 9 mars 1989 portant fixation de certaines modalités d'application du décret précité.

La circulaire du 20 décembre 1968 relative aux dépôts de titres étrangers, devises étrangères et titres de créances sur l'étranger modifiée par les circulaires des 27 novembre 1986 et du 17 juillet 1987, la circulaire du 27 novembre 1973 relative aux dépenses et recettes d'escale des navires français à l'étranger modifiée par les circulaires du 22 septembre 1976 et du 27 février 1981, la circulaire du 24 octobre 1978 relative aux opérations sur les marchés à terme étrangers modifiée par les circulaires du 5 février 1985, du 21 mai 1986 et du 4 juillet 1986, la circulaire du 5 février 1981 relative aux garanties entre la France et l'étranger n'ayant pas le caractère d'investissement direct, la circulaire du 27 novembre 1986 relative à l'utilisation des cartes de crédit, la circulaire du 3 juin 1988 relative aux opérations commerciales et financières avec l'étranger réalisées par les résidents pour leur propre compte ou dans le cadre d'un mandat de gestion contractuel et la circulaire du 25 juillet 1988 relative aux relations financières avec l'étranger en matière d'assurance sont abrogées.

Les investissements directs restent régis par la circulaire du 21 mai 1987 relative aux investissements directs français à l'étranger en France.

La présente circulaire sera publiée au **Journal officiel** de la République française.

Pour le ministre et par délégation:
Le directeur du Trésor,
J.-C. TRICHET

NOTE NO. 16 OF THE FRENCH POSTAL MINISTER REGARDING THE ISSUANCE OF AN ECU STAMP - 1988

1993 sera l'année du grand rendez-vous européen: la France ne doit pas le manquer. Lors de l'émission du timbre commun franco-allemand (consacré au 25e anniversaire du traité sur la coopération franco-allemande), M. Gard Longuet, ministre délégué chargé de la Poste et des Télécommunications, déclarait que "L'Europe de la Poste est une nécessité, parce que, dans le cadre du grand marché européen unifié de 1993, les communications prendront une importance cruciale."

Sans attendre l'échéance de 1993, la Poste française a décidé de participier, dès maintenant, à cette sensibilisation à l'idée européenne par l'émission, à titre symbolique, d'un timbre en Ecu.

L'Ecu (en anglais ECU, initiales de European Currency Unit) est une unité monétaire de type "panier de monnaies" composée d'une quantité fixe de la monnaie de chaque Etat membre (à l'exception pour l'instant de la peseta et de l'escudo). Ces quantités, qui peuvent faire l'objet de révision suivant des règles très strictes, ne sont évidemment pas identiques pour toutes les monnaies, mais ont été établies de manière à refléter l'importance économique relative au sein de la Communauté de chacun des Etats membres.

La valeur de l'ecu ne découle pas directement de son évolution sur les marchés des changes, mais résulte par calcul de l'évolution sur ces marchés des monnaies qui le composent. A côté de son utilisation "officielle" en tant qu'unité monétaire du Système Monétaire Européen, l'Ecu connaît une utilisation "privée" due à l'initiative des différents opérateurs économiques.

La Poste française a souhaité donner une large diffusion à l'émission d'un timbre en Ecu, afin que non seulement les citoyens français, mais aussi ceux des autres pays de la CEE qui reçoivent des lettres de France, soient touchés par cette action.

Pour répondre à l'objectif d'atteindre un public aussi vaste que possible, le choix s'est porté sur le timbre de série courante de 2,20 F. Ce tarif permet d'affranchir les lettres jusqu'à 20 grammes au départ de la France pour tous les pays de la Communauté depuis le 1er janvier 1988. Le montant en Ecu correspondant à ce prix: 0,31 Ecu ([1]) sera apposé sous forme de surcharge, étant néanmoins entendu que le prix de vente de ce timbre continuera à être fixé uniquement en francs et que la mention du montant en Ecu n'a qu'un caractère symbolique.

La valeur en Ecu des tarifs postaux dans d'autres pays: 0,30 Ecu pour le timbre de 13 francs belges et 0,39 Ecu pour le timbre de 0,80 mark par exemple, montre que dans chaque pays de la CEE, le tarif afférent dans la monnaie nationale ainsi que sa modulation peuvent différer sensiblement. Cette différence, jointe aux changements de parité entre les monnaies composantes. explique les éscarts qui apparaissent lorsque ces prix nationaux sont convertis en Ecu.

Le timbre-poste ne peut pas, à lui seul, anticiper les mouvements d'unification nécessaires en matière de définition des produits postaux, de détermination des gammes de tarifs, de monnaies enfin, pour arriver à la création d'un véritable timbre européen.

(1.) Concrètement, la variation des différentes monnaies, dans le cadre de marges de fluctuation déterminéees au sein du SME, entaîne une variation de la valeur du franc par rapport à l'Ecu. Ainsi, au 1er janvier 1988, 1 franc français valait 0,1430 Ecu, soit 0.3146 Ecu pour 2,20 francs. Au 16 janvier 1988, 1 franc français valait 0,1434 Ecu, soit 0,3154 Ecu pour 2,20 francs. Au 22 février, le même calcul donne 0,3149 pour 2,20 francs.
C'est pour tenir compte de ces variations que la valeur exprimée en Ecu sur le timbre a été limitée à la deuxième décimale, soit 0,31 Ecu.

Ministère des Finances

Administration de la T.V.A., de l'Enregistrement et des Domaines. Aliénation d'immeubles domaniaux. Publications faites en exécution de la loi du 31 mai 1923, p. 3300.

Exécutifs — Ministère de la Région wallonne

Circulaire ministériel du 4 mars 1987 relative à la transmission au gouvernement provincial des délibérations et des arrêtés des autorités communales, p. 3301.

Ministerie van Financiën

Administratie van de BTW, Registratie en Domeinen. Vervreemding van onroerende domeingoederen. Bekendmakingen gedaan ter uitvoering van de wet van 31 mei 1923,

LOIS, DÉCRETS ET RÈGLEMENTS

MINISTERE DES FINANCES

F. 87 — 450

25 FEVRIER 1987. — Arrêté royal relatif à la frappe de pièces de monnaie libellées en Ecus, commémoratives du 30e anniversaire de la signature du Traité de Rome instituant la Communauté économique européenne

BAUDOUIN, Roi des Belges,

A tous, présents et à venir, Salut.

Vu l'article 74 de la Constitution;

Vu la loi du 12 juin 1930 portant création du Fonds monétaire, notamment l'article 12;

Voulant commémorer le 30e anniversaire de la signature du Traité de Rome, instituant la Communauté économique européenne;

Vu la loi sur le Conseil d'Etat, coordonnée le 12 janvier 1973, notamment l'article 3, § 1er modifié par la loi du 9 août 1980;

Vu l'urgence;

Considérant la nécessité d'émettre ces pièces pour le 25 mars 1987, date du trentième anniversaire de la signature du Traité de Rome;

Sur la proposition de Notre Ministre des Finances;

Nous avons arrêté et arrêtons :

Article 1er. Il sera frappé des pièces en or de 50 écus et des pièces en argent de 5 écus.

Art. 2. Les pièces en or présentent les caratéristiques suivantes :

titre : 900 millièmes;
poids de la pièce : 17,27 grammes;
diamètre : 29 millimètres.

La tranche est lisse.

Elles sont émises suivant les besoins constatés, par voie de souscription dont la limite est fixée au 31 décembre 1987.

Art. 3. Les pièces en argent présentent les caratéristiques du florin Carolus d'argent de 1540, à savoir :

titre : 833 millièmes;
poids de la pièce : 22,85 grammes;
diamètre : 37 millimètres.

La tranche est lisse.

Elles seront émises au nombre de deux millions maximum.

Art. 4. Pourront également être ultérieurement frappées des pièces en or de 50 écus et des pièces en argent de 5 écus de qualité de frappe particulière, dont les caractéristiques seront conformes à celles décrites respectivement aux articles 2 et 3.

Art. 5. Les pièces porteront au droit l'effigie de Charles-Quint, telle que figurant sur les florins Carolus d'argent. L'empereur y est représenté en buste, la couronne en tête et la cuirasse sur la poitrine.

WETTEN, DECRETEN EN VERORDENINGEN

MINISTERIE VAN FINANCIEN

N. 87 — 450

25 FEBRUARI 1987. — Koninklijk besluit betreffende het slaan van in Ecus uitgedrukte muntstukken ter herdenking van de 30e verjaardag van de ondertekening van het Verdrag van Rome houdende oprichting van de Europese Ekonomische Gemeenschap

BOUDEWIJN, Koning der Belgen,

Aan allen die nu zijn en hierna wezen zullen, Onze Groet.

Gelet op artikel 74 van de Grondwet;

Gelet op de wet van 12 juni 1930 tot oprichting van een Muntfonds, inzonderheid op artikel 12;

De 30e verjaardag van de ondertekening van het Verdrag van Rome houdende oprichting van de Europese Ekonomische Gemeenschap willend herdenken;

Gelet op de wetten van de Raad van State, gecoördineerd op 12 januari 1973, inzonderheid op artikel 3 § 1, gewijzigd bij de wet van 9 augustus 1980;

Gelet op de dringende noodzakelijkheid;

Overwegende de noodzaak deze muntstukken in omloop te brengen vóór 25 maart 1987, verjaardagdatum van de ondertekening van het Verdrag van Rome;

Op de voordracht van Onze Minister van Financiën,

Hebben Wij besloten en besluiten Wij :

Artikel 1. Er worden gouden muntstukken van 50 ecus en zilveren muntstukken van 5 ecus geslagen.

Art. 2. De gouden muntstukken vertonen de volgende kenmerken :

gehalte : 900 duizendsten;
gewicht van het muntstuk : 17,27 gram;
diameter : 29 millimeter.

De muntrand is effen.

Zij worden uitgegeven volgens de behoeften die zullen vastgesteld worden aan de hand van intekeningen waarvoor de uiterste datum op 31 december 1987 is vastgesteld.

Art. 3. De zilveren muntstukken vertonen de kenmerken van de zilveren Carolusgulden van 1540, namelijk :

gehalte : 833 duizendsten;
gewicht van het stuk : 22,85 gram;
diameter : 37 millimeter.

De muntrand is effen.

Er worden maximaal twee miljoen muntstukken uitgegeven.

Art. 4. Er worden ook later gouden muntstukken van 50 ecus en zilveren muntstukken van 5 ecus van bijzondere slagkwaliteit geslagen. Hun kenmerken stemmen overeen met deze die respectievelijk bepaald zijn in artikel 2 en 3.

Art. 5. De muntstukken dragen op de voorzijde de beeldenaar van Keizer Karel, zoals hij voorkomt op de zilveren Carolusgulden. De Keizer is er afgebeeld in buste, gekroond en met het harnas op de borst.

Les inscriptions entourant l'effigie sont les suivantes « Carolus D.G. ROM. IMP. HISP. REX. DUX. BURG. CO. F. » soit in extenso, Carolus Dei Gratia Romanorum Imperator Hispaniarum Rex Dux Burgundiae Comes Flandriae. Elles sont complétées par la marque de l'atelier de Bruges de l'époque, à savoir une fleur de lis.

La gravure de la pièce originale a été retouchée par Paul Huybrechts, maître graveur.

Au revers : la valeur nominale entourée de douze étoiles figurant les pays membres de la Communauté économique européenne, le millésime 1987, la marque de l'atelier monétaire de Bruxelles, une tête d'ange, et à l'exergue les inscriptions Belgique - België -Belgien.

La composition est l'oeuvre de Fernand Brose, maître graveur héraldiste.

Art. 6. Toutes les pièces visées par le présent arrêté ont cours légal en Belgique.

Art. 7. Notre Ministre des Finances est chargé de l'exécution du présent arrêté.

Donné à Bruxelles, le 25 février 1987.

BAUDOUIN

Par le Roi :

Le Ministre des Finances,
M. EYSKENS

De inschriften rond de beeldenaar zijn de volgende : « Carolus D.G. ROM. IMP. HISP. REX. DUX. BURG. CO. F. » hetzij in extenso, Carolus Dei Gratia Romanorum Imperator Hispaniarum Rex Dux Burgundiae Comes Flandriae. Zij worden aangevuld met het teken van het toenmalig atelier van Brugge, een leliebloem.

De gravure van het oorspronkelijke stuk werd geretoucheerd door Paul Huybrechts, meester graveerder.

Op de keerzijde : de nominale waarde omringd door twaalf sterren die de leden van de Europese Ekonomische Gemeenschap voorstellen, het jaartal 1987, het teken van het muntatelier van Brussel, een engelhoofd, en in de afsnede de inschriften België - Belgique - Belgien.

De schikking is het werk van Fernand Brose, meester graveerder wapenkundige.

Art. 6. Al de door dit besluit beoogde muntstukken hebben wettelijke koers in België.

Art. 7. Onze Minister van Financiën is belast met de uitvoering van dit besluit.

Gegeven te Brussel, 25 februari 1987.

BOUDEWIJN

Van Koningswege :

De Minister van Financiën,
M. EYSKENS

MINISTERE DES AFFAIRES ETRANGERES, DU COMMERCE EXTERIEUR ET DE LA COOPERATION AU DEVELOPPEMENT

F. 87 — 451

Convention sur les droits politiques de la femme, faite à New York le 31 mars 1953 (1) Adhésions et retrait d'une réserve

Par une communication reçue le 17 décembre 1985, le Gouvernement néerlandais a notifié au secrétaire général qu'il avait décidé de retirer la réserve suivante, formulée lors de la ratification de la Convention susmentionnée :

(Orginal : français)

« Cete ratification est subordonnée à la réserve que la succession à la Couronne conformément aux dispositions constitutionnels y relatives soit exclue de l'application de l'article III de la Convention. ».

Ledit retrait a pris effet le 17 décembre 1985, date de la réception de la notification.

Dépôt de l'instrument d'adhésion de la Colombie : le 5 août 1986 (entrée en vigueur : le 3 novembre 1986).

Dépôt de l'instrument d'adhésion de l'Angola : le 17 septembre 1986 (entrée en vigueur : le 16 décembre 1986).

MINISTERIE VAN BUITENLANDSE ZAKEN, BUITENLANDSE HANDEL EN ONTWIKKELINGSSAMENWERKING

N. 87 — 451

Verdrag betreffende de politieke rechten van de vrouw, opgemaakt te New York, op 31 maart 1953 (1). — Toetreding en intrekking van een voorbehoud

Bij kennisgeving ontvangen op 17 december 1985, heeft de Nederlandse Regering de secretaris-generaal medegedeeld dat zij beslist heeft het navolgend voorbehoud, gemaakt bij de bekrachtiging van voormeld Verdrag, in te trekken :

(Origineel : Frans).

« Deze bekrachtiging behelst het voorbehoud dat de troonopvolging overeenkomstig de desbetreffende grondwettelijke bepalingen niet onder de toepassing van artikel III van het Verdrag valt. »

Gezegde intrekking is van kracht geworden op 17 december 1985, datum van ontvangst van de kennisgeving.

Neerlegging van de toetredingsoorkonde van Colombia : 5 augustus 1986 (inwerkingtreding : 3 november 1986).

Neerlegging van de toetredingsoorkonde van Angola : 17 september 1986 (inwerkingtreding : 16 december 1986).

F. 87 — 452

Accord relatif au transport aérien régulier entre le Royaume de Belgique et la République du Mali, et Annexe, signé à Bruxelles le 9 mai 1985

Le Gouvernement du Royaume de Belgique, d'une part, et le Gouvernement de la République du Mali, d'autre part, étant parties à la Convention relative à l'Aviation Civile Internationale ouverte à la signature à Chicago le 7 décembre 1944, aux fins de développer la coopération internationale dans le domaine du transport aérien,

Aux fins de créer les bases nécessaires pour exploiter des services aériens réguliers,

VERTALING

N. 87 — 452

Akkoord betreffende het geregeld luchtvervoer tussen het Koninkrijk België en de Republiek Mali, en Bijlage, ondertekend te Brussel op 9 mei 1985

De Regering van het Koninkrijk België, enerzijds, en de Regering van de Republiek Mali, anderzijds, Partijen zijnde bij de op 7 december 1944 te Chicago voor ondertekening opengestelde Overeenkomst inzake de Internationale Burgerluchtvaart, met het doel de internationale samenwerking op het gebied van luchtvervoer te bevorderen,

Ten einde de grongslagen te leggen, voor de exploitatie van geregelde luchtdiensten,

(1) Voir *Moniteur belge* du 2 septembre 1964.
Voir *Moniteur belge* du 23 juin 1967.

(1) Zie *Belgisch Staatsblad* van 2 september 1964.
Zie *Belgisch Staatsblad* van 23 juni 1967.

F. 87 — 492

3 MARS 1987. — Arrêté royal relatif à la détermination de la contre-valeur en francs belges des pièces libellées en écus

—

BAUDOUIN, Roi des Belges,

A tous, présents et à venir, Salut.

Vu l'article 74 de la Constitution;

Vu la loi du 12 juin 1930 portant création du Fonds monétaire, notamment l'article 12, inséré par l'arrêté royal n° 509 du 5 février 1987;

Vu la loi sur le Conseil d'Etat, coordonnée le 12 janvier 1973, notamment l'article 3, § 1er, modifié par la loi du 9 août 1980;

Vu l'urgence;

Considérant la nécessicité de connaître pour le 25 mars 1987, le mode de calcul de la contre-valeur en francs belges des pièces libellées en écus;

Sur la proposition de Notre Ministre des Finances,

Nous avons arrêté et arrêtons :

Article 1er. La contre-valeur en francs belges des pièces libellées en écus est obtenue par la multiplication de la valeur nominale de ces pièces par le dernier cours de l'écu, en francs belges, sur le marché réglementé, tel que publié dans le *Journal officiel des Communautés européennes.*

Art. 2. Notre Ministre des Finances est chargé de l'exécution du présent arrêté.

Donné à Bruxelles, le 3 mars 1987.

BAUDOUIN

Par le Roi :

Le Ministre des Finances,

M. EYSKENS

F. 87 — 493

6 MARS 1987. — Arrêté ministériel déterminant le prix d'émission des monnaies libellées en écus

—

Le Ministre des Finances,

Vu la loi du 12 juin 1930 portant création d'un Fonds monétaire, notamment l'article 12 inséré par l'arrêté royal n° 509 du 5 février 1987;

Vu la loi sur le Conseil d'Etat, coordonnée le 12 janvier 1973, notamment l'article 3, § 1er, modifié par la loi du 9 août 1980;

Vu l'urgence;

Considérant la nécessité de déterminer pour le 25 mars 1987, le prix d'émission des monnaies libellées en écus,

Arrête :

Article 1er. Le prix d'émission des pièces d'or libellées en écus est fonction de leur valeur intrinsèque, majorée d'une prime. Cette valeur intrinsèque est calculée quotidiennement en fonction du cours de l'or établi chaque jour à Londres et du cours du dollar en francs belges sur le marché réglementé à Bruxelles.

Le prix d'émission ainsi obtenu, appelé ci-après cours, est publié quotidiennement dans la presse.

Art. 2. En cas de fluctuation importante du cours de l'or exprimé en francs belges, le cours quotidien des pièces visées à l'article 1er peut être suspendu.

Art. 3. Pour les ventes des pièces visées à l'article 1er réalisées en cas de suspension de cotation, c'est le premier cours suivant la période de suspension de cotation qui est d'application.

N. 87 — 492

3 MAART 1987. — Koninklijk besluit tot vaststelling van de tegenwaarde in Belgische frank van de in ecus uitgedrukte muntstukken

—

BOUDEWIJN, Koning der Belgen,

Aan allen die nu zijn en hierna wezen zullen, Onze Groet.

Gelet op artikel 74 van de Grondwet;

Gelet op de wet van 12 juni 1930 tot oprichting van een Muntfonds, inzonderheid op artikel 12, ingevoegd bij het koninklijk besluit nr. 509 van 5 februari 1987;

Gelet op de wetten op de Raad van State, gecoördineerd op 12 januari 1973, inzonderheid op artikel 3, § 1, gewijzigd bij de wet van 9 augustus 1980;

Gelet op de dringende noodzakelijkheid;

Overwegende de noodzaak om tegen 25 maart 1987 de berekeningswijze te kennen van de tegenwaarde in Belgische frank van de in ecus uitgedrukte muntstukken;

Op de voordracht van Onze Minister van Financiën,

Hebben Wij besloten en besluiten Wij :

Artikel 1. De tegenwaarde in Belgische frank van de in ecus uitgedrukte muntstukken wordt bekomen door de nominale waarde van deze muntstukken te vermenigvuldigen met de laatste in Belgische frank uitgedrukte koers van de ecu, op de gereglementeerde markt, zoals gepubliceerd in het *Publicatieblad van de Europese Gemeenschappen.*

Art. 2. Onze Minister van Financiën wordt belast met de uitvoering van dit besluit.

Gegeven te Brussel, 3 maart 1987.

BOUDEWIJN

Van Koningswege :

De Minister van Financiën,

M. EYSKENS

N. 87 — 493

6 MAART 1987. — Ministerieel besluit tot vaststelling van de uitgifteprijs van de in ecus uitgedrukte muntstukken

—

De Minister van Financiën,

Gelet op de wet van 12 juni 1930 tot oprichting van een Muntfonds, inzonderheid op artikel 12, ingevoegd bij het koninklijk besluit nr. 509 van 5 februari 1987;

Gelet op de wetten op de Raad van State, gecoördineerd op 12 januari 1973, inzonderheid op artikel 3, § 1, gewijzigd bij de wet van 9 augustus 1980;

Gelet op de dringende noodzakelijkheid;

Overwegende de noodzaak om tegen 25 maart 1987 de uitgifteprijs van de in ecus uitgedrukte muntstukken vast te stellen,

Besluit :

Artikel 1. De uitgifteprijs van de in ecus uitgedrukte munt stukken is functie van hun intrinsieke waarde, verhoogd met eer premie. Deze intrinsieke waarde wordt dagelijks berekend in functie van de koers van het goud die elke dag te Londen wordt vastgesteld en de koers van de dollar in Belgische frank op de gereglementeerde markt te Brussel.

De aldus bekomen uitgifteprijs, hierna koers genoemd, wordt dagelijks in de pers gepubliceerd.

Art. 2. In geval van belangrijke schommelingen van de in Belgische frank uitgedrukte koers van het goud, kan de dagelijkse koers van de in artikel 1 beoogde muntstukken worden geschorst.

Art. 3. Voor de verkoop van de in artikel 1 beoogde muntstukken die plaatsvindt op een ogenblik dat de koers is geschorst, is de eerste koers die volgt op de periode tijdens dewelke de koers was geschorst, van toepassing.

Art. 4. Le prix d'émission des pièces visées à l'article 1er est payé au moment de l'achat ou de la souscription.

Pour les ventes réalisées en cas de suspension de la cotation, le prix d'émission est payé aussitôt que le cours visé à l'article 3 est connu.

Art. 5. Le rachat par les établissements financiers des pièces visées à l'article 1er s'effectue en fonction du cours quotidien calculé selon les modalités prévues à l'article 1er, déduction faite d'une commission de 3 % pour frais.

Art. 6. Une demande d'admission à la cote pour le 1er janvier 1988 sera introduite auprès de la Bourse de Bruxelles.

Art. 7. Le prix d'émission des pièces d'argent libellées en écus est fixé à 500 francs belges.

Art. 8. Le rachat des pièces visées à l'article 7 se fait sur base de valeur nominale en écus dont la contre-valeur en francs belges est établie conformément à l'article 1er de l'arrêté royal du 3 mars 1987.

Art. 9. La Banque Nationale de Belgique centralise les pièces d'argent rachetées par la Régie des Postes, au prix de rachat que celle-ci a payé au détenteur.

Art. 10. Le Fonds Monétaire rachète les pièces d'argent centralisées par la Banque Nationale de Belgique au prix de rachat que celle-ci a payé au détenteur.

Art. 11. Le présent arrêté entre en vigueur le jour de sa publication au *Moniteur belge*.

Les articles 1 à 5 cesseront d'être en vigueur le 1er janvier 1988.

Bruxelles, le 6 mars 1987.

M. EYSKENS

MINISTERE DE L'INTERIEUR ET DE LA FONCTION PUBLIQUE

—

F. 87 — 494

23 DECEMBRE 1986
Arrêté royal portant répartition entre les provinces du crédit de l'article 43.14 de 1986

—

BAUDOUIN, Roi des Belges,

A tous, présents et à venir, Salut.

Vu la loi du 31 octobre 1986 ouvrant des crédits provisoires pour l'année budgétaire 1986, destinés à assurer la marche des services publics;

Vu l'article 43.14 de la Section 56, Titre I du budget du Ministère de l'Intérieur et de la Fonction publique;

Considérant qu'il s'impose de promouvoir des actions de coordination au niveau provincial entre les pouvoirs locaux et provinciaux;

Vu l'arrêté royal du 5 octobre 1961 portant organisation du contrôle administratif et budgétaire;

Vu l'arrêté royal n° 5 du 18 avril 1967 relatif au contrôle de l'octroi et de l'emploi des subventions;

Vu l'arrêté royal du 26 avril 1968 réglant l'organisation et la coordination des contrôles de l'octroi et de l'emploi des subventions;

Vu l'accord de Notre Ministre du Budget du 23 décembre 1986;

Sur la proposition de Notre Ministre de l'Intérieur et de la Fonction publique,

Nous avons arrêté et arrêtons :

Article 1er. Un montant de 551 998 551 francs figurant à l'article 43.14 du projet de budget du Ministère de l'Intérieur et de la Fonction publique pour l'année 1986 sera réparti par ressort provincial, selon les modalités fixées à l'annexe au présent arrêté.

Ces montants serviront à favoriser la coopération et la coordination entre les pouvoirs, notamment en matière d'utilisation de l'informatique, de sécurité et de prévention.

Un plan définitif de répartition sera établi par province par Notre Ministre de l'Intérieur et de la Fonction publique sur proposition des gouverneurs de province.

Art. 4. De uitgifteprijs van de in artikel 1 beoogde muntstukken wordt betaald op het ogenblik van de aankoop of van de intekening.

Voor de verkoop die plaatsvindt op een ogenblik dat de koers is geschorst, wordt de uitgifteprijs betaald zodra de in artikel 3 beoogde koers is gekend.

Art. 5. De wederinkoop door de financiële instellingen van de in artikel 1 beoogde muntstukken gebeurt tegen de dagelijkse koers berekend volgens de in artikel 1 bepaalde modaliteiten, verminderd met een kommissieloon van 3 % voor de kosten.

Art. 6. Bij de Beurs van Brussel wordt een aanvraag ingediend om de in artikel 1 beoogde muntstukken vanaf 1 januari 1988 in de notering op te nemen.

Art. 7. De uitgifteprijs van de in ecus uitgedrukte zilveren muntstukken is op 500 Belgische frank vastgesteld.

Art. 8. De wederinkoop van de in artikel 7 beoogde muntstukken gebeurt tegen hun nominale waarde in ecus, waarvan de tegenwaarde in Belgische frank overeenkomstig artikel 1 van het koninklijk van 3 maart 1987 wordt vastgesteld.

Art. 9. De Nationale Bank van België centraliseert de door de Regie der Posterijen wederingekochte zilveren muntstukken tegen de prijs van wederinkoop die de Regie aan de houder betaald heeft.

Art. 10. Het Muntfonds koopt de door de Nationale Bank van België gecentraliseerde zilveren munststukken weder in tegen de prijs van wederinkoop die deze aan de houder betaald heeft.

Art. 11. Dit besluit treedt in werking de dag waarop het in het *Belgisch Staatsblad* wordt bekendgemaakt.

De artikelen 1 tot 5 houden op van kracht te zijn op 1 januari 1988.

Brussel, 6 maart 1987.

M. EYSKENS

MINISTERIE VAN BINNENLANDSE ZAKEN EN OPENBAAR AMBT

—

N. 87 — 494

23 DECEMBER 1986
Koninklijk besluit tot verdeling onder de provincies van het krediet van artikel 43.14 van 1986

—

BOUDEWIJN, Koning der Belgen,

Aan allen die nu zijn en hierna wezen zullen, Onze Groet.

Gelet op de wet van 31 oktober 1986, waarbij voorlopige kredieten worden geopend voor het begrotingsjaar 1986, die bestemd zijn om de werking van de openbare diensten te verzekeren.

Gelet op artikel 43.14 van Sectie 56, Titel I van de begroting van het Ministerie van Binnenlandse Zaken en Openbaar Ambt;

Overwegende dat het geboden is op provinciaal niveau een coördinatie tussen de lokale en provinciale besturen in de hand te werken;

Gelet op het koninklijk besluit van 5 oktober 1961 tot regeling van de administratieve en begrotingscontrole;

Gelet op het koninklijk besluit nr. 5 van 18 april 1967 betreffende de controle op de toekenning en op de aanwending van de toelagen;

Gelet op het koninklijk besluit van 26 april 1968 tot inrichting en coördinatie van de controles op de toekenning en op de aanwending van de toelagen;

Gelet op het akkoord van Onze Minister van Begroting van 23 december 1986;

Op de voordracht van Onze Minister van Binnenlandse Zaken en Openbaar Ambt,

Hebben Wij besloten en besluiten Wij :

Artikel 1. Een bedrag van 551 998 551 frank ingeschreven in het artikel 43.14 van het ontwerp van begroting van het Ministerie van Binnenlandse Zaken en Openbaar Ambt voor het jaar 1986 wordt omgeslagen per provinciaal ambtsgebied, volgens de modaliteiten vastgesteld in de bijlage van dit besluit.

Die bedragen zijn bestemd voor het bevorderen van de samenwerking en de coördinatie tussen de besturen, inzonderheid inzake de aanwending van de informatica, de veiligheid en de preventie.

Op voorstel van de provinciegouverneurs zal door Onze Minister van Binnenlandse Zaken en Openbaar Ambt per provincie een omslagplan worden opgemaakt.

APPENDIX C

TIMETABLE FOR THE ECU

TIMETABLE

1958	
January 1	The Treaty of Rome establishes the European Economic Community among Belgium, West Germany, France, Italy, Luxembourg and the Netherlands.
1970	
March 6	The Werner Report on the realization of economic and monetary union (EMU) in the EC.
1971	
February 9	Agreement of the Council of Ministers on the realization of EMU before 1980.
1972	
October 19-21	EC Summit in Paris resolution to form EMU.
1973	
January 1	Denmark, Ireland and the United Kingdom join the EC.
March	Dollar crisis resales in the end of the system of fixed, but adaptable exchange rates in the Bretton Woods System.
April 3	Establishment of the European Monetary Cooperation Fund and the European Unit of Account.
1975	
March 4	Proposition by the Monetary Committee for the adoption of the Unit of Account (EUA) in the form of a basket of EC currencies.
March 18	Adoption of the EUA by BIS.
April 21	Adoption of the EUA for payments under the Lomé Conventions with the ACP nations.
November	All Saints' Day manifesto by nine leading European economists recommending an EC central bank and the issuance of "Europa" as currency for Europe.
December 5	First contacts with private banks regarding the opening of EUA accounts for the Commission.
1976	
April 7	Opening of the first accounts for the Commission.
July 20	Accounts exist in Belgium, Luxembourg, Italy, France and Great Britain.

1978

April 3	Quotation of maritime freight rates in EUA.
December	Council Resolution establishing the European Monetary System (EMS). Central bank agreement on the EMS operating procedures.

1979

March 13	EMS becomes effective among Belgium, West Germany, Denmark, France, Ireland, Italy, Luxembourg and the Netherlands. Introduction of the ecu as successor to the EUA.
September	First revision of the ecu basket and first realignment of the central rates.
November 30	Second realignment.

1980

January 1	St. Gobain begins invoicing in ecus.

1981

January 1	Greece joins the EC. The ecu replaces the EUA in all activities of the EC institutions.
February 23	First certificate of deposit in ecus.
March 23	Third realignment.
April 14	Italy conveys foreign currency status to the ecu.
April 21	First public ecu bond issue by SOFTE.
July	First syndicated ecu bank credit.
October 5	Fourth realignment.

1982

January	Opening of sight and time deposits.
February 5	First meeting of the ecu clearing group.
February 22	Fifth realignment.
February 23	Italy issues ECU 500 million in securities.
March 1	Belgium conveys foreign currency status to the ecu.
March 21	France conveys foreign currency status to the ecu.
June 14	Sixth realignment.
September	Savings accounts in ecus.

1983

March 21	Seventh realignment.
May 5	Eighth realignment.

May 24	Communication by the Commission on the promotion of the private use of the ecu.
September	Visa credit cards in ecus.

1984

February 2	Spanish banks permit ecu accounts.
March	Almost all EC member states treat the ecu as a foreign currency.
March 15	Official quotation of the ecu at the exchanges in Milan and Rome.
March 19	St. Gobain issues "Titres Participants".
June 4	Official quotation of the ecu at the exchange in Paris.
July	The EC institutions begin to pay their free-lance interpreters in ecu.
July 14	Greece conveys foreign currency status to the ecu.
September 3	First quotation of the ecu at the exchange in Brussels.
September 17	Second revision of the ecu basket and incorporation of the drachma.
	First ecu quotation in Copenhagen.
	Ninth realignment.
October	Use of ecus for debt payment of Latin American countries.
December	First "Yankee issue" of ecu bonds in the United States.
	St. Gobain expresses its accounts and its 1989 balance in ecus.

1985

January 3	Official ecu quotation in Oslo.
January 24	Official quotation of the ecu in Athens.
February	First dollar issue with an option to change into ecu instruments.
May	Public utility contract between Gasunie and Gaz de France in ecus.
	Ecu-based stock index by Deutsche Gesellschaft für Anlageberatung.
June	First "Samurai issue" of ecu bonds in Japan.
June 20	Ecu traveler's checks issued by Société de Chèque de Voyage en ECU and American Express.
July	OECD establishes CIRR rate for ecu.
July 1	First ecu quotation in Amsterdam.
July 22	Tenth realignment.
August 15	First quotation of the ecu at the exchange in Lisbon.

September 15	Ecu traveler's checks issued by Thomas Cook and Euro Traveller's Cheque International.
September 17	Founding of the ECU Banking Association.
September 22	Plaza Agreement; G-5 agree on stable exchange rates.
October 1	First ecu quotation in Stockholm.
November 12	"Other holder" status introduced for non-European monetary institutions.
December 5	Ecu/dollar option of the European Options Exchange.

1986

January 1	Spain and Portugal join the EC.
January 2	Quotation of the ecu at the exchange in Vienna.
January 7	Ecu/dollar futures contract at FINEX.
January 15	Ecu/dollar futures contract at CME.
February 12	Ecu/dollar option at Philadelphia Stock Exchange.
March 21	ECU Banking Association establishes ECU clearing system.
April 7	Eleventh realignment.
August 4	Twelfth realignment.
October 1	Ecu Clearing System begins operations.

1987

January 12	Thirteenth realignment (last realignment except technical realignment in January 1990).
February 22	Louvre Agreement: G-7 achieve agreement on closer cooperation to bring about exchange rate stability.
March 25	Ecu coins issued by the Royal Belgian Mint.
June 16	Deutsche Bundesbank permits the use of ecu in Germany.
July 1	European Single Act proposing a single market in the EC before the end of 1992 becomes effective.
	Quotation of the ecu at the exchange in Madrid.
September 8	Basel-Nyborg Agreement: the EC Central Banks reach agreement on the reinforcement of the EMS.

1988

June 28	The European Council in Hannover decides to pursue Economic and Monetary Union (EMU) and establishes the Committee for the study of EMU to study concrete steps to achieve further economic and monetary integration.

1989

April 22	Last session of the Committee Commission and presentation of the Report on the EMU.

June 16	Spanish peseta joins the Exchange Rate Mechanisms with 6 percent fluctuation margin.
June 26-27	Consideration of the Committee report during the European Summit in Madrid. European Council sets the beginning of the first stage toward EMU for July 1, 1990.
September 21	Third and last revision of the ecu basket, inclusion of the escudo and the peseta.
October 28	Three month ecu interest rate future at LIFFE.
November 9	The Iron Curtain crumbles with the fall of the Berlin Wall.
December 8-9	The European Council in Strasbourg affirms its support for EMU and calls an Intergovernmental Conference for 1990.

1990

January 8	Italian lira decreases fluctuation margin in EMS from 6 to 2.25 percent and corresponding technical realignment.
March 21	The Commission presents its initial report in the EMU and proposes a single currency - the ecu - and a single central bank - Eurofed.
March 29	Establishment of the European Bank for Reconstruction and Development.
March 31	The Council of Ministers supports Eurofed but does not agree on ecu.
April 28	The European Council in Dublin affirms support for EMU.
June 1	British "Hard Ecu" proposal.
June 25-26	European Council sets the Intergovernmental Conference for December 13, 1990.
July 1	Beginning of Stage I of the EMU.
August 21	Report on Economic and Monetary Union by the Commission.
October 8	British pound joins EMS exchange rate mechanisms with a 6 percent margin.
October 18	10-year ecu future at MATIF.
October 19	Report "One Market, One Money" by the Commission.
October 22	Norway links krona to the ecu.
October 26/27	Special Meeting of the European Council in Rome: all member states except Great Britain agree on time table for the EMU.
November 27	The Committee of EC Central Bank Governor submits draft statute for the EC Central Bank.
December 8	Draft statute for ESCB and European Central Bank by the Governors of the EC Central Bank.
December 13	Start of Intergovernmental Conference on EMU.

December 15	European Council Meeting in Rome.
1991	
March 6	LIFFE introduces ecu bond futures contract.
May 10/11	Informal Council of Ministers meeting agrees on "staggering" of EMU introduction.
May 17	Sweden links krona to the ecu.
June 7	Finland links marka to the ecu.
June 28/29	European Council Meeting in Luxembourg acknowledges drafts of the new EMU treaty and central bank statute submitted by the Intergovernmental Conference.
October	EC and EFTA create the European Economic Space (EES).
December 11	European Council in Maastricht agrees on new treaty for the EMU, introduction of an EC central bank and single currency before January 1, 1999. British and Danish governments have certain "opt-out" rights.
1992	
February 7	EC member states sign new EMU treaty in Maastricht.
April	Portuguese escudo joins exchange rate mechanisms of the EMS with a 6 percent-fluctuation margin.

APPENDIX D

OFFICIAL AND PRIVATE INSTITUTIONS

BELGIUM

GOVERNMENT

MINISTRY OF FINANCE
12 rue de la Loi
B-1000 Brussels
tel. 32 (2) 233-81-11

BANKING

COMMISSION BANCAIRE
99 ave Louise
B-1050 Brussels
tel. 32(2) 535-22-11
fax 32(2) 535-23-23
telex 62107

BANQUE NATIONALE DE BELGIQUE
5 blvd Berlaimont
B-1000 Brussels
tel. 32(2) 221-21-11
fax 32 (2) 221-31-01
telex 21355

STOCK EXCHANGE

LA BOURSE DE FONDS PUBLICS DE BRUXELLES ET LA COMMISSION DE LA BOURSE
Palais de la Bourse
Place de la Bourse
B-1000 Brussels
tel. 32(2) 509-12-11
telex 21374

DENMARK

GOVERNMENT

MINISTRY OF FINANCE
Christiansborg
Slotsplads 1
Dk-1218 Copenhagen K
tel. 45 33-92-33-33
fax 45 33-32-80-30
telex 16140

BANKING

DANMARKS NATIONALBANK
Havnegarde 5
Dk-1093 Copenhagen K
tel. 45 33-14-14-11
fax 45 33-14-59-02
telex 27051

TILSYNET MED BANKER OG SPAREKASSER
Nørre Voldgade 94
Dk-1358 Copenhagen K
tel. 45 33-15-56-46
fax 45 33-93-56-46
telex 19457

STOCK EXCHANGE

KØBENHAVNS FONDBØRS
Nikolaj Plads 2
P.O. Box 1040
Dk-1007 Copenhagen K
tel. 45 33-93-33-66
fax 45 33-12-86-13
telex 16496

FRANCE

GOVERNMENT

MINISTRY OF ECONOMY,
FINANCE AND THE BUDGET
139 rue de Bercy
F-75572 Paris Cedex 12
tel. 33(1) 42.60.33.00
telex 217068

BANKING

BANQUE DE FRANCE
39 rue Croix des Petits Champs
F-75001 Paris
tel. 33(1) 42.92.42.92
fax 33(1) 42.96.04.23
telex 220932

STOCK EXCHANGE

LA BOURSE DE PARIS
4, place de la Bourse
F-75080 Paris Cedex 02
tel. 33(1) 40.26.85.90

COMMISSION DES OPERATIONS
DE BOURSE (COB)
Tour Mirabeau 39-43
F-75739 Paris Cedex 15
tel. 33(1) 45.78.33.33
telex 205238

MARCHE A TERME DES INSTRUMENTS FINANCIERS (MATIF)
176 rue Montmartre
F-Paris 75002
France
tel. 33(1) 40.28.82.74

GERMANY

GOVERNMENT

MINISTRY OF FINANCE
Grauerheindorfer Str. 108
D-5300 Bonn 1
tel. 49(228) 682-0
telex 886645

BANKING

DEUTSCHE BUNDESBANK
Wilhelm-Epstein-Str. 14
D-6000 Frankfurt/Main 50
tel. 49(69) 158-1
fax 49(69) 5601071
telex 414431

STOCK EXCHANGE

ARBEITSGEMEINSCHAFT DER
DEUTSCHEN WERTPAPIER-
BÖRSEN
Biebergasse 6-10
D-6000 Frankfurt/Main 1
tel. 49(69) 299903-0
fax 49(69) 29990330

WERTPAPIERBÖRSE FRANKFURT
Postfach 100811
D-6000 Frankfurt/Main
tel. 49(69) 2197-0
fax 49(69) 2197455
telex 411412

GREECE

GOVERNMENT

MINISTRY OF FINANCE
Odos Karageorgi Servias 10
Athens
tel. 30(1) 3224071
telex 216373

BANKING

BANK OF GREECE
Odos El. Venizelou 21
102 50 Athens
tel. 30(1) 3201111
fax 30(1) 3232239
telex 215102

STOCK EXCHANGE

ATHENS STOCK EXCHANGE
Odos Sophocleous 10
105 59 Athens
tel. 30(1) 3211301
fax 30(1) 3213938
telex 215820

IRELAND

GOVERNMENT

DEPARTMENT OF FINANCE
Government Buildings
Upper Merrion Street
Dublin 2
tel. 353(1) 767571
fax 353(1) 789936
telex 30357

BANKING

BANK CEANNAIS na hEIREANN
(Central Bank of Ireland)
P.O. Box 559
Dame St
Dublin 2
tel. 353(1) 716666
fax 353(1) 716561
telex 31041

STOCK EXCHANGE

THE STOCK EXCHANGE (Irish Unit)
24-28 Anglesea St
Dublin 2
tel. 353(1) 778808
telex 93437

IRISH FUTURES AND OPTIONS EXCHANGE
Ferry House
48 Lower Mount Street
Dublin
tel. 353(1) 614977

ITALY

GOVERNMENT

MINISTRY OF FINANCE
Viale America EUR
00144 Rome
tel. 39(6) 5997
telex 614460

BANKING

BANCA D'ITALIA
Via Nazionale 91
00184 Rome
tel. 39(6) 47921
fax 39(6) 4747820
telex 630045

STOCK EXCHANGE

COMMISSIONE NAZIONALE PER
LE SOCIETA E LA BORSA
(CONSOB)
Commission for Companies and the
Stock Exchange)
Via Isonzo 19
00198 Rome
tel. 39(6) 84771
telex 612434

ROME STOCK EXCHANGE
Borsa Valori
Via dei Burro 147
00186 Rome
tel. 39(6) 6792701

LUXEMBOURG

GOVERNMENT

MINISTRY OF FINANCE
3 rue de la Congrégation
1352 Luxembourg-Ville
tel. 352 47-81
fax 352 47-52-41
telex 2790

BANKING

INSTITUT MONÉTAIRE
LUXEMBOURGEOIS
63 ave de la Liberté
2983 Luxembourg-Ville
tel. 352 47-88-88
telex 2766

STOCK EXCHANGE

BOURSE DE LUXEMBOURG SA
11 ave de la Porte-Neuve
B.P. 165
2011 Luxembourg-Ville
tel. 352 47-79-36-1
fax 352 47-32-98
telex 2559

THE NETHERLANDS

GOVERNMENT

MINISTRY OF FINANCE
Korte Voorhout 7
2511 VB The Hague
tel. 31(70) 3428000
telex 33141

BANKING

DE NEDERLANDSCHE BANK NV
Westeinde 1
P.O. Box 98
1000 AB Amsterdam
tel. 31(20) 5249111
telex 11355

STOCK EXCHANGE

EUROPEAN OPTIONS EXCHANGE
P.O. Box 19164
1000 GD Amsterdam
tel. 31(20) 5504550
fax 31(20) 230012
telex 10955

VERENIGING VOOR DE EFFECTENHANDEL (Amsterdam Stock Exchange)
Beursplein 5
1012 JW Amsterdam
tel. 31(20) 5234567
fax 31(20) 248062
telex 12302

PORTUGAL

GOVERNMENT

MINISTRY OF FINANCE
Rua da Alfândega
1100 Lisbon
tel. 351(1) 877555
telex 12143

BANKING

BANCO DE PORTUGAL
Rua de Comércio 148
1000 Lisbon
tel. 351(1) 362931
fax 351(1) 364843
telex 16554

STOCK EXCHANGE

BOLSA DE VALORES DE LISBOA
Rua dos Fanqueiros 10
1100 Lisbon
tel. 351(1) 879416
fax 351(1) 8877402
telex 44751

SPAIN

GOVERNMENT

MINISTRY OF ECONOMY, FINANCE AND TRADE
Ministerio de Economìa, Hacienda y Comercio
Alcalá 9
Madrid 14
tel. 34(1) 2326124
telex 48387

BANKING

BANCO DE ESPAÑA
Alcalá 50
28014 Madrid
tel. 34(1) 4469055
telex 27783

STOCK EXCHANGE

BOLSA DE MADRID
Palacio de la Bolsa
Plaza de la Lealtad 1
28014 Madrid
tel. 34(1) 5892600
telex 49184

UNITED KINGDOM

GOVERNMENT

HM TREASURY
Parliament Street
London SW1P 3AG
tel. 44(71) 270 3000
fax 44(71) 270 5653
telex 9413704

BANKING

BANK OF ENGLAND
Threadneedle Street
London EC2R 8AH
tel. 44(71) 601 4444

STOCK EXCHANGE

THE INTERNATIONAL STOCK EXCHANGE OF THE UNITED KINGDOM AND THE REPUBLIC OF IRELAND
London EC2N 1HP
tel. 44(71) 588 2355
fax 44(71) 628 1037
telex 886557

THE LONDON INTERNATIONAL FINANCIAL FUTURES EXCHANGE (LIFFE)
Royal Exchange
London EE3V3PJ
tel. 44(71) 623 0444

EC GOVERNMENT

COMMISSION OF THE EC
200 rue de la Loi
B-1049 Brussels
Belgium
Directorate-General II
(Economic and Financial Affairs)
tel. 32(2) 235-11-11
fax 32(2) 235-01-22
telex 21877

EC COUNCIL OF MINISTERS
170 rue de la Loi
B-1048 Brussels
Belgium
tel. 32(2) 234-61-11
telex 32(2) 21711

STATISTICAL OFFICE OF THE EC
Information Office
Batiment Jean Monnet
rue Alcide de Gasperi
l-2920 Luxembourg
Luxembourg
tel. 352 4301-4567

OTHER INSTITUTIONS

EUROPEAN INVESTMENT BANK
100 blvd Konrad Adenauer
L-2950 Luxembourg
Luxembourg
tel. 352 4379-1
fax 352 437704
telex 3530

COMMITTEE OF EC CENTRAL BANK GOVERNORS
(also BIS)
Centralbahnplatz 2
CH-4002 Basle
Switzerland
tel. 41(61) 2808080
fax 41(61) 280 09100
telex 962487

APPENDIX E

PRIVATE ECU-RELATED ORGANIZATIONS

ECU BANKING ASSOCIATION
4, rue de la Paix
F-75002 Paris
France
tel. 33(1) 42.96.93.50
fax 33(1) 42.96.35.56
telex 220164

ASSOCIATION FOR THE MONETARY UNION OF EUROPE
26 Rue de la Pépinière
F-75008 Paris
France
tel. 33(1) 45.22.33.84
fax 33(1) 45.22.33.77
telex 282438

ECU ACTIVITIES
M. Pierre Guimbretière
Clos Manuel 3
B-1150 Brussels
Belgium
tel. 32(2) 762 1869
fax 32(2) 763 0897

CENTRE ECU ET PROSPECTIVE D'INTEGRATION MONETAIRE EUROPEENNE (CEPIME - ICHEC)
2 boulevard Brand Whitlock
B-1150 Brussels
Belgium
tel. 32(2) 739 39 83
fax 32(2) 739 38 03

APPENDIX F

INTERNATIONAL EXCHANGE MARKETS

GREAT BRITAIN

LONDON INTERNATIONAL
FINANCIAL FUTURES EXCHANGE
The Royal Exchange
London EC3V3PJ
tel.: 44(71) 623 0444

FRANCE

MARCHE A TERME DES
INSTRUMENTS FINANCIERS
176 rue Montmartre
Paris 75002
tel.: 33(1) 40288274

NETHERLANDS

EUROPEAN OPTIONS EXCHANGE
P.O. Box 19164
1000 GD Amsterdam
tel.: 31(20) 5504550

LUXEMBOURG

BOURSE DE LUXEMBOURG, S.A.
11 avenue de la Porte-Neuve
2011 Luxembourg-Ville
tel.: 352 4779 361

UNITED STATES OF AMERICA

CHICAGO MERCANTILE
EXCHANGE
30 South Wacker Drive
Chicago, IL 60606-7402
tel.: 1(312) 930 1000

CHICAGO BOARD OF TRADE
141 West Jackson Boulevard
Chicago, IL 60604
tel.: 1(312) 435 3500

NEW YORK COTTON EXCHANGE
FINEX
4 World Trade Center
New York, NY 10048
tel.: 1(212) 938 2702

PHILADELPHIA BOARD OF
TRADE
1900 Market Street
Philadelphia, PA 19103-3595
tel.: 1(215) 496 5000

APPENDIX G

BOND PROSPECTUS

Prospectus

THE KINGDOM OF BELGIUM

ECU 150,000,000

$8^{1}/_{8}$% Bonds Due 1994

The issue price of the Bonds is $101^{3}/_{4}$ per cent. of their principal amount.

Principal of and interest on the Bonds will be paid as described under "Terms and Conditions of the Bonds — Payments". Payments will be made without deduction for Belgian withholding taxes, as described under "Terms and Conditions of the Bonds — Tax Status".

Interest will be payable annually in arrear on February 28 in each year, commencing on February 28, 1990.

The Bonds will mature on February 28, 1994.

Application has been made to list the Bonds on the Luxembourg Stock Exchange.

The Bonds will initially be represented by a temporary global certificate to be deposited with a common depositary for both CEDEL S.A. and Morgan Guaranty Trust Company of New York, Brussels office, as operator of the Euro-clear System on or about February 28, 1989. The temporary global certificate will be exchangeable for definitive Bonds in bearer form not earlier than 90 days following completion of distribution of the Bonds, as determined by Kredietbank N.V., and upon certification as described under "Terms and Conditions of the Bonds — Principal amount, Form and Denomination".

Kredietbank International Group

Banque Paribas Capital Markets Limited | **Credit Suisse First Boston Limited**
Morgan Stanley International | **Nomura International Limited**

Swiss Bank Corporation
Investment Banking

Algemene Bank Nederland N.V. | **Amsterdam-Rotterdam Bank N.V.**
ASLK-CGER Bank | **Bank Brussel Lambert N.V./Banque Bruxelles Lambert S.A.**
Bank of Tokyo Capital Markets Group | **Banque Générale du Luxembourg S.A.**
Banque Internationale à Luxembourg S.A. | **Berliner Handels- und Frankfurter Bank**
Coöperatieve Centrale Raiffeisen-Boerenleenbank B.A. | **Creditanstalt-Bankverein**
Daiwa Europe Limited | **Deutsche Bank Capital Markets Limited**
Generale Bank | **Long Term Credit Bank of Japan (Europe) S.A.**
Mitsubishi Finance International Limited | **New Japan Securities Europe Ltd.**
The Nikko Securities Co, (Europe) Ltd. | **Sanwa International Limited**
Shearson Lehman Hutton International, Inc.

The date of this Prospectus is February 23, 1989

In connection with the issue or sale of the Bonds (as defined in General Information below), no person is authorized to give any information or to make any representation other than those contained in this Prospectus and, if given or made, such information or representation must not be relied upon as having been authorized by The Kingdom of Belgium (hereinafter referred to as the "Issuer") and the financial institutions named in "Underwriting" below (hereinafter referred to as the "Managing Underwriters").

The delivery of this Prospectus at any time does not imply that the information herein is correct as of any time subsequent to the date of this Prospectus.

The Issuer has warranted to the Managing Underwriters, inter alia, that all information contained in this Prospectus is true and accurate in all material respects, that this Prospectus does not contain any untrue statement of any material fact and is not misleading in any material respect, that this Prospectus does not omit to state any material fact necessary to make the statements herein, in the context in which they are made, not misleading and that all reasonable inquiries have been made with all due diligence to ascertain facts and to verify the accuracy of all such statements. The Issuer accepts responsibility accordingly.

The distribution of this Prospectus and the offering of the Bonds in certain jurisdictions may be restricted by law; persons into whose possession this Prospectus comes are required by the Issuer and the Managing Underwriters to inform themselves about, and to observe, any such restrictions.

This Prospectus does not constitute and may not be used for the purposes of an offer to sell or solicitation of an offer to buy Bonds by anyone in any jurisdiction in which such offer or solicitation is not authorized or to any person to whom it is unlawful to make such offer or solicitation.

The Managing Underwriters may over-allot or effect transactions in the open market or otherwise with a view to stabilizing or maintaining the market price of the Bonds at levels above those which might otherwise prevail in the open market. Such transactions, if commenced, may be discontinued at any time.

The Bonds may not be offered or sold, directly or indirectly, to residents of, or corporations or other legal entities having their domicile in, The Kingdom of Belgium or the Grand Duchy of Luxembourg except, provided that the offer or sale does not constitute an offer to the public in The Kingdom of Belgium, to (i) a bank which is so resident or domiciled, provided that such bank shall notify l'Institut Belgo-Luxembourgeois du Change of its purchase forthwith on the purchase taking effect by notice in writing containing a certificate to the effect that the consideration payable in respect of such purchase has been funded through a financial market situated outside The Kingdom of Belgium and the Grand Duchy of Luxembourg, (ii) a broker, similar intermediary or institution of international standing whose business involves dealing in securities or managing customers' funds, which is so resident or domiciled and payment for whose purchase is effected through an approved bank ("banque agréée") and through the free exchange market ("marché libre"), as defined by the regulations of l'Institut Belgo-Luxembourgeois du Change and (iii) an insurance company which is so resident or domiciled in circumstances where the Bonds in question are to be held in an "assurances-compte réglementé" in accordance with such regulations. Each Managing Underwriter has agreed that it has not taken, and will not take, any steps which would constitute a public offer in the Kingdom of Belgium and will procure that any purchaser from it of any of the Bonds falling within (i), (ii) and (iii) undertakes to comply with the provisions of this paragraph (including this sentence).

The Bonds have not been and will not be registered under the Securities Act of 1933 of the United States of America. Accordingly, the Bonds may not be offered or sold directly or indirectly in the United States or to U.S. persons (as defined below) as part of the distribution of the Bonds. Notwithstanding the completion of such distribution, any offers or sales in the United States or to U.S. persons must be made in compliance with the registration requirements of such Securities Act of 1933 or pursuant to an exemption therefrom; none of the Issuer or any of the Managing Underwriters makes any representation in respect of or has assumed any responsibility for the availability of any such exemption; and the availability of any such exemption would depend on the facts and circumstances existing at the time of such offers or sales.

Each Managing Underwriter has represented and agreed that (a) it has not offered or sold and will not offer or sell, as principal or agent, directly or indirectly in the United States or to, or for the benefit of, any U.S. person (i) at any time, any Bonds acquired by it in connection with the distribution of the Bonds, or (ii) prior to the Exchange Date, any Bonds however acquired by it and (b) it will cause each purchaser (other than a retail purchaser) of Bonds acquired by it in connection with the distribution contemplated hereby to represent and agree that such purchaser has complied and will comply with the foregoing (a) and further to agree that it will obtain from any person or entity (other than a retail purchaser) to whom it sells any of such Bonds substantially the same agreements.

As used herein, "United States" means the United States of America (including the States and the District of Columbia), its possessions, its territories and all areas subject to its jurisdiction, "U.S. person" means a citizen or resident of the United States, a corporation or other entity organized in or under the laws of the United States, or an estate or trust the income of which is subject to United States federal income taxation regardless of its source, and "Exchange Date" means the date 90 days following the completion of distribution of the Bonds (as determined by Kredietbank N.V.).

Bonds will carry a legend reading as follows: "Any United States person who holds this obligation will be subject to limitations under the United States income tax laws, including the limitations provided in Sections 165 (j) and 1287 (a) of the Internal Revenue Code."

In this Prospectus all references to "$" are to United States dollars and all references to "BEF" are to Belgian francs, unless otherwise specified.

For statistical purposes only, the middle rates of exchange as of February 15, 1989, as quoted by Belgian banks, were ECU 1 = $ 1,1310 and ECU 1 = BEF 43,6875.

This Prospectus does not constitute an offer or invitation by or on behalf of the Issuer or the Managing Underwriters or any of them to subscribe or purchase any of the Bonds.

Table of Contents

Underwriting

The following Managing Underwriters have agreed to underwrite the Bonds by an Underwriting Agreement dated February 23, 1989.

Kredietbank N.V.

Banque Paribas Capital Markets Limited
Credit Suisse First Boston Limited
Morgan Stanley International
Nomura International Limited

Swiss Bank Corporation

Algemene Bank Nederland N.V.
Amsterdam-Rotterdam Bank N.V.
Algemene Spaar- en Lijfrentekas/ Caisse Générale d'Epargne et de Retraite
Bank Brussel Lambert N.V./ Banque Bruxelles Lambert S.A.
Bank of Tokyo Capital Markets Limited
Banque Générale du Luxembourg S.A.
Banque Internationale à Luxembourg SA
Berliner Handels- und Frankfurter Bank
Coöperatieve Centrale Raiffeisen-Boerenleenbank B.A.
Creditanstalt-Bankverein
Daiwa Europe Limited
Deutsche Bank Capital Markets Limited
Generale Bank
Long Term Credit Bank of Japan (Europe) S.A.
Mitsubishi Finance International Limited
New Japan Securities Europe Ltd.
The Nikko Securities Co, (Europe) Ltd
Sanwa International Limited
Shearson Lehman Hutton International, Inc.

General Information

The present issue of ECU 150,000,000 8 1/8 per cent 1989-1994 Bonds (herein referred to as the "Bonds"), the terms and conditions of which are set forth hereinafter, has been duly authorized, pursuant to a Royal Decree dated February 20, 1989.

The Bonds are issued pursuant to a fiscal agency agreement (the "Fiscal Agency Agreement") dated February 23, 1989 made between the Issuer and Kredietbank S.A. Luxembourgeoise (the "Fiscal Agent"), the text of which may be examined at the principal office of the Fiscal Agent in Luxembourg (as such terms are defined in the terms and conditions of the Bonds).

SELLING AND UNDERWRITING

The Managing Underwriters have, pursuant to the Underwriting Agreement dated February 23, 1989, jointly and severally agreed with the Issuer, subject to the satisfaction of certain conditions, to purchase the Bonds at 101 3/4 per cent. of their principal amount, less a selling concession of 1 1/4 per cent. of such principal amount. The Issuer will pay the Managing Underwriters a combined management and underwriting fee of 5/8 per cent. of the principal amount of the Bonds in respect of management and underwriting services and ECU 45,000 in or towards reimbursement of certain expenses. The Managing Underwriters are entitled to terminate, and to be released and discharged from their obligations under, the Underwriting Agreement in certain circumstances prior to payment to the Issuer.

The Bonds will initially be represented by a temporary global certificate, without coupons, which will be deposited on behalf of the subscribers of the Bonds with a common depositary (the "Common Depositary") for CEDEL S.A. ("CEDEL") and Morgan Guaranty Trust Company of New York, Brussels office, as operator of the Euro-clear System ("Euro-clear") on or about February 28, 1989. Upon deposit of the temporary global certificate with the Common Depositary, CEDEL and Euro-clear will credit each subscriber with a principal amount of Bonds equal to the principal amount thereof for which it has subscribed and paid. The temporary global certificate will be exchangeable for definitive Bonds each with five coupons attached not earlier than the date (the "Exchange Date") 90 days after the completion of the distribution of the Bonds as determined by Kredietbank N.V. On or after the Exchange Date, a holder of record of Bonds may obtain definitive Bonds on presentation of a certificate to the effect that (i) the beneficial owner is not a U.S. person and (ii) the beneficial owner is not a resident of The Kingdom of Belgium or the Grand Duchy of Luxembourg or a corporation or other legal entity having its domicile in The Kingdom of Belgium or in the Grand Duchy of Luxembourg other than (a) a bank which is so resident or domiciled provided that such bank shall notify l'Institut Belgo-Luxembourgeois du Change of its purchase forthwith on the purchase taking effect by notice in writing containing a certificate to the effect that the consideration payable in respect of such purchase has been funded through a financial market situated outside The Kingdom of Belgium and the Grand Duchy of Luxembourg or (b) a broker, similar intermediary or institution of international standing whose business involves dealing in securities or managing customers' funds which is so resident or domiciled and payment for whose purchase is effected through an approved bank ("banque agréée"), and through the free exchange market ("marché libre"), as defined by the regulations of l'Institut Belgo-Luxembourgeois du Change, or (c) an insurance company which is so resident or domiciled in circumstances where the Bonds in question are held in an "assurances-compte réglementé" in accordance with such regulations.

Delivery will be without charge (save for any costs of postage and postal insurance) to the persons receiving such Bonds.

ECU ACCOUNTS

The Fiscal Agent has undertaken, for the benefit of the holders of Bonds (hereinafter referred to as the "Bondholders"), to open and maintain on its books ECU accounts for any Bondholder who so requests, so long as the European Currency Unit is used in the European Monetary System.

LEGAL MATTERS

In connection with the Bonds matters of Belgian law are passed upon by Messrs. De Bandt, Van Hecke & Lagae, Brussels, and matters of Luxembourg law are passed upon by Messrs. Elvinger, Hoss & Prussen, Luxembourg.

LITIGATION

The Issuer is not involved in any litigation, arbitration or administrative proceedings relating to claims or amounts which are material in the context of the issue of the Bonds, nor so far as it is aware is any such litigation, arbitration or administrative proceedings involving it pending or threatened.

CLEARING

The Bonds have been accepted for clearance through CEDEL (reference No. 246085) and Euro-clear (reference No. 59122).

Use of Proceeds

The net proceeds from the sale of the Bonds, expected to aggregate approximately ECU 149,767,500, will be applied to the general financing and debt requirements of the Issuer.

Terms and Conditions of the Bonds

PRINCIPAL AMOUNT, FORM AND DENOMINATION

The aggregate principal amount of the Bonds will be ECU 150,000,000. The Bonds will be serially numbered and issued in bearer form in the denominations of ECU 10,000 and ECU 100,000. Title to the Bonds passes by delivery.

INTEREST

(a) The Bonds will bear interest from February 28, 1989 at a rate of 8⅛ per cent per annum payable annually in arrear on February 28 in each year. The first payment of interest will be made on February 28, 1990. Interest will be paid against surrender of the appropriate coupon subject to and in accordance with the provisions of "Payments" below. Title to the coupons passes by delivery. Interest will cease to accrue on each Bond on the due date for redemption thereof unless, upon due presentation thereof, payment of principal is improperly withheld or refused. Any overdue principal of any Bond shall bear interest at a rate of 8⅛ per cent per annum (after as well as before judgment) until paid or, if earlier, the full amount of moneys payable has been received by the Fiscal Agent and notice to that effect has been given in accordance with the provisions of "Notices" below.

(b) Interest in respect of a period of less than one year will be calculated on the basis of a 360-day year of 12 months of 30 days each and, in the case of an incomplete month, the number of days elapsed.

REDEMPTION AND PURCHASE

(a) *Final Redemption*

Unless previously redeemed, pursuant to the provisions set forth below under "Tax Status" and "Acceleration of Maturity", or purchased and cancelled, the Bonds will be redeemed at their principal amount on February 28, 1994.

(b) *Purchases*

The Issuer may at any time purchase Bonds at any price.

(c) *Cancellation*

All Bonds redeemed or purchased as aforesaid will be cancelled (together with all unmatured coupons surrendered therewith).

VALUE OF THE ECU

Subject to the provisions under "Computation of Equivalents of the ECU" below, the value of the ECU is equal to the value of the European Currency Unit that is at present used in the European Monetary System and which is at present valued on the basis of specified amounts of the currencies of ten member countries of the European Communities ("EC") as shown below.

Pursuant to Council Regulation (EEC) No 3180/78 of December 18, 1978, as amended by Council Regulation (EEC) No 2626/84 of September 15, 1984, the EC European Currency Unit is at present defined as the sum of the following components:

0.719	German mark
1.31	French francs
0.0878	Pound sterling
140	Italian lire
0.256	Dutch guilder
3.71	Belgian francs
0.140	Luxembourg franc
0.219	Danish krone
0.00871	Irish pound
1.15	Greek drachmas

This basis may be changed by the EC, including changes in the components, in which event the basis of valuation of the ECU will change accordingly.

PAYMENTS

Payment of interest and reimbursement of principal shall be made to the holder, upon surrender of the Bond or coupon, as the case may be, at the main office of any of the paying banks, by credit or transfer to an ECU account or, in the event that the EC European Currency Unit is not used in the European Monetary System, by payment in a component currency of the ECU chosen for that purpose by the fiscal agent (the "Fiscal Agent") acting pursuant to the fiscal agency agreement dated February 23, 1989 (the "Fiscal Agency Agreement") between the Issuer, and Kredietbank S.A. Luxembourgeoise as Fiscal Agent, subject in each case to any applicable laws and regulations in effect in the country of payment.

With respect to any due date for the payment of interest and reimbursement of principal ("Maturity Date") on which the EC European Currency Unit is not used in the European Monetary System, the Fiscal Agent shall, without liability on its part, choose a component currency of the ECU in which all payments due on that Maturity Date with respect to Bonds are to be made. The amount of each payment in the chosen currency shall be computed on the basis of the equivalent of the ECU in that currency, determined as set forth under "Computation of Equivalents of the ECU" below, as of the fourth business day in Luxembourg prior to the Maturity Date. On the first business day in Luxembourg on which the EC European Currency Unit is no longer used in the European Monetary System, the Fiscal Agent shall, without liability on its part, choose a component currency of the ECU in which all payments with respect to Bonds or coupons related thereto having a Maturity Date prior thereto but not yet presented for payment are to be made. The amount of each payment in the chosen currency shall be computed on the basis of the equivalent of the ECU in that currency, determined as set forth under "Computation of Equivalents of the ECU" below, as of said first business day. Payments made in a country other than that of the chosen currency may be made by check or bank transfer.

If the Maturity Date is not a day on which banks are open for business and carrying out transactions in ECU or the chosen currency (as the case may be) in the place where the Bonds are presented for payment, no payment shall be made and no credit or transfer instructions shall be given in respect thereof until the next following such day in such place, and the holder shall not be entitled to any interest or other sums in respect of such postponed payments.

The initial paying bank will be Kredietbank S.A. Luxembourgeoise in Luxembourg. Additional paying banks may be appointed and the appointment of any paying bank may be terminated in accordance with the provisions of the Fiscal Agency Agreement, provided that notice thereof be published by the Fiscal Agent in accordance with the provisions under "Notices" below and that, as long as the Bonds are listed on the Luxembourg Stock Exchange, the Issuer shall maintain a paying bank in Luxembourg.

The Issuer will unconditionally undertake to pay interest on, and to reimburse the principal of each Bond at, the respective Maturity Date without discrimination as to nationality or domicile of the holders of Bonds or coupons, and without requiring the presentation of an affidavit of any kind or the fulfillment of any other formality, except as may be prescribed by applicable laws or regulations in the country in which such payment is made.

Each Bond presented for redemption is to be presented accompanied by all coupons appertaining thereto which are due after the date fixed for redemption. The aggregate face amount of all missing coupons due after such date (or in case of a partial payment of principal that proportion of the aggregate amount of the missing unmatured coupons that the principal paid bears to the principal due) shall be deducted from the principal to be paid on redemption, and the amount of principal so deducted will be paid upon surrender of the relevant missing coupons at any time before the expiration of a period of 5 years after the maturity date of such coupons.

The Issuer, the Fiscal Agent and any paying bank may deem and treat the holder of any Bond or coupon as the absolute owner thereof, for the purpose of receiving payment thereof, or on account thereof, and for all other purposes, whether or not such Bond or coupon shall be overdue and notwithstanding any notation of ownership or other writing thereon and neither the Issuer, the Fiscal Agent nor any paying bank shall be affected by any notice to the contrary and shall be required to obtain any proof thereof or as to the identity of the bearer.

COMPUTATION OF EQUIVALENTS OF THE ECU

In the event that the EC European Currency Unit is not used in the European Monetary System, the equivalent of the ECU in each of the component currencies as of any day (the "Day of Valuation") shall be determined by the Luxembourg Stock Exchange (the "Exchange") as follows.

The components of the ECU for this purpose (the "Components") shall be the currency amounts that were components of the EC European Currency Unit when the EC European Currency Unit was most recently used in the European Monetary System*. The equivalent of the ECU in U.S. dollars shall first be calculated as the sum of the U.S. dollar equivalents of each of the Components, and the equivalent of the ECU in each of the component currencies shall then be calculated on the basis of the U.S. dollar equivalent of the ECU, using the same rates as those used for determining the U.S. dollar equivalents of the Components as set forth below.

The U.S. dollar equivalent of each of the Components shall be determined by the Exchange on the basis of the middle spot delivery quotations prevailing at 2:30 p.m. Luxembourg time on the Day of Valuation, as obtained by the Exchange from one or more major banks, as selected by the Fiscal Agent, in the country of issue of the component currency in question**.

All determinations made by the Fiscal Agent or the Exchange shall be at their sole discretion and shall, in the absence of manifest error, be conclusive for all purposes and binding upon the Issuer and all Bondholders.

TAX STATUS

(a) All payments of principal and interest made by the Issuer will be made without withholding or deduction for or on account of any present or future taxes or duties of whatsoever nature imposed or levied by or on behalf of The Kingdom of Belgium, or any authority thereof or therein having power to tax, unless the Issuer is required by law to withhold or deduct amounts for, or on account of, such taxes or duties. In that event, the Issuer will pay such additional amounts as will result in the receipt by the persons entitled thereto of the sums which would otherwise have been receivable by them except that no such additional amounts shall be payable with respect to any Bonds:

(i) to, or to a third party on behalf of, a holder who is liable to the tax or duty in question by reason of his being connected with the Kingdom of Belgium, otherwise than merely by his ownership of any Bond or coupon; or

(ii) presented for payment in the Kingdom of Belgium; or

(iii) by or on behalf of a holder who would be able to avoid such withholding or deduction by making a declaration of non-residence or similar claim for exemption but fails to do so; or

(iv) presented for payment more than 30 days after the Relevant Date except to the extent that the relevant holder would have been entitled to such additional amounts on presenting the same for payment on such thirtieth day.

As used herein, the "Relevant Date" in respect of any payment means whichever is the later of (x) the date on which such payment first becomes due, and (y) if the full amount of the moneys payable has not been unconditionally received by the Fiscal Agent on or prior to such due date, the date on which, the full amount of such moneys having been so received, notice to that effect shall have been duly published in accordance with "Notices" below.

---

* In the event that the official unit of any component currency of the ECU is altered by way of combination or subdivision, the number of units of that currency as a Component shall be divided or multiplied in the same proportion. In the event that two or more component currencies are consolidated into a single currency, the amounts of those currencies as Components shall be replaced by an amount in such single currency equal to the sum of the amounts of the consolidated component currencies expressed in such single currency. In the event that any component currency should be divided into two or more currencies, the amount of that currency as a Component shall be replaced by amounts of such two or more currencies, each of which shall be equal to the amount of the former component currency divided by the number of currencies into which that currency was divided.

** In the event that no such direct quotations are available for a component currency on a Day of Valuation from any of the banks selected by the Fiscal Agent for this purpose, because foreign exchange markets are closed in the country of issue of that currency or for any other reason, the most recent direct quotations for that currency obtained by the Exchange shall be used in computing the equivalents of the ECU on such Day of Valuation; provided, however, that such most recent quotations may be used only if they were prevailing not more than two business days in the country of issue before such Day of Valuation. Beyond such period of two business days, the Exchange shall determine the U.S. dollar equivalent of such Component on the basis of cross rates derived from middle spot delivery quotations for such component currency and for the U.S. dollar prevailing at 2:30 p.m. Luxembourg time on such Day of Valuation, as obtained by the Exchange from one or more major banks, as selected by the Fiscal Agent, in a country other than the country of issue of such component currency. Within such period of two business days, the Exchange shall determine the U.S. dollar equivalent of such Component on the basis of such cross rates if the Fiscal Agent judges that the equivalent so calculated is more representative than the U.S. dollar equivalent calculated on the basis of such most recent direct quotations.

Unless otherwise specified by the Fiscal Agent, in the event that there is more than one market for dealing in any component currency by reason of foreign exchange regulations or for any other reason, the market to be referred to in respect of such currency shall be that upon which a non-resident issuer of securities denominated in such currency would purchase such currency in order to make payments in respect of such securities.

References herein to principal and interest on the Bonds shall be deemed to include any additional amounts which may be payable under this paragraph "Tax Status".

(b) If, as a result of any change in, or amendment to, the laws of the Kingdom of Belgium, or any district, municipality or other political subdivision or taxing authority thereof or therein affecting taxation, or any change in the official application or interpretation of such laws, the Issuer becomes or would in the future become obliged to pay additional amounts pursuant to the provisions under paragraph (a) hereof, the Bonds may be redeemed at the option of the Issuer, in whole but not in part, at any time (but not earlier than 15 days before the effective date of such change), at its principal amount together with accrued interest to the date set for redemption, upon not less than 30 days' notice to the Fiscal Agent.

STATUS OF THE BONDS

The Bonds will be direct, unconditional, unsecured, unsubordinated and general obligations of the Issuer. Subject to the provisions of "Negative Pledge" below, the Bonds will on issue rank and will at all times rank *pari passu* with all other unsecured and unsubordinated indebtedness of the Issuer from time to time outstanding and without any preference one over the other, by reason of priority of date of issue or otherwise.

NEGATIVE PLEDGE

The Issuer will not, so long as any of the Bonds remains outstanding (including Bonds in respect of which all amounts of principal and interest have been duly paid to the Fiscal Agent and remain available for payment subject to "Prescription" below), give or permit to be given or subsist or to be outstanding any security for any External Indebtedness now or hereafter existing of any person, whether by way of any mortgage, pledge, lien or other security interest, upon any of the present or future assets or revenues of the Issuer, without at the same time according to the Bonds the same security as is granted to such External Indebtedness or unless the Bonds are equally and rateably secured so as to rank *pari passu* with such External Indebtedness. "External Indebtedness" means indebtedness (including contingent obligations and liabilities) which is payable (or may be paid) in a currency other than the lawful currency for the time being of the Kingdom of Belgium or which is payable to any person domiciled, resident or having its head or principal place of business outside the Kingdom of Belgium.

ACCELERATION OF MATURITY

If any of the following events (an "Event of Default") should occur, the holder of any Bond may, upon written notice of acceleration to the Fiscal Agent, cause such Bond to become due and payable at its principal amount together with interest accrued to the date set for redemption, as of the date on which said notice of acceleration is received by the Fiscal Agent, unless prior to such date the Issuer shall have cured or otherwise made good such Event of Default in respect of all the Bonds:

(a) default in the payment of any principal when due (whether becoming due at maturity, upon redemption or otherwise) or default for more than five days in the payment of any interest in respect of the Bonds;

(b) default in the performance or observance by the Issuer of any other obligation on its part under the Bonds, which default continues for 30 days after written notice requiring such default to be remedied shall have been given by any Bondholder to the Fiscal Agent;

(c) any other indebtedness in respect of moneys borrowed by the Issuer shall become, or shall be capable of becoming or being declared, prematurely repayable following a default, or any security therefor becomes enforceable, or the Issuer fails to make payment or repayment of any such indebtedness at the maturity thereof (or when otherwise due) or at the expiry of any applicable grace period, or any guarantee of any indebtedness in respect of moneys borrowed given by the Issuer shall not be honoured when due and called upon;

(d) the Issuer is unable to, or admits its inability to, pay any External Indebtedness (as defined above) in respect of moneys borrowed as it falls due, or shall declare a moratorium on or readjustment of any of such indebtedness; or

(e) any consent, permission, authorisation, agreement, confirmation or exemption of any governmental authority required for the performance of the Issuer's obligations under the Bonds is revoked, modified or breached or becomes ineffective.

(f) a distress, execution or other process is levied or enforced upon or sued out against all or any material part of the property of the Issuer unless it is removed, discharged or paid out within 60 days or is being contested in good faith by the Issuer.

MEETINGS OF BONDHOLDERS AND MODIFICATION OF TERMS AND CONDITIONS

The Fiscal Agency Agreement contains provisions for convening meetings of the Bondholders to consider any matters affecting their interests, including modification of the terms and conditions of the Bonds and any provisions of the Fiscal Agency Agreement directly applicable to the Bonds. Any such modification must be authorised by an Extraordinary Resolution of the Bondholders (which means a resolution passed by a majority consisting of not less than seventy-five per cent. of the votes cast thereon). The quorum at any meeting will be two or more persons present in person holding or representing a clear majority in principal amount of the Bonds for the time being outstanding, and at any adjourned meeting two or more persons being or representing holders of the Bonds whatever the principal amount of Bonds so held or represented, provided that at any such meeting, the business of which includes the modification of certain of these terms and conditions, the necessary quorum for passing an Extraordinary Resolution is two or more persons holding or representing not less than two-thirds in principal amount of the Bonds for the time being outstanding. An Extraordinary Resolution duly passed at a meeting will be binding on all the Bondholders (whether present at the meeting or not). No modification to the Bonds and the Fiscal Agency Agreement can be adopted without the consent of the Issuer.

The Fiscal Agent may agree without the consent of the Bondholders to any modification of the Fiscal Agency Agreement or of the Bonds which, in the opinion of the Fiscal Agent, is not materially prejudicial to the interests of the Bondholders or for the purpose of curing any ambiguity or of curing, correcting or supplementing any defective provision therein or herein.

NOTICES

Any notice to Bondholders shall be validly given if published in the *Luxemburger Wort* (Luxembourg) and the *Financial Times* (United Kingdom) or, if either of said newspapers shall cease to be published or timely publication therein shall not be practicable, in such other newspapers as the Fiscal Agent shall deem necessary to give fair and reasonable notice to the Bondholders.

PRESCRIPTION

Claims against the Issuer for the payment of principal of the Bonds shall become void 10 years after the Maturity Date. Claims against the Issuer for the payment of interest on the Bonds shall become void 5 years after the Maturity Date.

REPLACEMENT OF BONDS AND COUPONS

In case of theft, loss, destruction, defacement or mutilation of any Bond or coupon, application for replacement thereof is to be made at the principal office of the Fiscal Agent. Any such Bond or coupon shall be replaced by the Issuer in compliance with such procedures and on such terms as to evidence and indemnification as the Issuer may require. Subject to applicable laws and stock exchange regulations, all such costs as may be incurred in connection with the replacement of any such Bond or coupon shall be borne by the applicant. Defaced or mutilated Bonds or coupons must be surrendered before new ones will be issued.

GOVERNING LAW, JURISDICTION AND WAIVER OF IMMUNITY

(a) The Bonds will be governed by and shall be construed in accordance with the laws of the Grand Duchy of Luxembourg.

(b) The Issuer will irrevocably agree for the benefit of the Bondholders and the holders of coupons that any suit, action or proceedings ("proceedings") arising out of or in connection with the Bonds may be brought in the courts of the Kingdom of Belgium and the Grand Duchy of Luxembourg, will submit to the exclusive jurisdiction of such courts and will waive any claim that any proceedings brought in any of such courts have been brought in an inconvenient forum. The Issuer will appoint the Ambassador of the Kingdom of Belgium for the time being in the Grand Duchy of Luxembourg, as its process agent for the receipt of any writ, judgment or other process in connection with such proceedings in the Grand Duchy of Luxembourg, and will agree that any writ, judgment or other process shall be sufficiently and effectively served on it if delivered to the said process agent at his official address for the time being in the Grand Duchy of Luxembourg or in any other manner permitted by law. The Issuer will irrevocably and generally consent in respect of any such proceedings to the giving of any relief or the issue of any process in connection with those proceedings including, without limitation, the making, enforcement or execution against any assets whatsoever (irrespective of their use or intended use) of any order or judgment which may be made or given in those proceedings (except that the obligations of the Issuer may not be subject to enforcement by way of attachment, seizure, garnishment or any other compulsory enforcement against its properties or assets located within The Kingdom of Belgium). Subject to the exception in the previous sentence, the Issuer will irrevocably agree not to claim and will waive, in connection with any proceedings which may be commenced in any of such courts with respect to any Bond or coupon appertaining thereto, any immunity which it might be entitled to claim for itself or which might be attributed to it (whether on grounds of sovereignty or otherwise) from suit, from the jurisdiction of any of such courts, from attachment prior to judgment, from set-off (to the fullest extent permitted by applicable law), from attachment in aid of execution of a judgment or from execution of a judgment or from the giving of any other relief or issue of any process.

FISCAL AGENT

Kredietbank S.A. Luxembourgeoise,
43 Boulevard Royal,
L-2955 Luxembourg

PAYING BANK

Kredietbank S.A. Luxembourgeoise,
43 Boulevard Royal,
L-2955 Luxembourg

LISTING AGENT

Kredietbank S.A. Luxembourgeoise,
43 Boulevard Royal,
L-2955 Luxembourg

LEGAL ADVISORS

as to Belgian Law
De Bandt, Van Hecke & Lagae
Brussels

as to Luxembourg law
Elvinger, Hoss & Prussen
Luxembourg

PART XIX.

INDEX